DEATH IN THE OUTBACK

The desert night was more than just dark. It was pitch black, without a breath of wind; and yet some of the trees near the lights of the campsite started moving—waving as if there was a breeze.

Lindy called to Michael. "A dingo's in the tent!"

She hurried toward the low railing, realizing that something awful might have happened. She knew that dingoes were wild animals and, if it had been her baby's cry that they had heard, the child might have been disturbed.

When she got to the railing, she could see inside the tent. Azaria's blankets were scattered everywhere. Lindy instantly felt sick. Instinct told her the baby was gone, but hope told her it was not possible. She scrambled into the tent and felt inside the cot. The baby was no longer there. . . .

MOTHER ON TRIAL

THE MYSTERIOUS DEATH OF AN OUTBACK BABY

RICHARD SHEARS

ST. MARTIN'S PRESS/NEW YORK

This St. Martin's edition of *Mother on Trial* is the revised version of a book titled *The Dingo Baby Case,* first published by Sphere Books (Australia) in November, 1982.

MOTHER ON TRIAL

ISBN: 0-312-91343-5   Can. ISBN: 0-312-91344-3

Printed in the United States of America

First St. Martin's Press mass market edition/December 1988

10 9 8 7 6 5 4 3 2 1

Prologue

"The Spirit Take Him . . ."

On the Sabbath, on the road through the Wilderness leading to the hallowed and mysterious place where it all began, he walked the last few kilometers of his life.

It was too hot to be out in the desert with a backpack, out in the heart of summer in the blazing heat of midafternoon. Sometimes he paused and swayed, giving the appearance of a man who had had too much to drink. His eyes gave a different impression. Glassy and lifeless, they had the faraway stare of a drug addict, but David Brett had no narcotics running through his veins. Neither was there any food in his stomach, for the Lord had taught that the only way to cast out the Devil which possessed him was by prayer and fasting.

In the distance, its brutish shape distorted by the heat waves rising from the red sand and stunted brush, his destination loomed.

The Rock.

It lay in the middle of God's harshest land like a huge beast at rest, a place of worship for 30,000 years since the aboriginal tribes made their way to the mainland from the islands of Southeast Asia. Awestricken, they saw it as the creation of their mythological ancestors. They gave it the name Uluru.

The day that David chose to walk toward that shimmering miragelike monolith was Australia Day, 198 years after the landing of the crews and convicts of the First Fleet. If there was one true symbol of the Dreamtime that had survived the intrusion of an alien culture, it was the Rock, immobile, indestructible, guarded by the spirits of time.

At 4:30 in the afternoon of that Sunday, January 26, 1986, Sharon Grey, a Conservation Commission ranger, noticing David's small backpack as he entered the Uluru National Park, advised him that camping was no longer permitted in the area; it was now administered by its traditional aboriginal owners. There were new rules, and if he wanted to put up a tent, he would have to return to the tourist complex at Yulara, twenty kilometers away. Yes, he understood that, he said, then headed on toward the Rock.

Its hue was deepening to blood-red when David reached the place he had selected to begin his climb. More than five hundred million years of erosion had carved deep folds in its surface and the rain that tumbled down over its sides onto the plain gave it a cloak of moss and lichen. David began climbing up over this growth, an antlike creature on the back of a silent monster 335 meters high and 9 kilometers in circumference. It was cooler now, but no one can climb the Rock without pouring sweat.

A visiting aboriginal couple, Tanya Armstrong and Edwin Edwards, of Ernabella, South Australia, watched him for a while. They were on their way to the sunset viewing area where they could observe the colors change minute by minute to a deep purple, but their curiosity was aroused by the lone figure slowly working his way up an area not designated for climbing; the proper route to the top, where there were steps and chains to help, was farther around to the west. They studied his slow progress for some minutes then proceeded on their way.

David was doing quite well. He was now a good one hundred meters up—as high, perhaps, as the Lord when he took Peter, James, and John to a mountain and was transfigured before them, his face shining like the sun, his raiment as white as the light.

So many kilometers across the world, so many empty rooms, so much conflict with Beelzebub.

"Can't you see him?" asked David and put a cigarette lighter to the chair. "Out! Out!"

Julian Richards laughed at his friend. Magic mushrooms affected people in different ways. Silly David thought the Devil was in the chair. Then David was up and running through the door and out into the streets of 1980 Bournemouth, England, his lighter an Olympic torch—no, the flames of Hades!—blazing the way. Julian ran after him. Bloody hell, he thought. The law will have us if he isn't stopped. But David was running fast, his flame touching trees, park benches, doorways.

"Burn! Burn!"

His eyes were wild and if he could have breathed fire he would. Julian didn't like it. He thought he knew David pretty well from all the work they'd done at the mine in Australia, but that night something was different about him. It was more than the hallucinogenic effect of the drug. Hey, whatever it was came right out of his friend's being, like out of his soul. Like he was possessed.

The night had a profound effect on Julian. The image of David trying to burn down Bournemouth kept him awake for months afterward; really spooked him for about two years.

David Brett had grown up in Kent, staying on at school until he was eighteen before announcing to his parents and two sisters that he didn't want to go to university; he wanted to travel, working his way around the world. It was 1973, when the last of the hippies were heading across Asia to Europe, when the final platoons of American soldiers were leaving Vietnam but at a time when bombs were exploding in London railway stations. Britain became embroiled in the fishing war with Iceland, eighteen miners were killed in Derbyshire, and fifty holidaymakers died in a fire at an Isle of Man entertainment center. The one bright event in a gloomy year of angry politics and sudden death was the wedding of Princess Anne and Captain Mark Philips. Still, it was not enough to satisfy the restless, those who believed it was time to leave Britain and her troubles behind for a while.

David Brett was one of them. He was in a youthful, rebellious mood, unable to see much of a future for himself from the perspective of small-town Hartley. His attitude at that time was reflected in a visit he made with a friend to a tattooist in Chatham when he asked for an engraving that was to be sadly prophetic. Pulling down his trousers and pointing to his buttock he asked to be branded with a Union Jack, the words *Born to Lose* underneath. He also wanted the words *British Made* added, but the patriotic tattooist felt that would be defamatory to the flag. So his friend borrowed the latter caption for himself and the words were tattooed under the image of a tiger's head.

Marked by his own doing, David crossed the Channel for Europe. Strumming his guitar, he worked in restaurants, factories, and at any odd job he could find to keep him and his music on the road. Then he decided on something completely new and headed for Australia.

He landed a job in the iron ore mines at Mount Newman, in northwestern Australia. That was where he met Julian. They got on well together, two Poms on a godforsaken landscape, and shared more than a few beers in the throat-parching heat.

When Julian went back to England for a visit in 1979 Dave wasn't very far behind. He carried close to £10,000 when he arrived back on his doorstep in Hartley, Kent, in June 1980. The one significant change he found at home was the absence of his father; he and David's mother, Doreen, had parted. But Doreen and David's younger sisters, Gina and Yvonne, were delighted he had returned from his foreign adventures, his skin tanned, his conversation filled with the tales of a traveler who had worked his way around the world. David had hoped to use some of the money he'd brought back to help his sisters set themselves up in a boutique, but it was agreed that 1980, with Britain going through a period of economic depression and with higher duty and taxes being imposed in the budget, wasn't a good year for it. David hung around for a while, at a bit of a loose end, then teamed up with Julian, his mate from the outback. They reminisced about the mine, ate their magic mushrooms because it was the thing to do at the time, and talked about heading back Down Under.

One of Julian's close friends was an Irish girl, Annette Riordon, and one day in Colchester, Essex, he introduced her to David. David liked her a lot and they started seeing each other, but it was a purely platonic relationship. For David Brett had come to realize that he was gay.

In November 1981 David returned to Australia. On his previous trip he had hoped to buy property in the Queensland mining town of Mount Isa, where he had worked for a while, but he told Julian that it hadn't worked out.

Mount Isa . . . The Brett family would not realize as David spoke of the tiny community in the middle of the Australian nowhere, that it was where a tragedy had begun, a terrible event that was, through a bizarre progression of events, to involve David.

When he returned Down Under David went straight to Perth, in Western Australia, and stayed for a month with Nina Castle and her husband, whom he had met previously through their daughter, an employee at the Mount Newman mine. The Castles had liked David the moment he'd introduced himself. A nice young man, they thought. And yes, they could understand why he didn't enjoy the burning outback. If he found a place to live in Perth he'd certainly be close to the sea, which he said he much preferred.

For the next three years, David played his guitar and drifted around the west and southwest coast, stopping off in Albany and Esperance, finding work to pay his way. In May 1982 he met up with his sister Gina, who had bought a combi van for a six-month tour of the country. When she left for England, he purchased the van from her and continued his own travels. But it was Perth that drew him back and in December 1984, the month he thought he might return home for a Christmas reunion with his family, he decided to stay on. He moved into a flat on the top floor of the eight-story Lakeview Apartments in Davies Road, Claremont, an outer suburb.

Until May 1985, Doreen Brett assumed all was well with her 31-year-old wandering son. He'd phoned home at Christmas and again in April to wish them well. But David was having serious problems. On May 7 he wrote in his tiny, spidery handwriting to tell his mother that something strange was happening and that he hoped to return home to England soon. This puzzled his family. It was unlike their Dave to be so vague. He followed the letter with a phone call asking his mother not to post a parcel to him at his flat but to send it care of the local post office.

Then his voice took on a note of urgency. "You're not going to believe what's happening to me. It's really freaking me," he said.

"What is it, Dave? Tell me!" Doreen implored, but David didn't elaborate.

On a Saturday morning in June that year, Mr. and Mrs. Castle were shopping at the local supermarket when David approached them, distraught.

"I need some help," he said. "Please . . . you've got to help me."

They took him home to the house he was so familiar with and over a cup of coffee David stunned them with his words.

"I'm possessed by a demon," he said. "It's in my stomach. It's living in my stomach."

The Castles glanced at one another. They'd always thought David was a levelheaded young man. He must, they agreed later, be having a nervous breakdown of some sort. They told a young woman friend who attended a local church about the troubled Englishman and she said she would mention the curious affair to her minister.

Pastor Milton Gabrielson got his name from his Norwegian grandfather who came to Australia the previous century. The pastor's father was a butcher by trade. He embraced Christianity and brought his children up to love the Lord. When the Congregational minister heard about David he thought he knew what was wrong. Convinced that demonic influences were active in our world, Pastor Gabrielson believed that many who displayed signs of mental torment were possessed. The only way to help was to challenge the evil spirit to leave the body. He believed in particular that spirits entered those who had gone against the principles of wholesome living and had, perhaps, taken drugs. Demons, he was convinced, took advantage of the temporary weakness of the mind to enter the body.

The foundation for his beliefs was, of course, the work of Christ who, as the Gospels taught, met a man called Legion who had been driven by the devil that possessed him to wander into the wilderness. Christ commanded the spirits to depart from Legion and they entered a herd of pigs which then, according to Luke, "ran violently down a steep place into the lake, and were choked."

Before David Brett was referred to him, Pastor Gabrielson had been called to attend a disturbed man whose home was filled with what to a Christian might seem idolatrous objects: stuffed snakes, African totems, Indian gods. Brought back from various countries as souvenirs, they had, Gabrielson believed, been used for worship and their influence had affected the owner. The pastor helped the owner burn all the items then performed an exorcism after which the man expressed "a great feeling of freedom."

Back in Hartley, Mrs. Brett and her daughters were desperately worried. So worried, in fact, that Doreen sent David a ticket to fly home. Her son's most recent phone call had been a great shock.

"I'm seeing a priest for an exorcism," he said. "But if I don't arrive home you'll know that I've been sacrificed."

"David . . . I don't know what's happening to you

out there, but come back," begged Doreen. "Come back, *please,* on the next plane!"

Pastor Gabrielson met David at the Castles' home in the Perth suburb of Bentleigh on June 6. The Englishman sat in the lounge, fidgety, uncertain. His eyes were glazed, his face white. The first thing Gabrielson thought was that David was in the grip of an evil power. Not crazy or suffering a breakdown; but certainly under the influence of something linked to the occult. He asked David to describe his troubles.

The Englishman spoke like a man struggling with some inner force. "They are chanting in the flat next door. They are trying to kill me. They wanted me to jump from the balcony. They chant, chant, chant. I can't sleep. The other night, I pulled the blankets over my head and my body lit up, shining bright and luminous. When I got into the shower, the Devil came in with me. I fought with him with the water flowing down around us."

Thirteen years a pastor, Gabrielson, along with a church deacon who had accompanied him to the house, listened intently as David told how his body emitted an evil smell one day, a traditional characteristic, the clergyman noted mentally, of the possessed.

"I know I'm going to be killed. They want me to die," David insisted. Pastor Gabrielson decided it was time to try to cast the evil out. With the lights remaining on so that he could look David straight in the eyes —"and stare at the spirit which possessed him"— he commanded the devil to leave the Englishman's body in the name of Christ.

Now David's eyes danced, first glaring, then glazing over. "I can't see!" he cried at one point as Gabrielson and his deacon prayed for his deliverance.

"In the name of Jesus Christ our Lord, we command

.you to leave," commanded Pastor Gabrielson. David's face contorted and his eyes rolled as the room filled with prayer.

And he said unto them, This kind can come forth by nothing, but by prayer and fasting . . .

After two hours of counseling, the minister and his assistant believed they had done all they could for the time being. But Gabrielson felt he had not been entirely successful. Whatever was troubling David, he believed, remained with him. More time was needed. In the meantime, he told David, he should find peace by reading the Scriptures and he would counsel him again.

But the opportunity did not arise. Two days later, after asking the Castles to sell his beloved combi van for him, David flew to England. His sisters were at Heathrow to meet him.

He stared at Yvonne. "Who do you see?" he asked.

"Why, I see you, Dave," she said. She thought to herself he looked like a man who had been to hell and back.

Back home he told his mother and sisters, "I died out there. They have my brain, you know. But I'll never go back. That's it."

Horrified by the change in her son, Doreen pressed him for information. But he told her he didn't want to risk the family's safety by bringing evil into the house. The only thing Doreen could think of was that David was going through a nervous breakdown. Perhaps drugs were involved, she thought, but when she challenged him he denied the charge. He had always been truthful with her, so she had no reason to doubt him. But each day increased the family's concern.

"That exorcism," he said. "It's just made things worse. It's taken all the good from me. I've only got evil left . . . only evil."

He began walking around the house. He was tormented by voices, by the faces of the devil, he told his mother.

When the unclean spirit is gone out of a man, he walketh through dry places, seeking rest; and finding none, he saith, I will return unto my house whence I came out.

And when he cometh, he findeth it swept and garnished.

Then goeth he, and taketh to him seven other spirits more wicked than himself; and they enter in, and dwell there: and the last state of that man is worse than the first.

Doreen persisted with her son, asking him again what had happened in Australia. More of his story emerged bit by bit.

There were two men living next door to him. One seemed more dominant than the other. Hearing David playing his guitar, the quieter man asked David to teach him. But after the lessons began, early in May, David realized the man wasn't paying any attention. Instead, he seemed to be studying David.

"What the hell's going on?" David said he had asked. Not long afterward, the chanting had begun, followed by banging on the wall. He felt certain that the bricks and mortar were going to fall in on him. Items started to vanish from his flat. As the days went by he lost his appetite.

During that first week at home, David received a phone call from Annette Riordon. She had finally made it to Australia and he had written to her in Sydney, where she was working as a waitress, from the Lakeview Apartments.

"Why don't you come on back to Australia?" she asked him now.

Doreen thought that Annette's call, followed by three others, unsettled her son. He phoned the Castles in Perth and asked them to go ahead with the sale of his van. Meanwhile he sat around the house reading the Bible and reciting the Lord's Prayer. His sisters and mother became so concerned about his unusual behavior that they finally sought medical help and in August he was admitted to a general hospital in Dartford, Kent.

"They can't find anything wrong with you," his mother told him when he came out eighteen days later. "No nervous breakdown, no physical problems. We think you just need a rest. Why don't you take a break, go up to the Lake District, somewhere quiet and peaceful?"

"No," said David. "I have to go back. I *must* go back!"

Realizing they could not stop him, his sisters drove him to the airport.

"You know," he told them as he loaded his luggage onto the scales, "I don't really want to go. It's just that I have to. And remember, if anything happens to me, you'll know I've been sacrificed."

His parting words alarmed the girls. They watched their brother turn to wave good-bye for the last time, and then he went through the emigration doors.

When he arrived in Perth he stayed with the Castles, who had not yet sold his van, which pleased him. He decided to use it. He rang his mother and said all was well and he now intended to drive the van to Sydney. Annette had offered him accommodation in her flat in Rosslyn Gardens, Kings Cross, and during the first few days of his arrival in Sydney he seemed happy enough. He sent Gina a card on August 30, wishing her a happy birthday, congratulating her on naming the day for her wedding, and telling his family that "things so far seemed to be going OK."

Annette cared a lot about David. There was no romance, but she enjoyed his company. She hadn't thought he was happy at home in Hartley and had offered to lend him $1,000 to come back to Australia. She was to think later how sorry she was to have even made the offer.

David continued to read the Bible and did some sketching as a means of relaxation. He wasn't a good communicator, but he and Annette got on all right until the day David decided he didn't want to be obligated to her. He reckoned, too, that he wanted to live closer to the water, so early in October he moved out and found accommodation in a flat in Dolphin Street, overlooking Coogee Bay. Located above a nightclub, the apartment was already home to Glen Langley, twenty-three, and Steve Grant, nineteen.

David settled in well, Steve thought, but there was, well, an edge about him that he couldn't place. Something sort of strange about the man who sat around with his Bible and his book about the Mormons. Two weeks after David moved in Glen left for an overseas holiday and that's when problems began for Steve. David became anxious, started drinking heavily, and got hold of some marijuana. One night when they were alone, Steve brought out a scrapbook of newspaper clippings he had been keeping. As David started looking through them a distant expression came to his face. He read the articles about a woman called Lindy Chamberlain who had been sent to jail for the murder of her baby, Azaria. All along she had claimed that a dingo, a wild desert dog, had taken the child. She maintained that one of the dingoes living around the base of Ayers Rock, the place the aborigines called Uluru, had entered the family holiday tent and run off with the baby. The more David read, the more anxious he became, it seemed to Steve.

"He went off into Disneyland," was the way Steve was to put it later.

David had found a job at a tilemaker's in the suburb of Mascot and it was there that he became friends with two young New Zealanders, Brett Burgerin and Greg Sullivan. Sometimes Brett, who was only seventeen, would come back to the flat with David. One night Steve came home to find that David and Brett had shaved their heads by candlelight.

David and Brett, thought Steve; funny how David Brett should become friends with a bloke called Brett . . . one of those funny things in life.

Steve became more uneasy in the face of David's increasingly odd behavior. One day, the Englishman flew into a rage and tried to hit Steve. Steve picked up his terrified Siamese cat and went home to his mother. A week later, in mid-December, Steve returned to the flat with his brother-in-law for support and they threw David out.

Brett thought he should offer David a bed at his own flat in Bondi, but he, too, was beginning to feel uneasy in the Englishman's presence. Still, Brett's eighteen-year-old brother Rod believed, they should do something to help him out, so they gave him the spare room. They all went out drinking a bit around the pubs in Bondi, but "Davo," as they called him, was worried because he'd been charged with driving the combi van under the influence. As it turned out, he was fined $900 and prohibited from driving for six months. The only way he could pay the fine was to sell his van, which put him in a bad mood.

The longer the brothers spent with David, the more

concerned about his behavior they became. He started talking about the demon in his stomach and he stopped eating, except to take some bread and water occasionally.

"He gave me the creeps," Brett was to recall later. "He started to tell me that I was evil and that he could see my eyes changing color. I didn't know what he was on about. But you should have seen his eyes; they were remote, dull. He was just sitting on the couch looking at the window and he was starting to get really skinny; you know, you could see his ribs poking through. We said to him, 'If you don't eat, mate, you're out because we don't want a corpse on our hands.' "

David sent a Christmas card home to Hartley on December 17. "Sorry not to have written, but trying to get myself into gear," he wrote. "Well, Gina, the old combi has finally gone. Unfortunately I got done for drunken driving and what with one thing and another had to sell it. Still, guess it taught me a lesson. Probably well needed. However, things are cool and I love you all. Bye Bye."

It was to be the last time he wrote home. Between Christmas and mid-January he packed up his gear and set out for Perth on four occasions. On each he returned to the flat within a few hours, never getting farther than Liverpool, twenty kilometers west. During these frustrated attempts to leave Sydney, which he said was too fast for him (indeed, someone had stolen his guitar while he was waiting for a taxi), he made a phone call to Annette, telling her he was going to Perth.

"I didn't know him," she was to say of that last conversation. "He seemed . . . different."

On January 15, 1986, David Brett said good-bye yet again to his flatmates. This time he didn't come back.

* * *

Bert Cramer is the only dairy farmer in the Alice Springs district. Of Lutheran background, he arrived in "The Alice" in 1957 looking for work. Now entering his sixties, he has always remembered how the locals took him in and has tried to help anyone who passes his way. Although not a regular churchgoer, he respects the Sabbath and believes in the unseen forces of good and evil.

In the afternoon of January 24 a man with a small pack arrived at the farm asking for milk. Bert gave him a pint, and the traveler asked if there were any spare jobs on the farm. Bert looked the stranger up and down. He was reasonably well presented, although he had a look in his eye that Bert couldn't quite place. His visitor said he'd done farm work before, although Bert reckoned from his hands that it must have been some time ago; they looked pretty smooth to him.

David Brett said he was quite willing to do anything. He was on the dole but he wouldn't mind a job of sorts, even if it paid only $50 a week. Bert told David he could follow him around, the best way of learning the routine of things. As they moved around the farm, unloading hay, checking the cattle, David asked: "Do you believe in evil spirits?"

Bert studied him for a moment. "As a matter of fact I do," said the farmer. "How did you know that? Why do you ask?"

"Because I have been exorcised," he said.

Bert wanted to question David a bit more about it. Just then the tea bell rang. Bert reckoned he would have to wait. He gave the Englishman a couple of chops and showed him to a shed that had been fitted out with a primus stove and a few utensils. It wasn't luxury accommodation, but David said he would be happy to stay there.

The next morning Bert found David sitting under a

tree, dressed in a gray shirt and pink shorts and staring at nothing. He hadn't eaten the chops; hadn't even cooked them.

"I won't be able to start work yet," said David. "But will it be all right if I come back and make a bit of a home out of that shed?"

"Yes, sure," said Bert. "But where are you going?"

David looked intently at Bert and the farmer thought the younger man wasn't quite seeing him; it was like he was looking right through him. Then David said he was going to Ross River, a cattle station-cum-tourist village about 120 kilometers east of Alice Springs.

Bert gave David a two-liter water bottle and said that if he was planning to walk he should go no farther than Emily Gap, the last water hole, about seven kilometers from Alice, and wait for a lift.

"You shouldn't walk anywhere in the desert round here," said Bert. "It's a dangerous business."

After David left, Bert had a long think about the visit. David had been like a man on a mission, someone who had been mysteriously guided to a place. And why, he wondered, of all the people he should have called on, should it have been he, one who immediately understood David's talk of spirits? It was something Bert was to think of for months to come.

Gary Glazebrook, manager of the Ross River Station, found David on the road about ten kilometers out from the complex. David said he was heading there to camp. Gary gave him a lift to the station and showed him the camping area. The next morning, however, there were no signs that David had spent the night there.

On the Sabbath, January 26, David bought a one-way ticket from Alice Springs to the tourist resort at Yulara. It was in the opposite direction of the Ross River Station. The bus arrived at 2 P.M. and David alighted with the other passengers. A couple of hours later local journalist Tony Wells saw a lone, hatless man walking unsteadily toward Ayers Rock. He wouldn't swear to it one hundred percent, but it seemed there was something weird about the man's eyes. . . .

David was two hundred meters up the rock now, unaware of Tanya Armstrong and Edwin Edwards, who were returning from the sunset viewing area and had stopped to watch him again. It was a little after 8 P.M. They thought they had better go and tell the rangers about him, a man climbing the rock so late in the evening and so far up.

David made his way up over the lichen. Some of the bits broke away as he climbed. It was certainly high up.

And the devil; taking him up into an high mountain, shewed unto him all the kingdoms of the world in a moment of time.

And the devil said unto him, All this power will I give thee, and the glory of them: for that is delivered unto me; and to whomsoever I will I give it.

If thou therefore wilt worship me, all shall be thine.

And Jesus answered and said unto him, Get thee behind me Satan: for it is written, Thou shalt worship the Lord thy God, and him only shalt thou serve.

Early in the morning of the following Sunday, February 2, Paul Robinson, a tourist from Victoria, was strolling around the base of Ayers Rock when he found a body. It was a gruesome sight. David's backpack was still attached but his right arm, left hand, and right foot were missing, apparently taken by dingoes.

Line searches of the area were carried out with the aid of Conservation Commission rangers and Northern Territory Emergency Service volunteers. As they spread out from where the shattered body had been found and walked through the nearby desert undergrowth, 150 paces maybe, a shout went up. Somebody had found something.

The searchers gathered around it. Cloth . . . a garment; woollen clothing of some kind, soiled and stained, as if it had been lying out in the weather for a long time. Somebody said it looked like a baby's jacket. Just then a strange feeling came over many of them. Some were to agree later that their blood had run cold as their minds went back five and a half years, to the time when a baby called Azaria, whose name means "for whom Jehovah aids," had vanished in the black night of the desert.

I

The Night a Baby Vanished

The road leading to the place where legends are born was, many frustrated travelers remarked, little better in 1980 than the animal tracks the explorer W. C. Gosse traversed in 1873. Probing the inland with his camels and billy-cans and salt beef, Gosse became the first white man to make the pilgrimage to the "Red Center" (Australia's vast central desert) and notice an enormous shape on the horizon. His excitement overflowed in his diary: ". . . what was my astonishment, when two miles distant, to find it was an immense pebble rising abruptly from the plain. . . . It is certainly the most wonderful natural feature I have ever seen."

The Chamberlain family, now bouncing along the desert road in their yellow Torana hatchback, would have liked to have made it to the rock campsite before nightfall. To see the monolith materialize from afar was part of the thrill and to have observed its fading colors at the end of what was their Sabbath would have held some significance, but there was really no way of judging time against distance on that road, 451 kilometers and a lot of it red dust. With the vehicle crammed with camping gear, the ride wasn't much fun. The one consolation was that they would now have more time at the rock, seeing that the rowdy groups who had turned up

1

in Alice Springs for the rodeo had driven them out of the nearby campsite a couple of days earlier than they had planned.

At the ranger station leading into the camping area Michael Chamberlain went through the formality of registering. Fit and blond, he carried an air of tranquility about him. He was what you might consider him to be; a man of the cloth. With him was his dark-haired wife, Lindy, and their two sons, Aidan, aged six, and Reagan, four. And snug in her blankets on Lindy's lap was a tiny baby.

Her name was Azaria Chantel Loren and Lindy had given birth to her a little more than nine weeks earlier.

The check-in formalities over, Michael drove the car past the rows of tents and camper vans looking for a space. The boys were fidgety after a day in the car, and when at last they found a space Aidan and Reagan were more than happy to help Michael get the tent up in the light of an overhead campsite lamp erected in a barbecue area some twenty-five meters away. There was a chill in the air, for it was the heart of the Australian winter, August 16. It was also the eve of a tragedy.

The campsite was about one kilometer to the east of the Rock, but on this blackest of nights, wedged between the end of the Seventh Day Adventist Sabbath and the beginning of the traditional Holy Day, it was impossible to see its enormous outline. But it would still be there in the morning, a backdrop for the tourist buses disgorging their passengers, just as it was there when the first birds flew, when dinosaurs roamed through thick vegetation and giant reptiles disturbed the inland sea.

The aborigines who made their way to the mainland more than 30,000 years ago from the islands of Southeast Asia were gripped with wonder; apart from its majestic presence, the Rock provided a source of food and water. They entered its caves for ceremonies, sharing them with eagles that nested in the nooks and crannies, and painted their legends in ochres and charcoal on the rough surface. These legends told of the Rock's creation, for the Yankuntjatjara tribe believe that this huge landmark was formed by the movements of their forebears. These mythical predecessors, the legends relate, were giant beings resembling the creatures of the Tjukjrapa age, although they behaved like humans.

There were the Liru, the poisonous snakes; the Kunia, carpet snakes; the Linga, sand lizards; and Itjari-tjari, marsupial moles. When they fought, made a fire, or performed a ceremony there arose, after their departure, a mountain range, a hill, or a valley—some form of geological phenomenon. Among these beings was the Kurrpan, an evil creature the size of a big dingo, sent out by sorcerers of the Wintalyka totem to harass and kill the people of the Mala totem. The myth tells how the sorcerers laid out a skeletal framework using a mulga branch for a backbone, forked sticks for ears, the teeth of a marsupial mole, the tail of a bandicoot, and women's hair. After songs had been chanted, the creature came alive and went off to hunt the Mala people, destroying most of the men and their families.

Rain falling on the Rock was shed onto the plain, so there was an abundance of fruit and water for the early inhabitants. A living pattern was established. On the western face of the Rock was a cave the men were not allowed to see; it was a hallowed area where the women went to conduct ceremonies. There was a cave, too, where the boys were taken for circumcision. Today tourists clamber through the deep cavities and recesses and end the day writing on postcards that they have visited such places as the Fertility Cave. For Uluru, by tradition, has been a monument to life.

It is most mysterious at dusk, and some who have watched its subtle change of hue to purple-gray just after sunset have sworn they have seen it move. If you look hard enough before the last of the light goes, they say, you can even see it breathing.

Mount Isa, 900 kilometers to the northeast, is a tough mining town. A plume of gray smoke constantly slashes the deep blue sky. To all appearances, the Chamberlains, so clean-cut, their blond-haired boys wearing T-shirts with their names on the back, were something of misfits in a locality where hard men drink to forget the drudgery of silver, copper, and lead production. In the 1950s it had been a bleak company town that had sprung up to house the few thousand employed in the copper mines. There were regular punch-ups in the pubs while the two cafés did a brisk trade in steaks for the brawny miners. As the town grew it cleaned up its image; new folk, like the Chamberlains, helped give it a more genteel air. A French restaurant opened and some of the pubs even managed to lay carpets. Nevertheless, it remained tough and the strangers stood out a mile, a handsome family.

Michael quickly threw himself into the life of the community, feeling he had an important message to get across. A keen runner, he wrote a weekly newspaper column under the heading "The Good Life." He was well qualified for this, as his physique showed the benefits of good living. His column discussed the advantages of health foods against alcohol and tobacco, and he took advantage of a radio program to further promote his beliefs on health. Their sixty Seventh Day Adventist parishioners enjoyed having such a young pastor in their midst—Michael was thirty-eight, Lindy thirty-four—and when Lindy gave birth to Azaria at the Mount Isa Maternity Hospital on June 11, 1980, the whole congregation prayed and gave thanks. Michael was overjoyed; his family was predominantly male and the couple, married for eleven years, were sure that the next child who came along would be another boy.

"You're kidding!" he exclaimed when told he was the father of a little girl. Lindy, too, was delighted. As a friend was to recall later: "It was the one she had always wanted, waited for. She put her whole heart into mothering her."

Because they saw the child as such a special gift they gave her a name which meant, by their interpretation, "blessed of God," or, by another meaning, "whom Jehovah aids." In the weeks to follow, Lindy, who firmly adhered to her husband's faith, settled down to writing to her friends, describing everything about the baby—she had fine brown hair, was nearly three kilograms at birth, and was exactly forty-seven centimeters long. Well aware that she wouldn't remain that small for long, Lindy put clothes on layaway at a local shop for when Azaria reached six months. And Michael, beaming like a man struck by a ray of heavenly light, told his friends and church associates that he was taking the whole family off for a holiday into the heart of the outback.

He had never been to Ayers Rock, but he'd heard Lindy talk about its fascination; she'd been there sixteen years earlier with her father, at the height of a drought, she remembered. She could still recall the day when one of the dingoes that roamed the area had come close to her and, although her father tried to scare it away, stood its ground defiantly, snarling.

On Wednesday, August 13, they packed their camping gear and set off for Ayers Rock. The car was cramped for a family of five, even if one was just a baby, but at least the vehicle was mechanically sound. They spent the first night at a tourist spot south of Tennant Creek known as the Devil's Marbles, a pile of huge red and black boulders. Michael, an avid photographer, with a camera bag full of lenses and filters, brought his single lens reflex out to take what was to be the first of many photographs he would capture over the next few days.

With their stay at Alice Springs cut short by the merrymakers at the Heavitree Park camping ground, and the long drive to Ayers Rock now behind them, the Chamberlains went to bed soon after their green and orange tent was erected. It had a ridged top and a low wall, with a built-in ground sheet and, although they were really packed in head to toe, they slept well. After all the driving, their holiday had now really begun.

Pushing out through the zippered flap in the morning, they were able to appreciate the lie of the land. They had found a good spot; the entrance faced the west, toward the barbecue area and the Rock, and the back looked on to Sunrise Hill, a nearby sand dune from which tourists take photographs of the first rays of sun striking the east face of the monolith. There were tents to the north and south of the Chamberlains; to the west of the row was a low post-and-rail fence that separated the tents from the barbecue area.

The boys were eager for breakfast, so the family made their way over to the barbecue where they were soon chatting with two of their fellow campers, Bill and Judith West of Esperance, Western Australia. With their twelve-year-old daughter Catherine, the Wests had driven some 1,200 kilometers from their sheep station to holiday at the Rock but one of their first experiences, they were to tell the Chamberlains as sausages sizzled on the grill, was rather alarming.

"We had an unusual experience yesterday," said Mrs. West. "Catherine was outside the tent, writing in her diary, when a dingo came close and actually put its mouth around her elbow."

Seeing the startled look on the Chamberlains' faces, she quickly assured them that Catherine had not been hurt. Then they got talking about children and Lindy brought Azaria over in her bassinet and told Mrs. West the meaning of the baby's name.

It was a great day for exploration—a big blue sky, not too hot. The Chamberlains drove around the perimeter before Michael, inspired like so many others before him, decided he was going to climb to the top. The safe route is just over a kilometer up and a painted line follows an anchored chain that gives a good handhold. A New Zealand athlete once baffled the locals by making it to the top in ten minutes, but for the average tourist it's a forty-minute haul. Michael, athletic and fit, made the summit with relative ease. He had left Lindy chatting with a woman tourist, Mrs. Florence Wilkin. When the boys disappeared, Lindy asked Mrs. Wilkin to mind Azaria for a moment while she went chasing after them. Mrs. Wilkin held the baby and noticed how contented she looked in her sleep, all dressed in pink. Not long afterward, Lindy handed Azaria to another couple, Gwen and Jack Eccles, grandparents from Victoria, while she headed up the rock after Michael and the boys. But she heard the baby cry and went back down to take her from the couple. Then she set off up the face again, this time carrying Azaria. Although her petite figure was rapidly returning, she was also carrying extra weight from the pregnancy and she managed to make it only thirty meters, to Chicken Rock, where the fearful usually change their minds and turn back down.

The movements of tourists such as the Chamberlains up and down the Rock had been monitored for a year by the Yankuntjatjara tribe who, the year earlier, had claimed Ayers Rock and the surrounding land. In 1980 the Aboriginal Land Commissioner, Justice Toohey, granted the tribe title to the area surrounding the Rock, but the giant landmark itself, he ruled, was alienated land. But there was nothing in the activities of the Chamberlains that morning to upset the guardian aborigines—they were simply a family enjoying themselves.

Michael and Lindy continued taking the children around the base of the Rock. Michael stopped to take pictures of the lichen and then they explored another area from the Dreamtime, the cavern known as the Fertility Cave. The boys shouted and laughed as their voices came echoing back. Then it was on farther west to the part of the Rock known as Maggie Springs, a natural waterhole also steeped in legend, fed by water pouring down the sandstone face after storms. The aboriginal Dreamtime legend says that if the waterhole became dry, the tribes would call "Kuka, Kuka" and the serpent guarding the waterhole would send a new torrent of water. It was at the waterhole that Lindy saw a dingo standing on a rock, silently watching them. It was a scene which was to become imprinted in her mind.

The Rock and its surroundings was territory for large numbers of dingoes, the wild desert dogs that came with the aborigines from the Asian continent thousands of years before the white explorers arrived in Australia. The tawny-colored dog with a distinctive bushy tail was not unlike a small German shepherd. But its haunts were the spinifex and rocks of the desert, its prey lizards, mice, and any small creature that moved. A cunning hunter, its habits were to be closely examined in the months and years to come as the world studied, dissected, and pronounced its varying verdicts on a tragedy that was soon to be played out in the heart of this scorched country, at the base of this awesome rock.

It had been a great day, and when they returned to the camping area young Reagan was ready for bed. Lindy, fighting her own tiredness, bathed him and his brother Aidan and sister Azaria and put the boys into their pajamas, while Michael wandered up onto the rise to take photographs of the sunset. His was one of many cameras that clicked in the warm red glow of the desert.

Reagan was out to the world as soon as he was in his sleeping bag. Lindy pulled up the zipper on the tent flap, then took Azaria and Aidan over to Michael, who was by now pottering around the barbecue, chatting with a few of the campers, including a young couple from Tasmania, Greg and Sally Lowe. The Lowes, Sally with her long plaited hair and brawny Greg, looking for all the part like a man who had stepped out of a timber mill, hit it off with the Chamberlains immediately. As Lindy sat on a rail at the barbecue nursing Azaria, they found out they'd all been to the same places during the day, which gave them plenty to chat about, and then they discovered, to their mutual astonishment, a coincidence with their babys' names. The Lowes, allowed a peek of Azaria's eyes and nose—all they could see above her blanket as Lindy held her—revealed how they named their baby Chantelle, a variant of Azaria's second name. Both mothers had never dreamed they would ever meet another child with a similar name.

Aidan wasn't interested in any of this. He'd had some food, but wanted more. He hung around the barbecue, sweeping the beam of a flashlight around the darkening sand. The light played on a mouse. As the shaft of light followed the tiny creature a dingo, a mangy, dusty specimen, wandered up to watch for a while. Suddenly the creature pounced, grabbed the mouse, and made off into the night. The Chamberlains were not only surprised; they were a little upset that a tiny creature had met its fate in the twinkling of an eye.

"How silently it moved," Lindy was to remember later. "How quickly it disappeared into the darkness with its prey."

"Hey," said Greg Lowe, "we didn't expect dingoes to come so close to the camping area." He and Sally made an instant decision to keep their little girl away from the bush area outside the railings, near where she was toddling about.

Azaria was now asleep in her mother's arms after patient rocking. It was time to take her back to the tent, Lindy told Michael—and Aidan would have to put his head down as soon as he had something else to eat.

He went with his mother back to the tent. Lindy, who was to be asked time and again what happened next, was to describe how she unzipped the tent flap and placed Azaria in the carry cot on the right-hand side, near the back of the tent. "She had both arms up beside her head with her face toward me. She stirred slightly and turned her face to the back of the tent. I tucked her in with the loose blanket securely. The blankets came up to within half an inch of the crown of her head."

Reagan, she was to recall, was still fast asleep. She ferreted around among the camping gear because Aidan was talking about wanting baked beans. She did not zip the flap up again, as she knew her son would be coming to bed as soon as supper was over. She then went to the car, found a can of baked beans, returned to the tent, and then proceeded on to the barbecue area.

It was now close to 8 P.M. Just how long she had been away at the tent putting Azaria into her bassinet and looking for baked beans in the car was to be a critical question, as critical as her actual movements. But now, as she stood at the barbecue holding the can opener, some of those with her were to say later that a sound penetrated the chilly night air. Sally Lowe heard it. Michael heard it. Aidan heard it—and he told his mother that he had heard Bubby, as the family referred to Azaria, cry.

"Was the baby settled?" Michael asked.

"I thought she was," said Lindy. But she said she'd go and check. She started walking back toward the tent, some twenty or twenty-five meters away, past the gas bottles. At that point, she was to relate time and again, she saw a dingo come out of the tent.

By her account, it was a youngish dog and it looked as though it had something in its mouth, or was playing with something at the tent entrance. From where Lindy had stopped momentarily in her tracks there was a full view of the tent area, but the railing and bushes hid the first meter or so up from the ground. She could therefore see the dingo only from its shoulders. From the tip of its nose downward, it was in darkness, but one thing she said she was sure of—it was shaking its head.

"Get out!" she yelled. "Go on—get out!"

Then she called to Michael: "A dingo's in the tent!"

She was to say later that she hurried toward the low railing, realizing that something awful might have happened. She knew that dingoes were wild animals and, if it was the baby's cry they had heard, the child might have been disturbed. By her account, when she got to

11

the railing, she could see into the tent. Azaria's blankets were scattered everywhere inside. Lindy instantly felt sick. Instinct told her the baby was gone, but hope told her it was not possible. She scrambled into the tent and felt inside the cot. She had been able to see the baby was no longer there, but she still felt inside, she was to tell police, just to make sure. In his sleeping bag, with the hood pulled up and his face in the pillow, young Reagan was still sleeping peacefully.

Her lips found words as she backed out. "The dingo's got my baby!" she cried.

Just then, she was to recall, she saw a dingo standing motionless and slightly behind the rear of the car. It had its back to her, but at a slight angle with its whole body visible. Its head was turned slightly, as if listening. As she approached, it ran swiftly at an angle to the right into the scrub, toward the sand hills. She didn't hear it move. The night was very quiet.

Hearing her cry, Michael, as she recalled the flow of events, had run straight from the cooking area into the scrub without a flashlight.

"It's no good. You can't see!" she cried. "You'll need a light." Then she shouted, shouted to anybody: "Has anybody got a flashlight? The dingo has got the baby. Has anybody got a flashlight?"

She remembered praying that other campers "wouldn't think I was drunk or joking." But three men came almost instantly with lights.

Michael came back and stood beside her. And suddenly, as they were to describe it, they felt the cold temperature of the desert night seep right into their bones. Pastor Chamberlain looked in the tent and, he was to tell police later, "all I could see was a horrible, lonely whiteness in that basket. . . . I was in a severe state of trauma. . . . I remember feeling very angry and frustrated." Frustrated because he did not have his keys to switch on his car lights.

Sally Lowe had found a flashlight and now thrust it into Greg's hand. He followed the beam into the stunted brush, looking for movement. Looking for a dingo with a baby in its mouth.

Then other lights flashed on as campers scrambled out of their tents. In hers, about thirty meters away, Judith West had heard Lindy's cry: "My God, the dingo's got my baby!" And minutes before she had heard a long, low growl—"a throaty growl," she was to remember—which she thought might have been a dog.

Michael Chamberlain, who likened the cry he had heard from the tent to that of a baby "squeezed for breath," ran to a tent from which he heard Christian music playing on a radio and, unceremoniously he thought, cried out: "A dingo has got our baby! If you have a flashlight, please come out and search. If you haven't, please pray."

Michael ran into the bush again to search, this time carrying a flashlight that seemed to him "pathetically inadequate." He stayed in the area searching, hoping, he was to recall, that Azaria might be under one of those bushes. "But all the time my heart was sinking."

Soon, as if the Lord had performed a miracle and created people out of bushes, some three hundred, many with flashlights, were running out into the darkness, their beams like dancing fireflies. It was more than just dark; it was pitch black without a breath of wind. Some of the searchers thought the atmosphere was "spooky."

Graham Seeley, who drives tourist buses for the Uluru Motel, one of the four resorts that were dotted around the Rock at the time, searched for a while, but thought things were creepy. Although there was no wind, some of the trees started moving, waving as if there was a breeze. Fired by the unimaginable, imaginations were running haywire.

Nurse Roberta "Bobbie" Downs, an attractive sandy-haired woman with big round spectacles, heard the story that was racing around the motels and the campsite. A dingo had taken a baby. Families were out searching, out there in that spinifex. She thought there was something eerie about the atmosphere that night. And her dog was unusually quiet. . . .

Instinctively, Nurse Downs got everything ready for an emergency and alerted the doctor in Alice Springs. She waited and waited, but nobody came to the clinic so finally she wandered across to Sunrise Hill where the search was being organized.

One of the local policemen, Senior Constable Frank Morris, who had arrived in the gray police four-wheel drive, its blue light flashing, went straight to the tent and crouched to look in as Lindy stood behind him. He saw the baby's empty bassinet, mattresses, and sleeping bags and thought how crowded it was. He also saw specks shining on a rug and concluded that he was looking at blood. Backing out, he found paw prints in the sand at the entrance. Although they faded out on the road he made up his mind that because the imprint of the claw was not visible, they were the prints of a dingo. Constable Morris found Nurse Downs and brought her across to Lindy, whom she thought was shocked and quite cold. But Michael turned down her invitation to go to a nearby hotel, telling her that they should wait while the search proceeded. Nurse Downs went to the motel anyway to see to a room. The Chamberlains were going to need it sometime, that was for sure.

The senior ranger at the Rock, Derek Roff, a white-bearded Yorkshireman who had been in the Kenyan police force before he came to the Australian outback, arrived at the camping ground within five minutes of receiving a phone call about the alarm. He found the Chamberlains near the tent that was now illuminated by a gas lamp young Catherine West had fitted to a pole. Michael stepped forward when Roff asked what the problem was.

"Our baby girl has been taken by a dingo and we are fully reconciled to the fact that we will never see our baby alive again. The dingo would have killed the child immediately, would it not?"

Roff needed more facts before he hit the panic button. He asked Lindy if she had seen anything in the dingo's mouth. No, she had not. In that case, was she sure the baby was not in the tent somewhere?

She led him across to the tent, where Reagan still lay in his sleeping bag, and knelt down among the scattered blankets. Her emotions cracked as she cried, "She's not here; she's not here."

Roff decided to get some organization into the search. He called the crowd that was stumbling around in all directions out in the brush to a briefing. About forty-five minutes ago, he told them, a small baby was taken from a tent and it was thought a dingo was responsible. The animal had headed southeast, he said. He instructed the volunteers to form a line search, so that each person was no more than a couple of yards from the next. Any clues at all would be helpful—clothing, tracks, anything. . . .

Smokey Paull didn't need to be told how to search. The bushy-bearded, longtime outback resident who had worked around the Rock for eight years on stations and driving graders, his Queensland blue heeler, Lucky, at his side, knew all about grid searches. He made sure he kept the volunteers in some form of order. He bent low to search for tracks that the dingo could have made in the dust. He went about his work dutifully, for he thought it quite probable that a dingo could have taken the baby. For a start, he didn't think there were any wild dogs in the district, although dingoes sometimes mated with domestic animals or feral dogs. But the offspring were such a menace that they were hunted down and shot. Smokey Paull's mind was open: dingoes would attack only for food, but wild dogs would kill for blood. And there were the mongrels that lurked around the aboriginal camps on the edge of the tourist camping areas. Paull knew there hadn't been much food about during that August, for it was very cold at night and the lizards, their staple diet, were still in hibernation. Dingo bitches were whelping and they would be hungry. If they had food, Paull considered as he pushed through the spinifex, and knew they were being followed, they would plant it and return for it later. He was also aware that dingoes were strong and could very well carry a baby a long way. He paused and listened. Apart from the movement of other searchers to the left and right of him there was no sound out there in the desert. If a dingo had taken baby Azaria, the child must surely be dead by now.

Up by their tent the Chamberlains stood with Sally Lowe, Judy West, and the woman who had been listening to the Christian music on the radio, Amy Whittacker. Judy had made the Chamberlains hot chocolate but Lindy had refused, saying she couldn't keep it down. Michael broke the tension of the moment by asking their fellow campers if it would be rude of them to go off by themselves for a minute. When they returned from what Judy thought was the barbecue area Michael said, "I'd like us all, if we could, to pray."

And then, placing his hands on his wife's head, he

16

said, "Let us all now remember that this is not the time for anger or for bitterness."

Aidan stood by the tent crying. "Don't let the dingo eat our baby," he sobbed. Sally Lowe tried to comfort him and led him in through the flaps. As she poked her head in she saw a smear of blood on a mattress. When Aidan noticed it he told her that Reagan was dead. But she quickly assured him he wasn't, reaching across to Aidan's younger brother to wake him. The action caused Aidan to think again about Azaria. He wailed: "The dingo has our Bubby in its tummy."

Police, rangers, and black trackers had now joined the campers in the search. Someone went to fetch the tribal statesman, Nipper Winmarti, who was now in his seventies with hair as white as salt. They knew his eyes weren't up to it anymore but he still had the bush skills developed over his long life. There was a better man than he, Captain Number Two, but it was so cold that no one could tempt him from his camp.

Like Smokey Paull, old Nipper knew a lot about dingoes and the legends that went with them. He had heard of bad spirits taking children from their mothers in the night, and now people were saying that a white baby had been taken. Nipper set to work and found a trail. But it faded.

Constable Morris spoke gently to Lindy, asking her to describe what the baby had been wearing. Everything was white, she told him. Azaria had on a disposable diaper with a plastic cover, a singlet, a jumpsuit, and booties. Morris decided to put the stark facts to them. They should understand that if the baby was not found quickly, she wouldn't survive in that bitterly cold temperature.

"There is nothing anyone can do about the will of God," said Michael. Then he added: "Our daughter

17

should be brought back to us, no matter what condition you find her in. We want her back."

As the night wore on and the temperature dropped ever farther, campers formed the opinion that Michael and Lindy Chamberlain were already resigned to the fact that Azaria was dead. But, as Lindy wept, Michael told Judith West's husband, William: "We can handle this; we are people of God."

Sometime after midnight Bobbie Downs came back to the tent area in the police truck along with an officer. Now the Chamberlains indicated they were ready to go with her to the motel. Their camping gear—an array of clothing, sleeping bags, blankets—was loaded into the bed of the vehicle. Lindy emptied away a solution from an ice cream container in which the baby bottle nipples were being cleansed. Although there was room for Lindy and the boys with the police driver in the truck cab, Michael and Bobbie couldn't fit. Michael told her to ride with him in the family Torana.

When she got in, Bobbie noticed Michael's camera bag tucked in behind his legs on his side. She offered to take it.

"It's OK," he replied. "I always keep it here."

Cold and pale, the family went into the Uluru Motel and closed their door on the evil blackness of the night.

II

Recall

The Rock had hardly changed from its dawn purple when words whizzed through the airwaves and hummed along telephone lines. The press was knocked out. It was sensational. A pastor's baby had been snatched by a dingo at Ayers Rock. It was almost too bizarre to be true. One of those stories you made up headlines about, knowing it could never really happen.

The staff at the motel were loath to allow the Chamberlains to be bothered by what they felt was unwelcome intrusion, but Michael entered the office and said he was quite willing to talk to the papers and television stations. "I felt at the time, because of the extraordinary nature of the tragedy, I should help where I could," he was to explain later.

Michael Chamberlain had in fact arranged to use the radio telephone that morning at 7 A.M. so that he and Lindy could notify their respective parents. It wasn't until 7:30 that he entered the office and it was clear to the staff that he and his wife accepted that Azaria was gone forever. He did not ask how the search had gone. First Lindy spoke to her parents. She gave it to them straight.

"Our baby was killed by a dingo last night," she said

softly into the telephone. But she lost her composure when she spoke to her brother and broke down in sobs.

Next, Michael telephoned his mother. The manager of the Uluru Motel, Alan Barber, couldn't help overhearing Michael: "Our daughter Azaria has been killed by a dingo and we don't expect to ever find her body."

Nurse Downs spent the morning with the Chamberlains. It was obvious to her that Lindy had been crying and was very upset. Once she found her weeping over a photograph of Azaria. "Nine weeks of joy," Lindy cried.

Michael, felt Bobbie Downs, was struggling to hold back his emotions for the sake of his wife. But both were equally pessimistic, believing the baby was gone.

Although the phones were running hot that morning, the calls weren't all directly for the Chamberlains. Some time between 8 and 9 A.M. Bert Couzens of Alice Springs received a call from Townsville. Bert and his wife Norma went to The Alice in 1980 to run the Seventh Day Adventist church there with its congregation of thirty. They had been in Papua New Guinea, the New Hebrides (now Vanuatu), and Fiji for twenty years as missionaries. The call Bert took that morning from Townsville was from Pastor Harold Parker and he had some sad news about two of their brethren.

"Yes, I've heard of the Chamberlains just a week ago from Judy Hughes, a church member who knows them from Mount Isa," said Bert. "She told us what fine folk they were. What's happened?"

"They're at Ayers Rock," said Parker. "A dingo or some other dog took their baby last night. There's been a search, but there's been no trace of the child. They need our prayers."

"Well, we're the nearest ministers," said Bert. "We'll set off for the Rock immediately."

When the Couzenses arrived after the long drive they found the Chamberlains standing among a group outside the Uluru Motel.

"We've given up hope," Michael Chamberlain said sadly and repeated the story he had already told many times to the enquiring reporters. He had told journalists that "we have given up hope that we will see our baby on this earth again, but we know we will see her in the resurrection."

After hearing the short, sharp cry from the tent, he said, "the next thing we saw was a dingo coming out of the tent where Azaria had been sleeping. It had something in its mouth, but it was too dark to see.

"My wife rushed into the tent and was shocked to see the baby was gone. We chased the dingo, but the terrain was too bad and there was no moon. The temperature was subzero.

"I'm an experienced bush walker and I'm sure the animal that took Azaria was a dingo. Whatever took her was smooth and powerful, with sharp teeth, because it bit through thick blankets."

As he repeated the story for the benefit of the Couzenses, Michael wept, although he still struggled to maintain his composure. Lindy, who filled in some of the story, had to stop sometimes in the middle of a sentence.

"I only hope the baby's death has not been prolonged," said Michael. He then asked Bert Couzens to do him a favor—get rid of the tent, burn it down, do what he liked, because he just didn't want to see it again. Michael saw the tent now as a morgue. He did ask, though, for the tent pegs, because they could be used with another tent they had left in Alice Springs. But Bert Couzens didn't have to worry about the tent—the police had already moved in before him to dismantle it. They did, however, hand over the tent pegs and later Couzens dropped them into the Chamberlains' Torana.

Michael gave a long interview to a reporter who flew up from Adelaide. "When we saw spots of blood in the tent," he said, "we realized it must have been a very quick event. The sharp, jagged marks in that thickly woven blanket. . . . We knew it was a powerful beast with sharp teeth. It was more than a domestic dog that did that, and it was confirmed in our minds that it was a very powerful, sly, and wily beast. It had probably stalked the baby. . . . It had premeditated it, we think."

Senior Constable Morris was also talking to the newspapers. He told of finding traces of blood inside the tent.

"There are tear marks in the blanket that was covering the baby in the basket," he said. "Whatever happened, there is no chance the baby could have survived the night in the freezing temperatures after it was taken. We have got to get that particular animal. We can't let it roam around the campground any longer."

Derek Roff, the chief ranger, also did some talking. Dingoes, he said, often roamed near the camping ground. "They are encouraged by tourists who feed them, despite notices we have erected saying that the animals should not be fed." Why, only two weeks earlier, he had reported to his superiors his concern about dingoes. They were a danger to children and babies in the area, and he had recommended that the public be educated that the animal was a hunter, a scavenger, and an opportunist. He had even gone so far as to ask to be provided with bullets, so that threatening dingoes could be shot.

The Chamberlains did not want to stay around at the Rock. Accepting the child's death, they made preparations to leave the following day, Tuesday. But Michael declared they would like to leave a memory behind. He and his wife would have a small monument to Azaria erected at the Rock.

Before they could leave, however, they had to repeat the story again, this time officially. Inspector Michael Gilroy and Sergeant John Lincoln had traveled down from Alice Springs to interview them.

Sitting in room 34 of the Uluru Motel, as Lincoln tended the tape recorder, Lindy gave Inspector Gilroy her full identification—Alice Lynne Chamberlain of Able Smith Parade, Sunset, Mount Isa. At first, she had difficulty remembering whether they had left for their holiday on the previous Tuesday morning or on Wednesday. She described how they had traveled in the car, stopping at the Devil's Marbles and at Alice Springs. She then came to their arrival at Ayers Rock.

"We stayed in the public camping area—right at the back of the camping area. The camp when we came here was fairly full and because of the baby we wanted to pick a quiet area and there were some spots at the back that were empty, so we stayed up there right next to the bush area. We have a four-man pup tent and the five of us were staying in that."

The police officer wanted to know where they had had a meal and when they had decided to bed down for the night.

"Well," said Lindy, fidgeting with her wedding ring, "I bathed the kids early because we wanted to see the sunset and it would be dark when we got back, so they were all in their pajamas ready to go to bed. We had climbed the Rock earlier in the day. Both the little boys had gone up and they were very tired, and as soon as we came back from the sunset Reagan, the second boy, said he was too tired for his tea. Actually, he went to sleep in the car on the way home, so I put him straight to bed

23

and zipped the tent up. The baby was a little bit troubled with the wind, and I had her in my arms."

Her husband, she said, got the tea in the barbecue area, which was directly opposite the tent. "He was cooking the tea and I was sitting on the rail, watching him cook the tea and calming the baby; and I got her off to sleep and I nursed her in my arms for about half an hour while she was asleep. While we were there we noticed a dingo coming to the barbecue area and it . . . there was a little mouse we were trying to see with the flashlight and it came right up to within eighteen inches or two feet of our feet. We were looking at it . . . a gentleman and another family having their meal. He and I were discussing this mouse and, all of a sudden, the dingo pounced on it right beside us and took it off, and we did not see the dingo again.

"My oldest son had his tea and said he was tired and wanted to go to bed. I said to him, 'Bubby's asleep and I will have to put her down before I have my tea, so I will take you both up,' because the light of the barbecue shone directly into our tent and you could see the kiddies in the tent from where we were, and it was very close and the night air out here carries—you can hear every little move they make. So I took them both up and I put her down in her carry basket and then he said he was still hungry after climbing the Rock—that's Aidan, the oldest boy—and he would like some more tea, so I said I would get him some. He was going to stay there and I said to him he may as well come with Mummy. And I unzipped the tent and he was still in the tent."

Lindy added, without interruption from Inspector Gilroy, that she walked to the car and got out a tin of baked beans.

"I thought baked beans would fill him up as an extra,

and I came back to the tent and said, 'Come on,' and we walked down to the barbecue area and I put the tin down and picked up the can opener; and my husband said to me: 'Is that Bubby crying?' I think. 'Didn't she go to sleep?' And I said: 'I don't know; I can't hear her' and I walked back up and I said: 'I will go and see anyway.'

"And I walked back up toward the tent and got half-way there—it wouldn't be any more than the distance of this room away from the tent—and I saw the dingo come out of the tent and the light didn't shine on the lower part of the tent in the front because the bushes blocked it. I saw the dingo from about shoulder up and he sort of looked as if he— I thought he had got a fright and heard me coming with having trouble getting out the tent flaps. He sort of had difficulty to get out, and I immediately—I didn't realize he was in there and I thought the crying—he has disturbed the baby; he might have savaged it. The thought went through my mind because I had heard of them bite—that they had been biting around here and then I, he— I yelled at it to get out of the road and it took fright and ran in front of our car which was parked right next to the tent. But I didn't sort of keep looking at it. I dived straight for the tent to see what had made the baby cry, and when I got in the tent her blankets were—the three, the bunny rug and the two thick blankets she had around her—were scattered from one end of the tent to the other. Some of them were on Reagan so the dingo must have walked on his feet; at least walked right past him."

Lindy was just talking on. The policeman let her continue.

"The baby was sleeping at his feet in her carry basket. It must have walked right past him to get to the baby and taken the baby out. It was empty. There was noth-

25

ing there, and I called my husband straight away. I came straight out of the tent and called to him at the door that the dingo had taken the baby, and chased it. I could still see it. I chased it into the bush and followed it and, as I got to the edge of the road, the light did not carry any further than that. I saw where it went into the bush and I realized it was no good. As soon as I called out to my husband 'The dingo's got the baby' he came running, and he ran straight up into the bush but he never stopped to get a flashlight, and realized it was dark."

There Lindy paused. Inspector Gilroy, asking his questions gently, said, "Could you tell me when you actually saw the dingo go across the road; do you mean the road across into the bush on the other side from where your tent was?"

Lindy replied: "The tent was pitched on the edge of the road. There was only tents on one side of it. The opposite side of the tent was bush and the tent was facing the fire, so it was behind the tent that the dingo went."

"And did you actually see anything in the dingo's mouth?"

"No, I didn't see anything in the dingo's mouth because that was below the level of the light. It sort of had its head down and coming out of the tent—I thought it was just shaking its head to get past the thing. It was obviously because it had a heavy— It (the baby) had a little toweling stretch suit on, and often my other two used to wear toweling suits and often when they were bigger and crawling I would pick them up by the back. They are very strong, and it is quite easy to pick them up by the back, in which case the toweling stretches and the baby would be maybe six inches from the mouth if he was carrying her like that. It looked to me to be a youngish dog and certainly a very fit dog. It didn't— It struck me as perhaps not being the one that was by the campfire earlier because it looked mangy and this one was very young and very strong."

At this point Michael Chamberlain said, "I thought it was the same dog, but it may not have been the same dog now that I think about it—not that I saw the dog."

"Are both of your minds clear that it was a dingo?" asked Inspector Gilroy.

Lindy said, "Yes, definitely. We have done a lot of camping out and seen a lot of dingoes—and we saw some more this afternoon—and we said to people to make sure that we knew that's what it was that we thought it was a dingo. We have asked others—a truck driver out here."

Michael said, "We saw them at dusk tonight and, just to make sure of our own sanity on this, we asked others, 'Now, do you think that is a dingo, because in our opinion that is a dingo.' And they said, 'Too right, that's a dingo.'"

Inspector Gilroy checked the Chamberlains' eyesight. "Do you wear optical lenses or glasses?" he asked.

"Both of us have excellent eyesight," said Lindy.

The police officer then asked Lindy to draw him a sketch of the area to show where the tent was, where the car was parked, and the direction the dingo had taken. As the sketch was being drawn, Michael said, "See, the thing is—the process of elimination. OK, if anyone says it is not a dingo, what would it be that could do that? That's my question. I believe it was. I didn't see it. My wife did. But what other creature would do that?"

"As opposed to a camp dog, an aboriginal dog . . . ?"

"That's right."

"Or a—"

"The alternatives are frightening. If there is an alternative."

Lindy asked how long it took to walk twenty-one meters, the distance from the barbecue area to the tent, and then answered her own question: "Not very long." She added: "My estimation would be—I was away from the tent a minute and a half, a few minutes at the most before I went back to check on her; and it was too late. So the dog must have been lurking behind the car, around the car, somewhere near, and we think now there was a— I know a lot of the dogs look alike, but we have seen a young, very nice-looking dog. At least there was another family walking around the Rock. My husband was not there but the two little boys were, and I had the baby in my arms over at the cave—in the afternoon. It was standing down looking and it was almost as if the dog had been casing the baby out. . . . She had just been bathed earlier and she smelt lovely and sweet and clean and—"

"Can you tell if there was a tear on the left-hand flap by the zip previously?" asked the policeman, trying to steer her away from a distressing subject.

Yes, said Lindy, the zip had been torn previously and the tent was open. "It had been shut before I went up, but I left it just for that little while because I intended to go straight back. I was going to tidy the camp out. I took one sleeping bag out so I could get up to the baby and back and my sleeping bag wasn't there and I was going to tidy it out right ready to hop straight into bed after tea because we were very tired ourselves."

Although he had been talking occasionally to Michael, Inspector Gilroy now formally asked him his full name. Michael told him, adding, "I am an ordained pastor of the Seventh Day Adventist church."

The police officer asked him about the baby's cry. Michael answered, "It was a short, sharp cry that I heard, and this is what attracted my attention. My wife ran, more or less—just walked up, actually, I think, didn't you?" His question was directed at Lindy.

"I walked the first ten meters until I saw the dog—" she began.

"And then," said Michael, "we knew there were real problems."

Inspector Gilroy asked Azaria's date of birth and was told June 11, 1980. To his question about Azaria's state of health, Lindy replied: "She had a tiny chest cold; not very much. She was very snuffly in her nose. The whole family is a little snuffly in the nose."

"Any medical problems since birth?"

"No, she's been fit and healthy," said Lindy.

The Alice Springs police officer wanted to know when the baby was fed prior to her going missing. Lindy said she was feeding the child while they were watching the sunset. "At half past six I started to feed her. She usually takes—she took her time last night. She sort of fed off and on over about an hour, so it would—"

"You were breast-feeding her?"

"I breast-feed her and comp feed her S26, and she would have had a feed of about two hundred to two-fifty milliliters, so she would have been very full of food."

Asked how dark it was when she saw the dog, Lindy said it was "fully dark." There was a half moon, but it was not giving any light. The only light source was from the barbecue area.

She had actually chased the animal?

"Yes, I chased the dingo. I yelled at it when I first saw it. I didn't chase it when I first saw it. I yelled at it

29

because I thought it had just been in the tent and I had called it soon enough. I had frightened it coming—and the baby's cry—I thought maybe it had bitten it like biting around here—more likely savaged it because I knew that the only thing that was out was a little head. She was in very thick blankets, double continental-weave, two-sided ones; and I dived straight in the tent first to see if there was anything I could do. I never thought of him taking her. I thought perhaps he had killed her in her little basket. I thought immediately that—we'd both done first aid, and my first thought was that if she was bleeding there might be some hope of saving her with some direct action. And then when I got in, it looked as if it was empty, and I went straight in and saw she wasn't there and knew that the dog must have it; and I sort of went straight out and I felt the things just in case it was—she was—under something that I couldn't see. She is so tiny. I knew in myself that she wasn't there, and I came out to chase the dog. He sort of waited just the other side of the car almost, because he hadn't seemed to have moved and as I came around the car he took off and he would have been ten to fifteen meters ahead of me, and when I came around the corner he moved fast."

Lindy said ten meters was the closest she got to the dog. Asked about Azaria's weight, her mother said that a week and a half before they went to Ayers Rock she was one ounce under nine pounds, but with the way she had been gaining she would say she was now ten pounds. Asked about the child's clothing, Lindy said she was wearing a Johnson's disposable diaper, a kind that had only been out a few weeks, and a little Bonds ribbed singlet. Her matinee jacket was a Marquise but the booties did not carry a brand name. And then, said Lindy, there was Azaria's little stretch suit. She was not sure whether that was Bonds or another brand, but it was one of the more expensive ones, "with the little pieces that flip over their hands when it is cold, and I had that folded over her hands so she was all rugged up to the neck."

Constable Morris, who had earlier briefed Inspector Gilroy, had made no mention of a matinee jacket and this was the first time he had heard of it. But he did not remark on the fact. His attention was taken by Michael who said he had wondered if "the animal that attacked her did have probably very sharp teeth, and again I think that this is another reason why probably the death of the child was very quick."

"We feel it was an instant death," said Lindy.

She then recalled the search, observing at first that "if she had been alive at all we would have heard some sort of whimper or cry from her, and there was nothing." She said that when she called to Michael he did not stop to get a flashlight. He ran, said, "Where?" and she said, "The dingo's gone in there."

Lindy continued: "I think I called out again that the dingo had my baby and then I said to Michael that there was no flashlight, that we would have to get [one] and the thought flashed through my mind that it was no good going to caravans and telling people, 'Could you please come and help,' so I just stood there and screamed out, 'If anybody's got a flashlight . . . dingo . . . baby!' They came immediately. There was—it was almost as if they had been sitting there with flashlights in their laps. There were four blokes out of their tents just immediately that went straight up and the man that was at the barbecue with us . . . he was there, just a few seconds afterward. And Michael went, rushed back, and got his flashlight and he went up and they combed the area, and the lady from the next caravan, she came out and said, 'Has anyone gone for the police?' I said, 'No, they're up there looking,' while it—you know—while it was close enough. Because we thought, well, he must have dropped her; at least we will get her body back, or maybe she's alive and unconscious. She went; her husband, I think he might have been in bed actually. He came out and hopped straight in the car and went for the police and they contacted the ranger and they were there, it can't have been any more than fifteen minutes, and by that time there would have been twenty or thirty people out searching. In an hour, there were nearly two hundred out there. We searched ourselves. About eleven to eleven-thirty P.M. we searched ourselves."

Michael Chamberlain said, "I'd like to pay tribute to the people who went out so quickly and so voluntarily and anyone who was able to go out appeared to be on the way out and it was very heartening to see it; very grateful." He added that Senior Constable Frank Morris was very good and they would like to commend him on his action.

"The nurse stayed with us," said Lindy, "and she's been here again this morning for about half a day. Everybody's been terrific to us."

The conversation with Inspector Gilroy was almost over. But he asked if there was anything else they would like to say. Yes, Michael had an observation.

"I have listened very carefully to a lot of people about their comments regarding this incident. I wouldn't be so unkind as to say that some would try and defend a dingo, and look at you and consider that you are a bit daft suggesting it's a dingo. But I have noticed that some of the more authoritative people have been the ones to try and knock the idea; not openly—through innuendos . . . well, not innuendos, but questioning;

32

whereas when you talk to the people who have lived here and know the dingo, none of them have been at all surprised."

Lindy had more to add on the subject: "The only thing that I can think of is that it's the campers trying to make pets of them. That's encouraged them to come in so close. They say that it's an aboriginal reserve and it's a protected area for the dingoes. It's their breeding ground, and we had read the notice in the toilets that said the dingoes belong to the aboriginals, and that they were protected and were around the aboriginal camp, but there had been incidents of biting and to not feed them; and it was obvious in the way that they came in so close and so friendly—it was only—there was one just out here tonight as well. But it was encouragement by humans that brought them in. . . ."

Michael had one more comment. "I like dingoes and I have to confess that when I saw those notices in the toilet, I was a bit blasé myself. As a matter of fact, I'm ashamed to admit that I even attempted to feed one of those dogs when it came into the barbecue last night, only about fifteen minutes before that happened, so I've got nothing against dingoes. The other thing is that my suggestion would be, even though expensive, but perhaps one of the alternatives to keep these dogs away would be to have a dingo-proof fence around the camping area."

That chilly Monday night, August 18, police and rangers maintained a vigil at the Rock. Their purpose: to shoot dingoes on sight. Some eighteen to twenty dingoes regarded the campsite area as their territory; the first to die was a young dingo that wandered within a few meters of a campfire, sniffing the ground for food. A single shot from a policeman's rifle brought it down.

Shortly afterward another dingo was shot down less than one hundred meters away. Two wild dogs were also included in the night's kill.

The purpose of the shoot was to provide carcasses for autopsies to search for traces of human remains—Azaria's remains. Ranger Iaw Cawood, who was spotlighting for dingoes—using a powerful beam to transfix them—told police working alongside him that local dingoes had lost their fear of man. They would feed out of the hand, but they were still a wild animal that would grab food whenever the opportunity arose.

He also made his feelings public: "They are not domestic dogs like many tourists seem to think. I don't know whether we will overcome the problem except to shoot all dingoes in the immediate area. But this is their natural environment and it will be an ongoing problem until people refrain from feeding them."

The Chamberlains greeted Tuesday with a short service in their tiny motel room, Michael quoting from the First Epistle of Paul to the Thessalonians:

> For this we say unto you by the word of the Lord, that we which are alive and remain unto the coming of the Lord shall not prevent them which are asleep.
> For the Lord himself shall descend from heaven with a shout, with the voice of the archangel, and with the trump of God: and the dead in Christ shall rise first:
> Then we which are alive and remain shall be caught up together with them in the clouds, to meet the Lord in the air: and so shall we ever be with the Lord.
> Wherefore comfort one another with these words.

The interviews over, their acceptance of the child's death plain to everyone, the Chamberlains were free to leave the Rock, free to go home. Pastor Couzens turned up and took photographs of the area, a record of the hopelessness of finding anything in daylight, let alone in the dark. He also asked Inspector Gilroy if he could take photographs of the shot dingoes, including close-ups of the head and jaws of one suspected of being the culprit, because Michael had said he wanted the pictures for a book so he could warn people about the dangers of dingoes. The request, however, was turned down—the shot animals already had been sent to Alice Springs to have the contents of their stomachs examined.

The Chamberlains packed their belongings "with a heavy heart," they were to say later, for among the collection of camping gear was Azaria's empty carry cot. Before leaving, they stopped at the local store—Lindy wanted to buy a few mementos, *not* souvenirs, she later insisted. They purchased, to the amazement of some, teacups and T-shirts with an Ayers Rock motif on them for Lindy's young nephew. Michael had taken pictures of some of those who had helped in the search, and he also snapped a shot of Nurse Bobbie Downs. Then they were ready.

Only two full days had passed since their baby daughter had disappeared, but Michael was to ask later, "What more could we do?" And Lindy was to tell friends that she was able to leave because she had found strength and comfort in a passage from one of the Seventh Day Adventists' handbooks, *The Great Controversy*, which read: "Little children are borne by holy angels to their mothers' arms. Friends long separated by death are united, nevermore to part, and with songs of gladness ascend together to the City of God."

Lindy and Bert Couzens had talked about that passage for a while. She had learned that the Couzenses had lost their own first baby, a boy, just a few weeks old, in Tasmania in 1947. They had cried in private, but not in public.

Before he turned the yellow Torana on the road to Alice Springs, Michael told the police that he and Lindy would return for the coroner's inquest.

"Then," he said, "we will look at the possibility of erecting a monument for our baby girl. A monument may serve as some sort of warning to the parents of other children who come to this area. We have accepted Azaria's death as the will of God. God has willed it, so that's how it must be. My faith has allowed me to accept this tragic incident. I don't think they will find any sign of our little Azaria. . . ."

III

That We Might Find Strength

During the confusion of that Sunday night when Azaria vanished, Judith West had offered Lindy Chamberlain a hot chocolate drink, but the bereft mother told her she was feeling too sick to drink it. If it had been coffee or tea she would have refused that, too, for the Seventh Day Adventist church advocates a life of strict temperance—no alcohol or tobacco and abstinence, whenever possible, from tea, coffee, and meat.

Lindy, who had lived in the Victorian towns of Horsham, Ararat, Benalla, Mildura, and Swan Hill, married Pastor Michael Chamberlain in 1969, when she was twenty-three. For her wedding she wore a white gown with a long train, an outfit that, as a qualified tailoress, she made herself. She knew the church would be moving Michael around from time to time and when they eventually ended up in Mount Isa she busied herself setting up what would be their home for the next few years. The house adjoined the Seventh Day Adventist church where Michael, adhering to the teachings of the staunch Protestant body, preached that the Scriptures provide the unerring rule of faith and that Christ's return is imminent.

In fact, His return had been at hand from the first half of the nineteenth century, when an American, William Miller, proclaimed that the world was nearing its end and that a fiery conflagration would usher in a new heaven and a new earth. Miller set a date for this terrifying conclusion—some time between March 21, 1843, and March 21 the following year. The deadline passed uneventfully, so another date was set for seven months later.

With the Apocalypse nearing, Miller gained a following of some 75,000, but when October came and went without fire, Miller began to lose support. However, one of his followers then claimed to have had a vision and he told those prepared to listen that he had seen Christ entering the second compartment of heaven. Hiram Edson claimed that his vision proved that Miller had not been wrong. He added, though, that there was to be no second coming; what his vision meant was that a judgment had begun in heaven to ascertain who among the dead were worthy of resurrection.

Meanwhile, others who had been influenced by Miller felt that Christ's second coming had simply been held up by their own failure to keep the seventh day—from sundown on Friday to sundown Saturday—as the Sabbath. Prominent among these was Ellen G. White, who was to die in 1915. Although she had had a poor education, she wrote forty-five major books and more than four thousand articles; one work, *Steps to Christ,* sold more than five million copies in eighty-five languages. Founded in the New England states, the Adventists moved west, and by 1863 they were fully organized with headquarters in Michigan.

The human body, their missionaries proclaimed, was a temple of the Holy Spirit. Salvation came by grace through faith alone. Today, Adventists believe that the "end of age" is still due; thus they have a responsibility to proclaim their message throughout the world and generally work for the growth of the church. At "the end," the righteous dead will be raised and, along with the righteous living, will be ushered into heaven where they will spend the Millennium. For the next thousand years Satan will be left on earth and at the end of this time Christ will descend, bringing with Him His saints to destroy the wicked with fire. A new earth will be created, and at its center will be the New Jerusalem.

As well as suggesting members pay tithes on their income, Adventists emphasize the need for care of the body and abstaining from foods forbidden in the Old Testament—pork and shellfish. The church is also against gambling and secret societies and discourages the use of jewelry and cosmetics. Members are also encouraged to avoid what they consider "worldly entertainments"—the movies, theater and television.

Adventists are very much concerned with the state of man after death, believing in "soul sleep." They interpret the biblical word *soul* as meaning the entire individual, not only the nonmaterial aspect of the body. In death, they say, the condition of man is one of unconsciousness. All men, good and evil alike, remain in the grave from death to the resurrection.

One Seventh Day Adventist writer has put it this way, and his words help to explain what Michael Chamberlain meant when he said he would see Azaria in the resurrection: "The teaching of the Bible regarding the intermediate state of man is plain. Death is really and truly a sleep, a sleep that is deep, that is unconscious, that is unbroken until the awakening at the resurrection.

"In death, man enters a state of sleep. The language of the Bible makes clear that it is the whole man which sleeps, not merely a part. No intimation is given that man sleeps only as to his body, and that he is wakeful and conscious as to his soul. All that comprises the man sleeps in death."

A Seventh Day Adventist book, *Questions on Doctrine,* points out that it is believed that the time interval between death and the resurrection is negligible, since there is no existence at all after death: "While asleep in the tomb, the child of God knows nothing. Time matters not to him. If he should be there a thousand years, the time would be to him as but a moment. One who serves God closes his eyes in death, and whether one day or 2,000 years elapse, the next instant in his consciousness will be when he opens his eyes and beholds his blessed Lord. To him it is death—then sudden glory."

It seemed to many who watched the Chamberlains during the thirty-six hours after Azaria vanished that they found great strength in their beliefs. They did not keep themselves in their motel room, locking themselves in with their misery, noted those who observed them. Instead, they spoke matter-of-factly to searchers, campers, and the police. They saw no hope of finding Azaria, but they listened carefully to all the reports that came in of dingo tracks around the camping area. One of the rangers had pointed out to them that the dingo marks were easily recognizable because the animal, careful to protect its valuable "killing" claws from damage, kept them curled up away from the ground, leaving only the imprints of the pads.

When the Chamberlains arrived back in Mount Isa, Michael's congregation was joined by the general community in passing on their sympathies. But it wasn't easy for the family to settle back into a normal life, for they were plagued by journalists whose news editors had become intrigued by the bizarre circumstances surrounding Azaria's disappearance. The Chamberlains were friendly, but kept their comments to a minimum.

Eight days after Azaria's disappearance, Wallace Goodwin, a thirty-four-year-old tourist from North Dandenong, Victoria, strolled along a narrow track leading through the scrub at the southwest corner of the Rock. Wandering with his wife and two children, Wally was intent on photographing the wildlife. Sometime around 4 P.M., close to a large boulder, he noticed a jumble of clothing. A closer inspection confirmed his immediate thoughts—here lay a bloodstained jumpsuit, diaper, singlet, and booties; these had to be the clothes of Azaria Chamberlain, the baby they were all talking about. His first horrifying impression, from the way the clothing lay, was that the child had been eaten out of the clothes. Just how the garments were positioned and the way they appeared to him when he stumbled across them was to be a matter of critical difference of opinion between him and Senior Constable Frank Morris. But there was to be no disputing the distance from the campsite—when measured it was just over four kilometers.

It was Morris whom Goodwin found when he hastened back to the police station to report his find. The policeman, ever aware that this was the most unusual case he had dealt with, brushed through the spinifex and shrubs, studied the clothing for a while, then looked at the whole area. Some twenty meters away was a narrow dingo lair, a refuge created by fallen boulders and ringed with dingo tracks. On the face of it, the mysterious disappearance of Azaria Chamberlain had been solved. The policeman turned again to the clothing. Just how many, if any, of the snaps were undone was to be a matter of dispute, as was the question of

41

whether the baby's singlet was inside the suit or beside it. But there was no disputing that the singlet was found inside out; neither was there any disputing the dried blood around the collar and the tears in the material around the neck area.

Goodwin noticed the policeman's hands were trembling as he felt into the jumpsuit; he thought this was because the officer expected to find a foot. The booties were still inside the legs, but that was all. No skin, no bones—not a shred of human evidence, apart from the bloodstains. Morris arranged the clothing as he remembered it lying and then arranged for official photographs to be taken of the scene. The baby's clothing was packed into plastic bags for dispatch to forensic scientists in Adelaide.

On the Monday, August 25, police, rangers, and black trackers carried out a careful search of the area in which the clothes had been found, heading first to the west then to the east. They reckoned they covered the ground pretty well—several hundred meters in each direction—but they found nothing of any great significance apart from parts of bone which the old tracker, Nipper Winmarti, suggested might be from an animal like a wallaby.

As with all unusual events with a number of loose ends, people began to express their own opinions about the case. Many—bush people and city people, police officers, mothers, animal experts—did a great deal of thinking. If a dingo had taken the child and eaten it—a gruesome thought, but one that had to be considered— where were the child's remains? Surely the animal wouldn't have eaten *everything*? There was also the question of the matinee jacket that Lindy belatedly recalled had been wrapped around the baby when she had been tucked into the cot—where was that? Why wasn't it found near the rest of the clothing? Or anywhere on an approximate route from the tent to the dingo lair? And the baby's singlet—why was it turned inside out? Some skeptics even suggested that the clothing did not look as though it had been ripped by a desert beast savaging its prey.

Among the officials who asked himself similar questions was Inspector Gilroy from Alice Springs. He'd been making his own inquiries based on a policeman's old-fashioned gut feelings, nothing more, and he had discovered that after Azaria's birth Lindy had complained about the child being unwell. Azaria, Lindy was said to have grumbled, suffered from a condition that caused frequent vomiting. The mother would not listen, Inspector Gilroy had been told, even when hospital staff assured her the baby was quite normal. She didn't care for the child, he had heard, and there was a time when she did not feed it for the best part of a day. And there was a doctor, it had been mentioned to Inspector Gilroy, who had been disturbed by Lindy's treatment of the baby and had out of curiosity looked up the meaning of the name Azaria in a dictionary of names and meanings. The name, so the doctor had spread the word, meant "sacrifice in the wilderness." Inspector Gilroy got to thinking about the people who had seen the Chamberlains during the day before Azaria disappeared. So far the police had not been able to locate one witness who actually saw the baby although there had been people who had seen Lindy holding a bundle in her arms.

As time was to prove, Inspector Gilroy's line of thinking was to clash with opposing opinions and facts, but in the meantime gossip was raging elsewhere. It was obvious, many skeptics felt, that this was not a simple case of a dingo grabbing a baby from a tent and dropping the child where the clothing had been found. One of the theories offered in the Ayers Rock vicinity was that if a dingo did take the child, it probably dropped the body when it realized it was being chased. The locals knew that was a dingo trick—drop the food, run away, then return later. However, before the dingo came back for its food this time, it was suggested, the body had been found by one of the camp dogs that hang around the aboriginal settlements. The dog may have taken the body home but its owners, not wanting to be implicated in the death of a child, had disposed of the body and tossed the clothing near a dingo lair. That would explain why the singlet was inside out; it had been pulled from the child, but someone had forgotten to put it back in order.

While all the theories and guesses were being bandied about, the Chamberlains tried to resume a normal life. They asked their church to pray for them, that they might find strength. And on August 27, the day after the search had failed to find further trace of the baby or her matinee jacket, the local congregation sang a song, written by Michael, to commemorate his daughter's disappearance. Sung to the tune "Shenandoah," the words ran:

> Azaria, we long to see you
> Across the wide blue yonder.
> Azaria, we long to hold you
> When we meet again one day
> On that sea and distant shore.
> Azaria we will be near you
> Though the world has had us parted.
> Azaria, we shall be with you
> When face to face with our dear Lord
> You shall stand on that great day.

At the Chamberlain home they had set aside a room to the memory of their daughter. In the child's bassinet they placed a wreath made from a wedding ring cushion.

"It reminds me," Lindy told callers, "of happiness, of weddings and fluffiness . . . of happy things. All that has brought us through this nightmare is the peace of God and the love of Jesus Christ, which surpasses all understanding. We prayed and asked for God's grace to give us strength, and He did. We have been amazed by the people around Australia who have prayed for us. It has been very uplifting."

Many thought, said Lindy, that they were "superpeople," but they were not. Azaria's death had given them a great insight into what "our Lord and Savior had to endure himself."

Not long after the discovery of the clothing, police called on the Chamberlains to go over again the circumstances of the night Azaria disappeared. They also informed the couple that an inquest would probably be held in late October or December.

That visit by the police fueled the first of the many stories that began to circulate, as they do in country towns. It was rumored that police had laid charges against Michael Chamberlain, although that was completely unfounded. One story followed another, one of the ugliest being that Azaria had fallen from a supermarket shopping cart; that as a result she was a spastic and had been sacrificed because she would never be of any use.

In fact, Azaria *had* been involved in an incident in a supermarket. She was sitting in the cart and Reagan had accidentally tipped it up as Lindy was going through the checkout. A woman yelled "Look out!" and Lindy dived for the cart but to no avail. Azaria hit the floor and the cart spun around and hit her across the top of the head. The baby had been taken straight to a baby clinic for a checkup, but nothing was found to be wrong with her. In fact her sight, coordination, and hearing were all normal, or slightly above.

The more the rumors circulated, the more the reporters called—and the stronger the rumors grew. The Chamberlains were caught in a web of malicious gossip, fired by their connection with the Seventh Day Adventist church, a relatively unknown denomination in Australia; there was even talk of strange religious rites. Sorcery had been afoot, said the rumor-mongers. The child had been dressed in black and sacrificed to atone for the sins of the Seventh Day Adventist church. That had to be right, because hadn't Lindy Chamberlain once dressed one of the children in black to go to the doctor? And that name Azaria, did it not mean something about sacrificing in the desert?

At the Mount Isa police station, anonymous letters arrived, some claiming to be from members of the Seventh Day Adventist church. Sinister rituals were again alleged, but Inspector Bob Gray and his colleagues did not take them seriously.

"It's just pub talk," he said. "Let's forget it. We'll never track down the crackpots."

Michael was even falsely linked with the murders of three people some time before. Lindy tried to scotch the rumors about the "black sacrifice." Yes, she had taken one of the children dressed in black to a doctor. "We have a black dress. I like black. I made it for Reagan," she tried to explain to deaf ears. At school, Aidan was catcalled by other children and on more than one occasion came home crying.

What was happening to the Chamberlain family perturbed members of the Seventh Day Adventist church.

Those who knew the couple closely worked hard at putting down the rumors. One of the elders of the church, Dave Simpson, answering those who spoke of desert sacrifices, went to great pains to explain that Azaria was one of the most energetic babies he had seen—that there was nothing abnormal about her.

"Yes," added Peter Patterson, a member of the Assembly of God, "they loved and wanted that child." And he tried to explain to the critics that the parents did not appear upset because of "their faith and the hereafter."

One local bookshop owner was so concerned about the spreading rumors that he wrote a letter of complaint to his local newspaper. He, too, pointed out that the Chamberlains' composure was due to their faith.

Throughout early September the rumors continued. Police officers rang. The press pushed for more information, keeping the Chamberlain name in the papers and on radio and television. The police's line of questioning seemed to harden. And one day a Mount Isa resident used a word that gave Lindy Chamberlain a shock.

"You know what the coroner's finding will be?" he said to her. *"Murder.* Not that I'm saying you're involved. It's just what I think the coroner will decide."

A police officer was also to mention the word to her as the official line of inquiry continued into the baby's disappearance.

For a while, Lindy did not repeat these stories to Michael, fearing it would upset him too much. And while the couple tried to go about their everyday lives in a town of wild gossip, police tried to come up with the answers to questions that still puzzled them. The bits of bracken found on Azaria's clothing did not, it seemed, match the vegetation it would have been carried through by a dingo on its way to the Rock. A series of experiments began, as bizarre as the case itself.

Forensic botanists arrived in Alice Springs, then traveled down to Ayers Rock with an unusual request for Senior Constable Frank Morris. They wanted him to run through the scrub dragging along a baby's jumpsuit. Senior Constable Morris shrugged and did as he was told. First, the jumpsuit was filled with towels so that it created the appearance of a child's effigy. The policeman was then asked to drag the weird shape through three specific areas—near the campsite, over a sand hill, and through mulga country close to where the clothing of Azaria was found. If a dingo had taken Azaria from the tent, it would have passed through these spots.

Senior Constable Morris ran into the shrubs, dragging the stuffed jumpsuit at the height a dingo might carry it in its mouth. Although far from conclusive, the strange experiment indicated to the botanists that stone particles and plant fragments in the missing baby's clothes did not come from where tourist Wallace Goodwin was walking when he stumbled across the bloodstained pile. Police scientists had not found any charcoal in Azaria's clothing, and there was much of it in the area after the 1976 bush fires. Neither were there any obviously pulled threads, a natural outcome of clothing catching on low branches. The forensic men were puzzled, for their tests suggested that Azaria's clothing had been rubbed vigorously in a sheltered area at the base of the rock.

Another gruesome experiment was to follow a month later, but the Chamberlains' friends noticed they were more involved with the memory of their child than concerned with what the police were doing. After a memorial service in Mount Isa, Michael and Lindy revealed they had lodged an application with the federal government to erect the monument at the Rock they had spoken of earlier.

Said Michael: "Apart from being a memorial to our daughter, it will be a continual reminder to tourists at Ayers Rock to leave dingoes in their natural state. It is only because of tourists feeding dingoes and trying to pat them for photographs that some people have been bitten. It has become acute only in the past two months. People should remember that man is the intruder, not the dingo."

Intent on examining what could have been possible and what may not have been possible in the desert on that fatal night in August, police went ahead with a second, grisly, experiment. A goat was humanely killed and then dressed in baby's clothes, its legs placed in the arm and leg holes. The strange creation was then tossed into a dingo's pen at Adelaide Zoo and a film was made of the dingo eating the goat and burying the carcass and clothes in various parts of the pen. Two inspectors from the RSPCA in Adelaide confirmed the experiment by issuing a statement: "The Society has established that the animals used to represent a human child being taken by a dingo were humanely destroyed prior to their being given to the dingoes, and no ill-treatment was involved." The RSPCA talked of more than one animal, and it transpired that a similar experiment had been carried out at a park in the Adelaide Hills.

Throughout that month of September, the rumors persisted. Fingers were pointed at the Chamberlains. There were sick phone calls. Life in the town was no longer enjoyable, and Michael Chamberlain's thoughts turned to the standing offer by the Seventh Day Adventist church to study for a master of arts degree at Avondale College, a church center at Cooranbong, near

Newcastle, New South Wales. He had been considering doing a master of public health course for a number of years because of his interest in a healthy life-style; now, it seemed, was the opportune time.

Right at the end of September, before the final arrangements were made for his transfer to the college, the Chamberlains had a caller, a man who was to play a significant part in their lives and their destiny. His name was Detective Sergeant Graeme Charlwood.

IV

"Nobody's Going to Believe Me . . ."

Detective Charlwood, with his sharp blue eyes and Mexican-style moustache, had spent the past three weeks looking into the background of the case, visiting Ayers Rock and studying all the statements the Chamberlains had made, publicly and to the police. Now, accompanied by two other officers, he sat behind a desk at the Mount Isa police station looking at the petite dark-haired mother he had driven in from her home. Nearby was the baby's cot and blankets he had collected from the Chamberlain home that morning.

Lindy had said she was quite happy to go over the events for him and she began by describing their holiday route from Mount Isa. They had hoped to arrive at the Rock to catch the sunset, but they were some three quarters of an hour late. In the morning, Michael was up with the sunrise and at 10 they had set off for the Rock, looking first at a feature on its face known as the Brain. They had then moved on to the climbing area. "My husband went up the Climb and I waited down with the kiddies. Then he took Aidan and Reagan up. Then we took some photographs. No, the photographs we took of Azaria were in between him coming down and the boys going up."

One of the pictures had been studied by Charlwood.

It showed Lindy holding the baby by her arms, her feet on the sloping rock. More than one person had suggested, after seeing that picture reproduced in an Australian women's magazine, that while Azaria had dark hair and was tiny, the baby in the picture seemed to have fair hair and looked rather well developed for a baby of nine and a half weeks.

Michael had ascended the difficult climb three times that day, said Lindy, and he was feeling tired. But on the way back toward the camp they stopped off at the Echo Cave.

"There were some tourists there, and a couple about, I suppose, mid-forties with a child of, I'd say, eight, and another about ten or twelve, walking around the rocks. We met them at the back of that Fertility Cave and we were standing there talking and looking around, and wondering what the aboriginal legend of the rock above was, and where the echo part of it was. And I looked—I sort of sensed as though I was being watched—and I looked up. . . . On a rock just above there was a dingo looking down over the top of us."

Lindy said she told her family, "Look what's watching us." She went on: "We all stood there for at least four minutes, maybe longer, watching this dog. There was a crevice just beneath where it was, and Reagan was moving around, and it struck me at the time it was odd, because he said, 'Where is it, mummy? I can't see.'

"The dog would usually follow movements with its eyes, but it didn't seem to take its eyes off me. It made me feel a bit creepy, which I thought of after. Azaria was with me at the time. She was with me, unwrapped and awake, sitting across my shoulder, looking about."

They got back to the camping area some half an hour before sunset. She bathed the children and then they went to the Sunset Strip to take pictures. By the time they returned Reagan was already asleep. She put him into a sleeping bag on his mattress in the tent while Michael started to prepare their tea. "Then I picked the baby out of the carry basket in the car, took the carry basket into the tent, and then carried her down to the campsite. She had wind. I was patting her; walked around with her for a while."

Lindy estimated the time now was between 7 P.M. and 8 P.M. Certainly, it was dark. Azaria, she guessed, would have been asleep for half to three quarters of an hour. She went on to describe meeting up with the couple who were to be identified as the Lowes and then she told Sergeant Charlwood of the incident with the dingo pouncing on the mouse.

"About a quarter of an hour after that, Michael and Aidan had both finished tea, and Aidan said he was tired and wanted to go to sleep. I hadn't had my tea; I wasn't very hungry. Michael said, 'You'd better put her down and have your tea.' So I said to Aidan, 'It's time I put Bubby down.' I was thinking to myself 'I'll spoil her.' He said, 'I'll come up with you.' I had the tent zipped up with Reagan there, because of what they'd said. . . ."

Lindy then told how they had left a rubbish bag containing Azaria's used diapers beside the stove and while they were away for a short time an animal—she didn't know whether it was a camp dog or a dingo—had tipped it over and spread the contents over the ground. "Of course, because of this, I thought, 'Well, they're scavenging for anything. If they go for diapers, you know?'"

Lindy, happy to continue with what was turning out to be a long and detailed question and answer session with the detective, described how she had walked up to the tent with Aidan after Michael had suggested putting the baby down.

"We both climbed in the tent and he got his parka off and dumped it near the door of the tent, where Reagan's was, and started to get himself into bed. I put Azaria down and tucked her in. I put her down in the things I had her wrapped in and just put a blanket over the top."

What was she wearing? Charlwood wanted to know.

"A throw-away diaper, a singlet, white stretch suit—it was all white, with white booties underneath—and a little white matinee jacket, with very pale lemon edging around the collar and cuffs. It was one of those matinee jackets that's just got two or three buttons on the yoke, and then none coming down, and the buttonholes were a bit loose. She was wrapped up as I showed you this morning, in the blue bunny rug and the larger of the two blankets. She slept with her arms up, and her head on the side and her arms would be this angle . . ."

"She had her arms level with her head?"

"Yes, or slightly back a bit."

Lindy told Charlwood that Aidan had then asked, "Is that all the tea I'm getting?" He was at the stage, she said, where periodically he decided he had hollow legs and ate a huge feast but was still hungry. She said she then told Aidan she would get him something else. Knowing he liked baked beans, she went out to the car.

"I went back to the car and got the baked beans out, came back to the tent. Actually the car door would hit the tent, so I was right beside the tent at that stage. I saw nothing in the area anywhere. There was not a sight or a sound of a thing."

Then, accompanied by Aidan, she headed for the barbecue, pointing out that for some reason or other she did not zip the tent up again behind her. "I was planning to get his food and then bring back the tray with me and let him have it in the tent. I had decided by then I didn't want anything much, probably just watch him, and then go straight to bed. And I walked back to the barbecue area. I can't remember now if we climbed the fence, but I think we might have. I was going to chase him, and he went one way, and I went the other, to see who got back fastest."

Charlwood listened carefully. Hidden in his desk drawer a tape recorder was running.

"We climbed over the fence, on the right side of the gas bottle, walked around on the side where we had our things, and the can opener was sitting right on top. I put the can of beans down, picked up the can opener, and my husband said to me, 'Bubby cried.' I sort of paused and said to him, 'Are you sure?' She was sound asleep. He said, well, he heard a cry. And the other fellow sort of indicated that he'd heard something— whether he'd heard a cry or not I don't know. So I said, 'Well, I'd better go and see.' I put the can opener down, walked back across the gas bottles, climbed the fence, and I was halfway between the fence and the post, on the way to the tent, and I saw the dingo coming out of the tent. And it had its head down, and it was in the light from about there up—" She indicated by bringing her hands toward her head the part of the dingo she could see.

Shaking her head, Lindy said, "And when I saw it, it was going like this to get out." But she couldn't see it properly because of the shadows and a bush that was in front of her.

Her thought was that the dingo had got hold of Michael's shoes, which had been right beside the tent door. It was a young dog, perhaps still a puppy, with a gold coat in beautiful condition—not one of the mangy ones.

The light was blinking on it, so it must have been a shiny coat, she said, and its neck was a rust color.

Charlwood tried to ascertain the exact moment that she had first seen the animal.

"It was still inside the tent, its head was out, and it was trying to get something through the doorway and swinging its head around, now with its head down. That's what made me think it was a shoe and I thought, 'He's got it by the shoelace and it'd be swinging and he can't get it through the door.' The dog wanted to get out. It [the tent] was unzipped, not only down the middle, but at both sides, across the bottom, and I yelled at it, because I thought it would drop the shoe. As soon as I saw it, I started to run and I yelled. I can't remember what I said, but I think I said, 'Get out!' or 'Go!' I think I said, 'Go on!' to it; sort of yelled, 'Go on, get out!'

"Then I realized. I thought to myself, 'The kids! There's no food in there.' The shoes . . . and I thought, 'Well, she cried, so he must have disturbed her.'

"And then it sort of flashed through my mind that they're wild. When she first went to sleep she would sleep very heavily, and he would have to actually touch her to disturb her. I thought, 'Well, a wild dog; it could have bitten her.' The only thing visible is her head. She'll need first aid. As soon as I reached the front of the tent, I could see the blankets scattered. Instinct told me that she wasn't there, the dog had her, but my head told me it wasn't possible. Dingoes don't do such things, and this was, you know, just beyond the realms of reason and I dived into the tent just to make sure.

"I could see from the door that she wasn't there. But my mind wouldn't accept it and I dived in; actually felt in the cradle for her, to make sure she wasn't there. And as I backed out of the tent I felt with my hands in the blankets that were scattered, and the sleeping bag, just in case I frightened it off and he dropped her and one of the blankets was completely covering her. Being so tiny, she didn't make much of a bundle and if he dropped her. . . . I briefly glanced at Reagan on the way out and he had his sleeping bag hood up. No damage to the sleeping bag. There was no skin showing anywhere on him and I remember it flashing through my mind: 'Well, he's all right,' because the dog couldn't see anything of him."

Lindy went on to describe how she backed toward the door of the tent, feeling for the baby as she went. Then she stood up in the opening and called to Michael that the dingo had taken the baby.

"As I was calling this, I started to run in the direction that the dingo had gone because as it came out of the tent—as I was running toward it—it went out the tent and across in front of the car, which from my direction was right, and ran off into the darkness. It was under the shadow of the fence at that stage, and I didn't look at it again. My interest was what was in the tent, because immediately my thought was to get out after it.

"I felt within myself that she was dead, because if she was alive I'd have heard a whimper or a cry or something, unless by some miracle she was unconscious and still alive."

Michael had called to her as she was running. "What?" he'd asked, and she had repeated: "The dingo's got the baby—quickly!"

All that had happened, she said, in the time it had taken for her to come out of the tent and around to the other corner of the car. The dingo was standing in the shadow of the car, she said, at the back left-hand corner. As soon as she had peered around the corner, it had taken off.

"It was standing with its back to me, with its head slightly turned at that stage. I couldn't tell you whether it had anything in its mouth or not. My mind refused to accept the thought that it had her in its mouth, although I knew that must be it. I didn't know what I was going to do when I caught it, but I was going to."

Detective Sergeant Charlwood put a question to Lindy. "At that stage, you could only see the back of the dingo and its head when it was at the back of the car?"

"Well," replied Lindy, "I could see all the dog in the shadow. . . . It would have been slightly on an angle, with its head partly turned and it took off at an angle."

When she told Michael the direction the dog had taken, her husband ran out into the scrub without his flashlight.

"I'd stopped, because I realized there was dead silence. You couldn't see a thing; you couldn't hear a thing. The light from the barbecue didn't show any more there. I realized that there was just no hope of finding it. We needed a flashlight. We'd searched for ours earlier; couldn't find the one we were using. We went to get our big one out. We've got one of those Big Jims. Something had been packed on the button and flattened the battery and the one we had was just about flat. That's why we were looking, because I realized that our flashlight was useless and it sort of went through my mind: *Nobody's going to believe me. They'll all think I'm either drunk or I'm joking if I go to the tents and tell them to come. It's just going to take too long.*

"I needed help now. So I just stood there and yelled as loud as I could: 'Has anybody got a flashlight?' because the dingo had the baby . . ."

Lindy said it was almost as if the campers had them on their laps. Three people with flashlights came almost immediately. She was asked which way and she pointed the direction the dingo had gone. The woman in the next tent sent her husband off for the police and ranger and then Michael returned from the scrub and he was given a flashlight.

"It was one of those fluorescent ones. And the only thing that did penetrate into his mind at the time was that they don't give enough beam. They shoot around, but it's not a beam. And we went to our car and looked for a flashlight and asked people if they had flashlights could they go and look. Michael went back out into the scrub."

The ranger and the police arrived and by this time, said Lindy, there would have been anywhere from thirty to fifty people out with lights. Within the hour, with people from bus tours who were staying nearby joining in, there would have been two hundred or more searching in different directions.

Michael had asked her whether she had checked to make sure Azaria was not in the tent. They went in and checked again and as they were crawling out "he shone the light on the end of his sleeping bag and I saw the drops of blood which I hadn't seen before."

Lindy said there were only half a dozen or so spots. Michael said to her: "Look, honey, she's bleeding, so I don't think there will be any hope."

Azaria had also been sniffling from the tail end of a cold. Lindy recalled how cold it was—cold enough to leave a film of ice on some water in a saucepan the night before.

"I said to him, 'With the cold she's got, if she's alive anywhere, we've got maybe three quarters of an hour, an hour and a half, for them to find her or she'll be— she'll be either—have very bad pneumonia, or she'll be frozen to death, with no blankets on or anything.'

"After about two hours we just hoped that we would never— We initially said to the police if they found anything of her, it didn't matter what it was, we wanted to see her. Then we decided that, if they found her, we'd like to see something of her clothes, but we didn't particularly want to see her in a morbid state at all. As the night wore on, the ranger said he felt that they wouldn't find anything. He said we'd be very lucky to find clothes; it'd probably taken it back to its den. Very occasionally they would save without killing. . . ."

Lindy said she told Michael that a mother's instinct led her to feel that it was a female animal that had taken her. Although there was no reason to say that, she felt it was like the first dingo they had seen at Maggie Springs that afternoon.

Michael said to her: "Now listen, you be careful. It's one thing to say what you saw and it's another thing saying what you suppose to be. If you go around saying it's the same as that dingo, there seem to be dozens of dingoes around here and they all look alike, you know. You're getting into the realms of probability."

Detective Sergeant Charlwood asked Lindy to repeat what the baby was wearing, so once again she went through the list: the booties, stretch suit, singlet, disposable diaper, and the matinee jacket.

"They've got them all back except that matinee jacket," said Lindy, "and it wasn't a tight one. It had light elastic around the wrists and the buttons were loosish. So there is as much chance of it being off on a bush, on the way from the Rock somewhere, as there would be down a den, and left away from the other clothes, I should think."

The interview was interrupted for a time while Lindy went to the bathroom. Turning back to the events of that night, she said that after calling that a dingo was in the tent she had glanced back and noticed Aidan was four to six feet behind her, following her back.

"Where he went then I don't know. He wasn't near the tent. He must have been coming, but he didn't get into the tent when I was there."

But she said that at some point he must have been near the tent or looked in as helpers came running up. He was the type of child, she said, who if he were to cut his foot would go hysterical, but that night he did not.

"In fact, it amazed me," said Lindy. "Shock, I suppose. He came running out and he screamed at me and he said, 'Mummy, don't let the dingo eat our baby!'

"He put into words what my mind wouldn't accept. There's no doubt in my mind that he was quite aware of what had happened and what was going on. I explained to him then that I wanted him to stay back. I didn't know whether to stay with him or go and look for her or what."

But the Western Australian woman had told her not to worry about her son—she would look after him.

"We went looking and Aidan was still standing there, but I was cold and he had taken his parka off to go to bed already and I said to him, 'I want you to go and get into bed,' and I told him what was happening and I said, 'There is nothing we can do. The policeman's coming soon; get into bed,' because if Reagan woke up he would be frightened."

But her younger son slept through the lot. She told Aidan: "I want you to be there so Reagan's all right because he knows you." Aidan wanted her to stay and she assured him that she would just be outside where she could see what was happening.

"I went out with Michael. We both went together looking and we came back about every half hour to check if the police had come back or if anybody had found anything. And we stayed close then, in case they wanted us; back and forth. We could hear them. People were doing other things. We were out by ourselves."

She and her husband had searched until 11:30 P.M., perhaps longer. They started packing up their things to go to the motel between 12 midnight and 12:30. They decided to pack everything, putting some of their belongings in the back of the police vehicle, throwing the remainder into the back of their own car. They finally "settled," she thought, at about half past one. "I was the last one. It was half past one when I looked at my watch, just before we climbed into bed."

She pointed out, though, that they had decided to ring her parents, Michael's parents, and Michael's boss as soon as possible in the morning so she went back to the kitchen that night and made arrangements to use the radio telephone when they got up. Then she went to bed.

In the morning she told Michael to have a shave—"it might help him to feel better"—and then they had made their phone calls. They had breakfast in their room and spent most of the morning on the phone talking to the press because, she said, the police had advised it would be better to talk to them rather than avoid them. Then they had driven to the airport and back to the campsite to take photographs of the area, which was almost deserted—there were now only two tents. The afternoon was spent around the motel and talking to an airline employee who had been out searching all night and who had been on a number of safaris.

They had tea with the owner of the motel and on Tuesday morning they searched out the ranger, Derek Roff, in the aboriginal camp—they'd decided to go across to the camp to thank the trackers who had helped with the search.

"The ranger took us all around the aboriginal camp and we had a look at all the native dogs to see if I could identify any of them. But they were all different sizes and shapes and complete bitzers [mongrels]. Sort of hound dogs. Black, like brindle, mostly; long trunks, odd-shaped, everything."

Asked about when she first spotted blood on any clothing, Lindy said she noticed some on the sleeves of Aidan's parka when he put it on the morning after Azaria disappeared. She showed it to Michael and to the policeman, Frank Morris, when he came to get the child's blankets.

Sergeant Morris had entered Charlwood's office during the interview and now asked about her tracksuit. Lindy said the night had been cold and she had put it on underneath her dress, followed by the jacket, with her parka on top. She also had on a pair of running shoes. When she had arrived home in Mount Isa she had noticed that the shoes were smeared with what looked like blackcurrant. She thought she must have crawled through a pool of blood somewhere. Then she recalled more blood, saying that the parkas belonging to both her sons, which had been spread out near the door of the tent, showed bloodstains. Aidan's was more stained than she had at first thought, and Reagan's had blood all up one arm, on the hood, and over the other sleeve.

She had also discovered, when they were back home, two or three spots of blood across the flap of her own sleeping bag, as well as some milk stains where she thought the baby must have vomited as the dingo took her. She and her sister had looked for blood on the baby's space blanket because they remember it had been over Reagan.

"It must have sort of walked over his head, and

walked around," she told Charlwood. "We turned it the opposite way to the light and you could see all the rip marks through it. But you could see a dusty pad print on the thing, once you realized what it was."

Referring to a mattress that had been in the tent, she said that when she inspected it she found marks on it. "They were big-looking marks. Whether the kids had split their milk in the car or not, no, it would have had to happen in the tent come to think of it . . ."

Continuing their questions and answers the following day, Detective Sergeant Charlwood confronted Lindy with a copy of the women's magazine with the photo on the front showing her holding the baby. Charlwood said the picture showed the baby's hair as being blond—was it a true representation of the hair color at the time the snap was taken?

"Are you sure it shows the hair as blond?" asked Lindy. "Doesn't it look slightly ginger?" Then she said, "I suppose you could say that it's blond. I would say it had a gingery color in it. Her hair was, actually, medium to dark brown, but was beginning to lighten and had almost a ginger sheen in the sun. The picture actually looks lighter than it really was. The base of the hair at the back was quite dark still."

The detective wanted to know if she or her husband or either of the two boys suffered any injury while they were at Ayers Rock. Only a few prickles in the feet, she said.

Now it was time for Detective Charlwood to lay on the emotional pressure. One by one he showed Lindy, for her confirmation of ownership, items the police were now keeping: her sleeping bag, which had since been to the local dry cleaner's to remove the bloodstain; Aidan's parka; Azaria's bloodstained singlet; and then the baby's jumpsuit, stained around the neck and cuffs.

This was followed by Azaria's disposable diaper and then her booties. It was then that Lindy began to weep.

After a short break, Detective Sergeant Charlwood turned to the evidence the scientists had come up with. Tests, he said, had been carried out on the clothing, one of which was to determine the presence of dingo or dog saliva. The tests were negative. Had she any comment?

"None that I can think of. It just makes me wonder how."

"Would you have expected saliva to be present?"

"He would have to use his mouth, I should think. I would have expected to have some on it—I presume dingoes have saliva."

"Further forensic tests have been carried out in respect of the holes present in the clothing. The results of these tests indicate that the holes were not made by either a dingo's or a dog's teeth. Is there any comment you would care to make?"

"Do your tests show what made them?"

"No, not conclusively at this stage."

"Are you trying to say that somebody murdered her?"

"I'm just putting to you the facts I have. I'm looking for answers."

"Would saliva wash out in the rain?"

"I don't know. There was no rain at Ayers Rock at the time of this incident."

But that was not what Inspector Gilroy had told them, she said. He had told them it had rained on the clothes.

The detective showed her a report from Dr. Andrew Scott, an Adelaide forensic scientist, who had concluded that blood scrapings taken from inside the Fertility Cave were from the same blood group as hers. Only 14 percent of the population was of the same group.

Asked for comment, Lindy replied, "The findings almost seem incredible to me. I am to consider that it was done by something other than a dingo. That brings in such a range of coincidences, with split-second timing, that it seems impossible. Reading about the blood group of Ayers Rock—the same as mine—almost sounds like a well-planned, well-thought-out, fantastic plan to set me up."

After responding that she had no idea who would want to do such a thing, she was shown another report, this time from a veterinary scientist, Dr. Harry Harding. Hairs found in the blanket from the tent, he felt, without being sure, were those of a cat.

As the interview reached its conclusion, Detective Sergeant Charlwood asked: "Do you know what happened to Azaria?"

Lindy replied, "From the information you are giving me I'm beginning to wonder if I know anything. But I feel certain within my own mind that it was a dingo."

Before she left the office, Lindy was asked to perform a strange and emotionally taxing duty—wrap a doll up exactly as Azaria was wrapped on that night six weeks earlier. She pulled the blankets around the doll, then placed it in the cot, its head on the tiny pillow. Then they let her go home.

But there was still Michael. He had been sitting outside, waiting for his wife to finish her interview. Now he came in and sat down.

He recalled that on the morning of August 17 he had awakened perhaps later than he should have, according to his wife, who told him he had missed the best part of the sunrise. He had then hurried with his camera equipment to a sandhill to the east of the tent and spent some half an hour or more shooting 35mm film. He returned to the tent, had breakfast with his family, and later they had traveled by vehicle to the Rock. They stopped and took pictures of the Brain, drove to the airstrip, returned, and moved slowly around to the official Ayers Rock walkway.

Revealing his love for photography, Michael said, "I was amazed at the beauty and stark contrast of the color of the Rock, especially through the filters I was using, and firstly took a wide-angled shot of the cars, tourist buses, and the Rock together. Lindy and the children scrambled up Chicken Rock. I then left them and moved quickly to the top of the Rock. I took several pictures using various filters and lenses; had another tourist take a picture of myself leaning against the monument, I suppose—I'm not sure what it is at the top. It had a book in it, which I signed. Then I proceeded even more quickly back down to the children and my wife.

"Aidan and Reagan wished to climb part of the Rock also, and this we did. On returning, we then traveled by our vehicle around to what is known as the Maggie Springs area, where my wife and children, with a coachload of young people, surveyed the area. It was getting reasonably late, about 4:30 or 5 o'clock I would imagine, and we then, after I had taken some photographs of the paintings [aboriginal paintings on the cave walls], proceeded by car back to the camping area. We prepared tea while talking to some people from Tasmania. I cooked; my wife attended to the baby. When we had eaten, it was approaching 8:30, or thereabouts, when the tragedy occurred."

Detective Sergeant Charlwood asked if, when Michael was in the Maggie Springs area, he had seen any dingoes. No, he had not—but his wife had. She had seen "what she considered a beautiful-looking dog, possibly a female." Michael added that the animal was close enough to cause some apprehensiveness. "I considered that she may have been unreasonably frightened, as I had not thought of dingoes particularly as creatures to be feared."

He thought she had related the sighting to him at Maggie Springs—but he could not be sure.

Detective Sergeant Charlwood then asked him about events that followed the family gathering at the barbecue.

"On or about 8:15 or 8:20," he began, "we all saw what we considered a rather mangy, forlorn specimen of a dingo, lurking just outside the barbecue enclosure. It appeared to be looking for food. It went into the shadows and then, without any warning, came back into the light of the barbecue area next to the gas bottles and pounced with frightening agility on a small, I guess you'd call it a field mouse, which we'd sighted a few minutes earlier. This had been seen by the Tasmanian people as well as ourselves. My wife, who had been nursing Bubby, then took her to the tent to lay her down to rest. I prepared some food for her while she was putting Bubby down as she had not eaten much prior to this.

"She returned to have something to eat and as she was eating I think I thought I heard a faint cry from the tent. I think my words were 'Is that Azaria crying?'

"My wife said she would check it out and as she was proceeding back and into the tent her voice startled me when she cried out in horror, 'The dingo's got my baby!'

"I was stunned and raced with the other man madly toward and into the tent to see if this was so—that is, if the baby was missing. The sequence of events following this for some minutes is a little unclear. I was in a severe state of trauma. I felt useless. I raced for my flashlight, I think, and it would not go. I think that I ran into the bush madly hoping that in the darkness I might see either the dog or Azaria. I remember feeling very angry and frustrated because normally I pride myself with having very effective lighting and also because my keys were not in my pocket I could not switch the ignition of my car on in order to use the hundred-watt searchlight that was in my glove box. My Tasmanian friend, who had somewhere got hold of a flashlight, had raced out into the bush in front of me and searched feverishly. I cannot remember much at the time for a few moments except that I came back to the tent in the hope that our eyes were playing tricks on us; in other words, that the dog might have left Azaria somewhere in an unlit corner under a rug or bag, perhaps. But not so.

"The moment of truth that she really was gone hit me and, realizing now that I could do nothing alone, cried out—I'm not sure if it was in my conscience or out loud —'Oh God, help me!' It was probably a silent cry and [I] raced along the southerly section of the road to alert any other camps that I could see to, if they had a flashlight, get out and start searching. I was led toward a tent on the end of the road where I had heard Christian music. I raced unceremoniously to the tent door and said two things: 'A dingo has got our baby—if you have a flashlight, please come out and search. If you haven't, please pray.'"

Later, when Charlwood told Michael that no dingo hairs had been found on the clothing or the camping gear, Michael asked him when dingoes moulted.

"August and September," said the detective. "They were moulting when Azaria disappeared. There was no saliva on the jumpsuit, either."

"I'd have thought desert creatures might not salivate much at all," said Michael.

Charlwood was interested in obtaining Michael's observations about the baby photograph on the cover of the magazine. The pastor pointed out that in reality Azaria's hair was darker than that showed in the picture and did not look as reddish. "I might add," he said, "that I had been experimenting with a fluorescent filter, light pink in color, and at the time of the photograph had forgotten to remove it, as I usually only used it as a contrast with my polaroid filter to shoot landscape and the rock."

Azaria's hair, he said, was fairly dark at birth and had got fairer as she grew. Asked whether any animals had been kept in his house Michael confirmed what Lindy had told Charlwood—that they used to have a Siamese cat, which they had lost or which had been stolen about the time of Azaria's birth.

"When was the last time you saw Azaria alive?" asked the police officer.

"The last time I saw Azaria alive was in Lindy's arms while nursing it sitting on the bench rail at the barbecue, just prior to putting her to sleep."

Charlwood asked: "Do you know what happened to Azaria?"

"No," said Michael. "Except on the evidence we have given you, I don't know."

Asked if he had anything at all to say in relation to Azaria's disappearance, her father said he had not— "Except for my continuing observation, and strong feeling, that she was killed by a dingo or wild animal. What other alternatives? God only knows."

The main interviews of husband and wife finally over, Michael made another statement to satisfy increasing public interest in the affair. Commenting on the whispers that the forensic tests had failed to confirm that his daughter had been taken by a dingo, he said it was possible a human being might have killed his daughter.

"It's a possibility that cannot be ruled out," he said. "We still believe a dingo was responsible, but we are unable to say for sure. If a person did kill our daughter, he or she would have been a maniac. I wouldn't want to suggest any human being could be involved in such a terrible thing. The person would have had to have followed us all day and I can't see anyone having done that. My wife saw something in the mouth of the dingo, or dog, leaving the tent. She could not positively identify it as Azaria, but we presumed it was her because she was missing. We still believe that was how she was killed, but we have to have an open mind about it."

Unable to remain in the poisoned atmosphere of Mount Isa, among the gossip and pointing fingers, the Chamberlains decided it was time to move. For the time being they would stay with friends in the north Queensland town of Innisfail. "The environment was stressful" was the closest Michael would come to saying it was the rumors that had driven them away.

The date for the inquest was set for December 15, 1980. The coroner would be Denis Barritt, SM, a 54-year-old former Victorian detective for seventeen years and a barrister for thirteen. He had gone to the outback in 1978 with his family of five because the area appealed to him.

The Chamberlains arrived in The Alice on December 14. It had been a grueling four months. The search, the police interviews, the press inquiries, the rumors—yes, most of all the rumors—and then yet more police questioning. Lindy remembered well the police questions; how some officers had been kind, sympathetic, while others had "heavied" her. She had even been asked if she would be willing to be hypnotized to help with her recall, but she had told them that under no circumstances would she consider such a thing—giving up

71

one's mind to the control of another was the power of the devil.

Some police officers, she felt, had already made up their minds about the case. Despite what she said, some of them, she believed, were thinking, "Oh, yeah, what's the real story about your daughter?"

Well, she had made her statement. No doubt it would all be read at the inquest that would begin the next day. Whether the police, the coroner, or the world believed what she had to say or not, she knew in her heart what the truth was. . . .

V

The Inquest

Even before the inquest began, members of the Seventh Day Adventist church went to great lengths to defend the Chamberlains against the "child sacrifice" rumors. Bert Couzens of Alice Springs told those who raised the issue that nothing in Adventist teaching remotely suggested the idea of sacrifice.

"It started as one of those stories," he said, "and it just grew and grew. Without asking any more questions, people believed the stories. Because our religion is not as well known as the others, people think we get up to all sorts of strange practices. I think they confuse us with other groups who do have rather outlandish beliefs. We have even been linked with the Jimmy Jones cult that resulted in all those suicides in Georgetown, which is quite ridiculous. If I had to sum up our basic beliefs, I'd have to say we follow the Ten Commandments. You know, one of the problems is that people watch too much television today. They expect a plot in real life. Sometimes things are so simple that there is no plot, no dramatic ending."

On the morning of the inquest, Lindy Chamberlain, in a lace-sleeved summer dress, and her husband, in a white short-sleeved shirt and tie, were accompanied to the courthouse by another churchman anxious to protect them. Pastor Wal Taylor, the Church's legal liaison officer in Sydney, repeated the defense of his faith. Adventists weren't strange people with strange customs, he said. The church adhered to the Last Days and Second Coming prophecies, which were generally disregarded by other denominations.

The Chamberlains were given places at the front of the court before Coroner Denis Barritt's bench. The bespectacled coroner sat on a blue chair and gazed around the packed courtroom before getting down to his first task: to establish that Azaria was in fact dead. Mr. Ashley Macknay, the deputy crown solicitor who had been nominated to assist the coroner, quickly cleared up any doubt by presenting the court with a fact that the police had kept from the public. Tests had shown, said Mr. Macknay, that the baby had lost at least 20 percent of her blood; and weather conditions on the night she disappeared made it unlikely she would have survived for long.

His next statement was a shock, despite the weeks of rumors. Referring to the forensic report, he said, "Examination of the clothing, the damage to the clothing, the absence of saliva, the absence of dog or dingo hairs, and the absence of pulled threads or other fragments suggests that the deceased was removed from her clothing by a person, rather than a dog or dingo."

Mr. Macknay paused, then went on: "Second, the damage to the clothing was more consistent with a person, rather than a dog or dingo. Thirdly, the site of the clothing suggests that the clothes were put in the place where they were found, rather than dragged there by a dog or dingo."

Mr. Barritt then made his decision on whether he had jurisdiction to examine the child's disappearance.

"I agree," he said, "that the nature of the damage to

the clothing, the nature of the manner in which the clothing was found, would indicate there has at some stage been human intervention in the disposal of the body, that the body cannot now be found and I find that the body is in a place from which it presently cannot be recovered and for these grounds I find I do have jurisdiction."

The first day was taken up with the coroner listening to a reading of the Chamberlains' statements to Detective Sergeant Charlwood. When she was called forward to give evidence on the second day, Lindy said she had become aware after Azaria disappeared that the child's name could be interpreted as meaning "sacrifice in the wilderness."

It was at this point that the family solicitor, Tom Dean, decided to clear up once and for all the meaning of *Azaria Chantel Loren.* At his request, Lindy explained that Azaria was Hebrew for "Blessed of God," Chantel was a name used by gypsies and meant "lead singer," and Loren was a Teutonic name meaning "branch of laurel."

How, the coroner wanted to know, were the names chosen? Because of their meaning or because she liked them?

"A little of both," said Lindy. "My husband tended to look for the meaning of names, but I liked them because of their sound."

She thought there was public confusion between the name Azaria and Azazel, which appeared close together in a book of unusual names. Azazel meant "bearer of sins." (It was not raised at the inquest, but one legend states that Azazel, who was associated with Mars, the god of war, descended to earth and taught men evil by showing them how to make weapons of bloodshed. Azazel was also connected with the Jewish scapegoat ritual.

Until 70 A.D. a goat was selected each year, formally loaded with the sins of the people, and sent into the wilderness to Azazel.)

Lindy was asked by Mr. Dean: "Are you a Christian?"

"Yes," she said, "I am a practicing Christian. Not just in name. Jesus means a lot to me."

"Was Azaria a planned child?"

"Very much a planned child. None of them were accidents."

Pastor Chamberlain followed Lindy into the witness box. As he spoke of the birth of the baby he suddenly put his head in his hands and sobbed: "Azaria was a most wonderful gift for us."

Had his wife projected a calm or collected exterior in the hours after the baby's disappearance?

He replied, "As far as exteriors are concerned, it was, of course, dark, so I did not look into her eyes to see if she was crying, but I felt that while she was with me she was deeply emotionally upset and we just tried to control each other. We prayed together and we walked with our arms linked together or hands together."

Michael agreed he was "fairly pessimistic" from the outset because if it were a dingo that had taken the baby "we thought that it would have been a fairly quick affair."

Asked when he concluded his daughter was not going to be found alive, he said, "Well, you know, time is a very important item for life and death when you see blood, and people were confirming all through the Sunday night to us that there was less and less chance of her being alive. . . . We tried to comfort ourselves with the idea that if she was dead, it was quick. This is what we prayed it would be."

Yes, he admitted, he had taken pictures of the campsite and put them on an aircraft for a newspaper. He felt he could talk to the media "because of the very unusual nature" of the disappearance.

And indeed the Azaria Chamberlain case was continuing to receive widespread publicity. With it came the inevitable crank calls. The Alice Springs telephone exchange intercepted at least six threatening phone calls, one male caller telling the switchboard operator he was going to "blow Mrs. Chamberlain out." The result was that when the Chamberlains arrived at the courthouse the following day they had a police escort.

Mr. Macknay told the court that an object similar in thickness to a knitting needle had pierced the baby's clothing. He turned to Michael Chamberlain and asked if he could offer an explanation for that damage.

"No," replied Michael.

When the white-bearded chief ranger, Derek Roff, was called, he told of finding dingo tracks and drag marks leading away from the camp on that night August 17. They had been discovered during a search of sand dunes southeast of the camping area. With aboriginal trackers, he had followed the tracks, which began about twelve meters from a road beside the tent. In the sand dunes, a drag mark of some kind was found, about eight or nine inches in width.

"It was slightly wavy," said Mr. Roff. "Associated with it were dingo treads. They were large pads and I am pretty confident they were dingo pads."

As the inquest proceeded into the next day, with evidence being given by people who were around the camp on the night—Mrs. West from Western Australia and Nurse Roberta Downs—Mr. Roff was called back to be asked: "Do you think it's possible a dingo did take the child?"

"Yes, it's possible."

"Do you think it was possible that the dingo hid in the scrub and doubled back to the area where the clothes were found?"

"It is quite possible."

The ranger was asked to read out a letter that had been sent to the coroner by Dr. Judith Best of Warwick, Queensland. In it she described how she was camping at the Rock the night before the baby's disappearance. She saw a wild dog force its way into a tent that had not been securely fastened and emerge with a bundle of green plastic in its mouth. It had then nuzzled into the bag, pulled out the contents—which appeared to be cake, bread, and meat—and ate them.

Then there was the evidence of Ranger Ian Marshall who said he had heard of an incident in which a dingo grabbed a child from a car at the camping ground. She was bitten as she was dragged out, but he believed the child was not otherwise injured.

A third ranger, Rohan Dalgleish, told the coroner that the area where Azaria's clothing had been found was searched meticulously by rangers down on their hands and knees. A patch of blood was found nearby, he said, along with a substance which appeared to be either feces or an intestine.

Waiting patiently to give evidence was an elderly white-haired aborigine with a flowing beard—Nipper Winmarti. Yes, he said through an interpreter, he found tracks on the night of Sunday, August 17, and they led away from the corner of the tent where Azaria had been left by her mother.

Coroner Barritt asked Mr. Winmarti to describe aboriginal legends relating to dingoes and children. Interpreter Pam Harmer listened carefully while Mr. Winmarti spoke, then explained that aborigines who had twins would leave the weaker one in the bush for the dingo spirit, considered evil. (In fact, aboriginal experts say a more realistic interpretation is that since a mother could not care for twins while traveling, the weaker child was smothered at birth.)

"Do you have any knowledge of bad spirits taking children from their mothers in the night?" the coroner asked the old man. Yes, said Mr. Winmarti, he had heard of this.

Asked Mr. Dean: "Have you ever heard of dingoes taking aboriginal children?"

"Never."

"What about camp dogs taking aboriginal children from your people's camp?"

"No."

Friday, December 19, was to be the last full day of the inquest before the Christmas adjournment. It was not without its revelations. Senior Constable Frank Morris, the first to inspect the clothing, said he approached the child's jumpsuit with apprehension because he thought it would contain remains. He had often had to deal with children's deaths, but on this occasion he was apprehensive. But he had overcome his fears, observed the clothing, made mental notes, then informed his senior officers. A small piece of intestine-like matter was found some ten to fifteen meters from where the clothes lay. It was collected for forensic examination.

Asked why he had disturbed Azaria's clothing before it was officially photographed, Senior Constable Morris said he was acting on instructions radioed from senior officers at Alice Springs. He had been asked to check if any remains were inside the clothes. He believed, he said, "the baby had been taken by a dog or dingo and I felt my priority was to find the baby and spare no time in doing that." In order to get his hand into the leg of the suit to retrieve a bootie, he had to undo "up to four studs."

Tracks close to where the clothes were found were about ten meters away, said the policeman. They had no particular direction and seemed to be those of an animal walking around between rocks. But fresh tracks had been found later, leading in and out of a dingo lair close by. The lair was kept under observation for several days following Azaria's disappearance and two dingoes had been shot. These animals were sent to Alice Springs for tests on their stomachs' contents. A further search of the area resulted in the discovery of two pieces of very fine bone about half a kilometer from where the clothes were found.

The policeman's next statement caused a murmur in the courtroom. Evidence of what appeared to be fresh digging by a dog or person was found in an area of the Fertility Cave at Ayers Rock. Several blood spots had also been found on rocks on a climb above the cave. A piece of this rock had been chipped off and sent to the scientists.

The day after Azaria's disappearance, said Senior Constable Morris, he collected from Michael and Lindy Chamberlain a sleeping bag and two blankets from their motel room. The blankets appeared to have several marks and tears on them. According to Michael Chamberlain, two marks had not been there before Azaria disappeared. Senior Constable Morris went on to say that a child's parka had been pointed out by the Chamberlains as having blood spots on it, but they had asked if they could keep it because of the cold night and he had agreed.

"Do you think it possible," Mr. Dean asked the policeman, "that a dingo might have taken the child and the child may have subsequently been found by some person and buried and the clothes dumped?"

"I believe a dingo could have taken the baby," said the policeman. "I have never experienced anything like that. It is feasible."

Several theories had been bandied around the region, he said, one suggesting that Azaria had been taken by a dingo and her body later found by a human and buried. He had heard variations on the theme, including suggestions that a dingo or dog had taken the baby and, in panic caused by shouting and flashing lights, dropped the mutilated body.

Senior Constable Morris, a resident at Ayers Rock for five years, said dingoes in the area were friendly and often treated as pets. But he had received a number of complaints, from one motel in particular, about a dingo that had been misbehaving. It had even been seen walking across dining tables at the motel. It had also been found under his bed and at another time had got into the police station and made a nice old mess. There had also been complaints, he said, about dingoes or camp dogs rummaging through tents at the Ayers Rock camping ground.

The recital of evidence ended there for the time being. The coroner wanted to visit Ayers Rock himself, where the inquest would continue in the ranger station, starting on February 9, 1981.

Although it had been an enlightening week, there was still much to come—in particular, the scientific evidence. The Chamberlains were not to know it then, as they left the courtroom in Alice Springs that Friday afternoon, that the months ahead were to be as traumatic as the night baby Azaria disappeared.

VI

Unanswered Questions

If anything, the inquest had served to deepen the mystery of Azaria Chamberlain's disappearance. It had raised more questions than there were answers. No one had been able to provide firm evidence that would answer the biggest query: Where was the baby? That she was dead was not disputed, unless a gigantic, sick hoax had been played. But to what end? No, it seemed the coroner had made the correct assessment: The child had died. Where, then, were the remains? Lying out there in the desert? Buried? In a dingo's lair? No one had been able to say, but certain facts seemed to speak for themselves.

Someone, the evidence suggested, had seen the baby after it was reported she had vanished from the tent. Because someone, the facts indicated, had taken the child from the jumpsuit. How else to explain the singlet being inside out? Unless a dingo had pulled the singlet off, gripping it by its lower edge and pulling it up over the baby's body before devouring the child. But why would a dingo go to all that trouble of completing stripping the baby before eating it? And if someone had placed the clothes at the base of the Rock, what was the reason . . . to incriminate a dingo?

Prominent on the list of unanswered questions was

whether a dingo was capable of entering a tent, pushing or pulling aside several layers of blankets, picking up a four kilogram baby in its mouth, and running off for several kilometers into the desert. Yes, the experts had generally agreed, it was possible. But was it probable? The animals had put their jaws around children's arms and they had cheekily stolen food. They had lost their fear of man, the provider of tidbits around the camping sites. But now had one dingo, driven by hunger and the knowledge that man would not harm it, carried out an unthinkable act? Dingoes, the coroner had been told, were capable of carrying large hares; some had been seen carrying lumps of flesh up to four kilograms in weight and still been able to keep their heads up. But, given that they had the strength to carry the child, was it in the nature of dingoes to eat live human beings?

Mr. Macknay had told the court that marks found on the clothing were not consistent with what a dog or dingo could cause. And he had said a hole that pierced the jumpsuit and the singlet had been caused by an object of a similar thickness to a knitting needle. Had something been thrust into the clothing while the child was wearing it? If a dingo had taken the baby, why was there no saliva on the jumpsuit? Was there any significance in the fact that the blood found at Ayers Rock came close to the same group as Lindy Chamberlain's? What was the small piece of intestine or feces found near the Rock? Just what had those bizarre, macabre experiments—dragging a baby's effigy through the scrub, feeding a goat dressed in baby clothes to a dingo —achieved? And who had rubbed the clothing vigorously in vegetation at the Rock's base, as was reported to police by scientists?

And where was the child's matinee jacket, the one Lindy said Azaria had been wearing? If that could be found, it would possibly explain the absence of saliva on the jumpsuit, for part of the jacket would have covered the suit. But there had been a massive search around the area where the jumpsuit had been found, a search carried out by expert trackers, for hundreds of meters around. There was no sign of the matinee jacket. Some searchers had even been down on their hands and knees, probing the earth. And there had been scores, hundreds, of tourists wandering through the area since the child's disappearance. Why hadn't they stumbled across the jacket? Had it snagged on a bush somewhere and been dragged from the child as the dingo ran on with its prey?

The missing matinee jacket was certainly a big mystery and it was to remain a key element in this strangest of events.

The gossip followed the Chamberlains throughout the remainder of December and into January. They tried to keep out of the limelight, staying at their new home at the Seventh Day Adventist College, Avondale, near Newcastle, north of Sydney. But the rumors reached the point where Lindy could stand it no more. She started disguising herself, making changes to her appearance and hiding behind dark glasses. The boys still came home from school in tears and the Chamberlains turned to their church friends for solace, often praying with them. And while the Chamberlains hid from a suspicious world, police, forensic scientists, and park rangers got on with their work, trying to unravel the great mystery. More than half the estimated twenty dingoes in the Ayers Rock area had lost their lives in recent months, Ranger Roff disclosed. Five had been shot before Azaria vanished because of attacks on children, another three and two camp dogs had been killed for analysis of their stomachs' contents after Azaria's disappearance, while another five or six had been destroyed because they were suffering from mange.

Michael and Lindy Chamberlain arrived in Alice Springs on February 6, 1981, in readiness for the inquest that was to resume at the Rock three days later. They flew in from Adelaide where they had engaged Phil Rice, a burly silver-haired Queen's Counsel, to represent them for the hearing. When they arrived at the dusty airstrip at Ayers Rock two days later, Michael wept. "It cut me up as we flew in and saw the Rock again," he said. "It was a terrible feeling. This is a traumatic experience."

He expressed sorrow that so many dingoes had been apparently wiped out since the tragedy, but their feelings about the animal being the culprit had not changed. "Azaria can't be brought back. However, in time we know we will see her again—we have no doubt about that."

Lindy was less affected by the return to the Rock. "Coming back here has not been as difficult for me," she said. "I think I have already dealt with it in many ways."

"Our faith," said Michael, "has given us our inner strength."

The couple relaxed later in the day and stood side by side watching Ayers Rock change its colors as the sun went down. Time stood still at the Rock, but sometimes it went full circle.

The makeshift coroner's courtroom was, in fact, set up in the national park visitors' center. Three friends of the Chamberlains, Seventh Day Adventists from Alice Springs, set up tape-recording gear. Coroner Barritt took his seat in front of a projector screen and facing the lawyers—Phil Rice, QC, and his instructing solicitor, Peter Dean, representing the Chamberlains; Ashley Macknay and his junior, Mike O'Loughlin, who were assisting the coroner; and the court clerk.

The first witness, Constable James Noble, who had driven Lindy to the motel in the police truck on the night Azaria disappeared, was asked by Mr. Rice if the area where the clothes were found had been cordoned off.

No, said Constable Noble, it had not. As far as he could remember there had been no instructions about keeping clear of the area. This meant, of course, that lay people as well as the experts had been free to roam all over the area. Constable Noble had been to the area himself and had collected samples of grass and twigs at random to help the scientists with their assessments.

Now the evidence was about to take a new turn. The court was to hear the conclusions of Dr. Rex Kuchel, a consultant botanist to the South Australian Police.

Coroner Barritt read out a number of conclusions from a report written by Dr. Kuchel after he had carried out field tests at the Ayers Rock campsite in October 1980 and laboratory tests at Adelaide University and police headquarters in Adelaide. The most striking fact from the doctor's report was his conclusion that there was a "distinct possibility" that Azaria's clothes had been buried and then dug up before being placed where they were found.

This was indicated by what he described as "considerable quantities" of reddish sand in the baby's jumpsuit. Dr. Kuchel had taken a number of soil samples and plant fragments from the clothing by vacuuming them. Although the clothes contained reddish sand, the soil he had taken from the southwest face of the Rock was dark in color, because there was a lot of charcoal in the area that came from burnt logs on the ground and trees, still standing, that had been damaged by fire at the base.

The bespectacled botanist was called before the coroner and asked by Mr. Macknay whether he could say, from his visual observations, whether the soil vacuumed from the jumpsuit was like that in the area where the clothes were found or the samples taken from the sandhill area behind the campsite. He replied that it was more consistent with the sand east of the campsite because of the absence of charcoal.

Dr. Kuchel's tests of vegetation found on the clothing had resulted in the identification of fragments from seven plants. These included spearhead grass seeds, common in the area, yet there were few on the jumpsuit. He would have expected clothing to pick up many more of the seeds. Another of his conclusions was that the jumpsuit and singlet had been deliberately rubbed vigorously against vegetation near the base of the Rock. His report read: "Plant material requiring a damp and sheltered micro-climate, principally *Parietaria debilis,* had been abraded into small fragments. Having regard to the size and quantity of the abraded fragments it is considered that this could only occur if the clothing had been deliberately rubbed vigorously where this material was growing in abundance."

There must, he told the court, have been considerable agitation to get the fragmentation.

Reference was then made to the experiment in which Senior Constable Morris carried a towel-filled jumpsuit through a number of areas near Ayers Rock. Dr. Kuchel, who had arranged the experiment, told the coroner: "One thing that struck me was that there were no pulled threads on the original clothing." The threads on the test garment were "extensively pulled, as one would expect," yet this clothing had been carried for less than 10 percent of the distance Azaria's body would have had to have been carried or dragged.

Dr. Kuchel drew four conclusions from his involvement in the disappearance investigation.

Sand particles and plant fragments on the baby's clothing had not come from the location where the clothing was found.

Azaria's clothes had not been dragged or carried by a dingo from the campsite to the place where they had been found.

The jumpsuit and singlet had been rubbed in vegetation.

Because of the considerable quantity of reddish sand found in the jumpsuit, there was a distinct possibility that the clothing had been buried and then dug up before being placed in the spot where it was found.

During the hearing of that day's evidence, there had been an interesting departure. The coroner adjourned during the morning to visit the place where Azaria's clothing had been discovered. The lawyers and other interested parties traveled in a convoy of vehicles to the southwest face of the Rock. The temperature was just over 104°F. The crowd scrambled over rocks and pushed through the scrub to a small clearing where shrubs and trees had been blackened by fire. The exact spot lay between two large boulders about two meters apart. Dr. Kuchel squatted down to show examples of vegetation. In front of him and Mr. Macknay stood Mr. Barritt, Mr. Rice, and Michael Chamberlain.

"This inquest is now in session," mumbled the coroner, although it was difficult for him to hear all of Dr. Kuchel's answers about vegetation as observers shuffled around and twigs broke underfoot.

When he continued his evidence back in the makeshift courtroom the following day, Dr. Kuchel was asked by the Queen's Counsel, Mr. Rice, if he made the assumption that at some stage the baby may have been buried in its clothing, or even that the clothing on its own had been buried. Yes, he did make that assumption —"It was the only way I could account for the relatively large amount of sand inside the jumpsuit."

Asked if he was aware that even domestic dogs sometimes buried their prey, Dr. Kuchel replied, "Oh, yes . . . but the fact that the clothing was found all together in one clump indicated that it could not have been put there by an animal."

But he conceded that Azaria's jumpsuit was significantly smaller than the one he had used. And his experiment did not include simulation of the missing matinee jacket Lindy said Azaria had been wearing. "I didn't know of the matinee jacket until a fortnight ago," the botanist explained.

Inspector Michael Gilroy, the Alice Springs officer who had led the investigation until Detective Sergeant Charlwood took over, was asked by QC Rice if he stuck to his initial belief that there was every possibility a dingo had taken the baby. The policeman replied, "I have changed my view several times."

He added, hesitatingly: "As far as I am concerned I can't really— Perhaps I will put it this way: the evidence I saw on the Monday [the day after Azaria disappeared] made it likely and possible that a dingo had taken Azaria Chamberlain."

"And you still hold that belief?" asked Mr. Rice.

Again, the policeman paused before replying. "I would say it's still a possibility."

Inspector Gilroy told the coroner that when he checked the tent the day after Azaria disappeared, he found "what appeared to be a very fine spray of what could have been blood . . . darkish, very small dots, not much bigger than pin heads." They were halfway up the side of the tent, on the right-hand side. Under the right-hand rear corner of the tent was a damp spot of sand about half an inch wide and four to five inches long.

The day's evidence had quickly dismissed at least two facets that observers, in the early stages of the inquiry, felt might have provided helpful clues. Bone fragments found between the campsite and the southwest base of the Rock were those of a rabbit; and stomachs of the dingoes shot after the disappearance contained no human remains.

There was to be other evidence that further lessened the probability of the dingo theory. But one statement read to the court between all the police and scientific evidence turned the thought of those attending the inquest back to the dramatic events surrounding the Chamberlains that tragic night.

The statement emerged from a police interview of Aidan, who was six when his sister was reported missing. He recalled the family's visit to Ayers Rock this way: "It was just about nighttime when we got to Ayers Rock. We pitched our tent, had tea, and then went to bed. My bed was at the side of the tent next to Daddy's. Then there was Mummy, Reagan, and Bubby was down at the bottom of Reagan's feet. When we got up next morning we had breakfast and then Reagan and I found some friends and we found a mouse that hopped. We found some dog prints and then my friend left. After that Mum, Dad, Azaria, Reagan, and me went for a drive and we found some caves after we climbed the Rock.

"I climbed the Rock with Daddy and Reagan while Mummy and Azaria climbed the Chicken Rock. After we climbed the Rock we found the caves and one of the caves had aboriginal drawings in it. When we were looking at the cave there was Mummy, Azaria, and Reagan. Daddy was taking some pictures.

"Just before we looked at the drawings, I saw a dingo near the cave. When we saw the dingo there was other people there, too. The dingo was on some rocks high above and I could see his head and neck. He was a goldy-brown. After we looked at the cave we went home. There was Mummy, Daddy, Reagan, and Azaria. After we got back to the tent Mummy bathed me after Reagan, and we put on our pajamas and Daddy held up Azaria. After we got dressed we went up the road in the car and had a look at the sunset. We all got out of the car and after the sunset we went back in the car. On the way back in the car Reagan and Bubby fell asleep.

"When we got back to the camp we got out of the car and I said to Mummy, 'I want tea.' Daddy went to the barbecue and got some tea. There was a man, a lady, and a little girl there, too. While we were in the tent, Mummy put Bubby down in the cot and then I went to the car with Mummy and she got some baked beans. I followed her down to the barbecue area. When we got to the barbecue area Mummy opened the tin of baked beans and Daddy said, 'Is that Bubby crying?' Mummy said, 'I don't think so.' Mummy went back to the tent and said, 'A dingo has got my baby.'

"Mummy shouted, 'Has anyone got a flashlight?' and Daddy went around and asked if anybody had one. When Mummy saw the dingo come out of the tent I was behind her, but I didn't see the dingo come out. I went to the barbecue area and got Daddy's flashlight. I gave it to Mummy and Daddy. After I gave them the light I stayed with a lady and then I went to bed. Bubby's blankets were spread over the tent and I saw some blood on them. And I saw some blood on a sleeping bag. I think it was Mummy's. I saw the tent post at the front of the tent. It was knocked over away from the thing that it sits in. Mummy told me not to touch it. I saw some blood on Reagan's parka . . . on the sleeve. There was some blood on the wristband of my parka. There was no blood on the parka before that night."

The simple words of a child. . . . In essence, they confirmed all that his parents had related.

The inquiry turned back to the scientific evidence, with Dr. Andrew Scott, head of the oral biology section of the Institute of Medical and Veterinary Science in Adelaide, saying he failed to find dingo hair or saliva on Azaria's clothes. He revealed, though, that blood on the clothes was the same group and type as Azaria's, as was blood on the tent and on a blanket and a parka. But further blood discovered on the outside of the tent and on a tent pole could have come from either a human or an animal. Then there was the blood found near Fertility Cave. He confirmed it was of the same type as that of Mrs. Chamberlain and 10 percent—not 14 percent as Detective Charlwood had told Lindy—of the white population. Dr. Scott said he had concluded that the baby's singlet, found with her jumpsuit, had been folded at some time. And a black substance discovered some fifteen meters from the clothing was not from a human but was of vegetable origin.

After the experiment at the Adelaide Zoo with the dead kid goat dressed in baby clothes, he had found saliva on the test clothes. He was of the opinion that rain would not have washed out any dried saliva on the original jumpsuit as there would be a tendency for a halo of saliva to spread over the clothing. However, he went on, it was possible that a matinee jacket prevented saliva reaching the jumpsuit and singlet.

When Mr. Rice asked if the whole of the jumpsuit had been painstakingly examined for saliva, Dr. Scott replied, "The only way to do that would be to cut the whole lot up."

Dr. Scott said the bloodstains on the baby's jumpsuit were heaviest around the collar, where the blood appeared to have flowed down to the left shoulder straps and at the rear of the right shoulder.

"If the baby," the coroner asked, "was put on its side in the bassinet and a dingo picked it up, carrying it somewhat off-center, even if by the head, could the bloodstains go to the left?"

Replied Dr. Scott: "Yes—the baby need not have been carried vertically; just the head higher than the feet."

The bloodstained parka belonging to four-year-old Reagan had come into direct contact with a bloodstained object, said Dr. Scott. That contact would have to have been made while the blood was still relatively fresh, within about three minutes.

It was Dr. Scott's opinion that the parka had been moved while the blood was smeared on it. The alternatives were that something was carried over the top of the jacket and the jacket moved—"and the obvious possibility was that the jacket moved while it was being worn."

The scientist told the court he had not found any blood on the parka belonging to Azaria's older brother, Aidan. And, referring to the singlet belonging to the baby, he said it had been soiled and there were evident crease lines where it had been folded when the soiling took place.

The scientific evidence being brought forward was intriguing the nation. Armchair detectives were making their own deductions. The evidence was shifting from

the probability of a dingo having taken baby Azaria
Chamberlain. What, then, were the alternatives? The
scientists had, in the main, been able to say what they
felt had *not* happened. But the evidence was too vague,
too circumstantial, to piece together a conclusive picture.

Although they hid it well, the pressure on Michael
and Lindy Chamberlain was immense. Their daughter
was dead, they had had death threats made against
them, and their claim that a dingo had taken Azaria
was in question. And, as if they had not faced enough
worry, there were more scientific witnesses waiting to
give evidence—evidence that would cast an even greater
shadow of doubt on their story.

It was not surprising that the couple, once again,
turned to prayer.

VII

Failure to Find is Failure to Look

Death threats against the Chamberlains continued when the inquest returned to Alice Springs. The couple moved from their hotel and were put under the watchful eye of Constable Frank Gibson.

The inquest was into its tenth day when Sergeant Frank Cocks of the South Australian Police Forensic Laboratory was called to discuss his findings following a microscopic examination of holes in the right collar and left sleeve of the jumpsuit. His forensic experience suggested to him the holes had been made with some sort of blade, possibly scissors. Explaining his reasoning, he said that where a sharp cutting action took place it was clear to see that fibers were cut, whereas when a tearing action was employed the fibers were frayed.

"This is readily distinguishable under a microscope," he said. The fibers of the jumpsuit had been cut with a sharp instrument—a "bladed" instrument—because they had not been frayed or torn.

Discussing the hole in the collar, he felt it may have been cut after the collar area had been folded over. This was because, as he put it, "one angle is completely cut through; then it goes off at another angle, where it is only partly severed." He went on: "If a bladed instrument like a knife was used, it would have to have been

95

done against a solid background. But I feel it was more consistent that the cut was made by a pair of scissors. If the jumpsuit was folded like that"—and, holding up the baby's bloodstained clothes, he folded it over—"it hasn't been done with a knife."

If the cut had been made before blood flowed, then the cut fibers would have had blood on them. "I can't see any other way because the blood just isn't there."

Turning to the hole in the sleeve, the police scientist conceded that some fibers had been frayed or torn, but a large majority showed sharp cutting. The frayed edges, he said, were consistent with the cut being incomplete and the rest being torn. The irregular nature of the cutting also suggested a pair of scissors may have been used.

When asked about animal hairs he had vacuumed from the baby's clothing, the sergeant said he had recovered only two from the singlet and four from the jumpsuit. Yet on the clothes used in the Adelaide Zoo experiment he had found "many hundreds of animal hairs."

The second witness that day, Dr. Kenneth Brown of the Oral Biology Department of the University of Adelaide, cast further doubt on the dingo theory by concluding that two holes and a "crumpling" on the singlet appeared to be inconsistent with the teeth marks of a dingo. Damage below the right armband on the front of the singlet, he said, "appeared as a crumpling, folding, stretching—as if something had been pushed from the opposite side. It was in an area of staining and appeared to have been set by the drying of the substance. It appeared to have been produced by an object which had a point—not a needle-sharp point—and appeared to have some length because it was pointed in a certain direction."

Dr. Brown told the coroner that he had carried out an experiment using the skulls and teeth of two dingoes and a singlet, trying to "copy" the damage to the original garment.

Asked Mr. Macknay: "The examination of that crumpling showed a linear shape, which was not consistent with the shape of the lower canine tooth of a dingo?"

"It was not." The holes in the back of the singlet, said Dr. Brown, appeared to have been produced by something other than teeth because of the direction in which the fibers had gone and the fact that they had been severed.

Yet another forensic witness that day, Dr. Antony Jones, from Darwin's Casuarina Hospital, was questioned by the coroner about blood flows. "If an instrument, say a meat skewer, was fed through the clothing, then the body, and then withdrawn, would you expect to find blood in the surrounds of that hole?" asked Mr. Barritt.

Dr. Jones replied, "When you are talking about a puncture of this kind, bleeding might be quite minimal. Certainly there might be a detectable amount, but it would require close examination."

The court adjourned for the weekend, the Chamberlains retiring to a secret address because, it was learned, there had been bomb hoaxes at their new hotel in addition to the death threats.

When the inquest resumed Dr. Kenneth Brown was called back and questioned further about holes in the jumpsuit and singlet. It was possible, he said, they could have been aligned. The hole in the back of the singlet, he said, had probably been made by an object the diameter of a knitting needle.

"What about the beak of a bird?" the coroner asked.

"Again, I doubt it. I would not say it was impossible."

"Could you describe something in common usage that could make such a hole?"

"Possibly a small screwdriver—like an electric screwdriver, where you have got a point with an edge that can sever."

Apart from questions about what had caused certain holes, whether the clothing had been cut or torn, another issue was whether a dingo could have actually taken baby Azaria from her tent. Dr. Alan Newsone, a senior research scientist with the Commonwealth Scientific and Industrial Research Organisation's Wildlife Research Division in Canberra, felt the odds had to be very long, but that the possibility could not be dismissed.

Les Harris, of the Dingo Foundation, went further. In a letter to the coroner, read during Dr. Newsone's evidence, he wrote: "Based on my knowledge of dingo behavior, and having a good understanding of the seriousness with which they view the matter of food, I would assess the probability that a dingo might have taken and consumed the baby as very high indeed."

Dr. Newsone, asked by Mr. Rice if the relationship between male and female dingoes was strong enough for them to go hunting together, said the dingoes around Ayers Rock had behavioral patterns different from any he had observed either in the wild or in captivity. They had access to a garbage dump and water supplies and were also fed by campers.

The thirteenth day of the inquest was to prove to be unlucky for a young policewoman, Myra Fogarty, twenty-five, of the forensic section of the Northern Territory Police Force. She had been with the department for thirteen months, although she had worked in the technical area only three months. She had, she told the coroner, received no formal forensic training. Her explanations were not enough to protect her from the wrath of the coroner when he read part of her report. In this, she said she had studied Azaria's blankets, a sleeping bag, and the tent and, although she had found blood traces on the tent floor, had not noticed any on the outside.

The last paragraph of her report stated: "Overall, there is a noticeable lack of blood on these items." The coroner wanted to know what she meant by that. Myra Fogarty said, "From the facts that I had heard, I had expected to find lots of blood and gore. I had expected to find it, but I didn't."

Mr. Barritt then asked: "Did you expect to find evidence of a violent attack by a dingo, which would have left pieces of matter all over the tent?"

"Yes."

"Then the purpose of that statement was to discount that theory and advance the theory of murder?"

"No. It was just not what I expected to find."

Mr. Barritt said, "The difficulty I have with that last paragraph is that the very areas of blood you failed to observe—if the blood could be shown to be the baby's— were the strongest evidence that could possibly exist to substantiate the account given by the Chamberlains. Would you agree that that is the likely possibility of the blood you failed to observe?"

"Yes, I suppose."

"There was nothing deliberate at all about your non-observance of that blood?"

"No."

"Were you taught anything about the objectivity that a forensic technician should adopt?"

"I observed my other counterpart as to what I should be doing. I was never given any formal training."

Mr. Barritt said he supposed Constable Fogarty, the last of thirty witnesses, was not taught to be totally objective. She replied, "It was a police report I put in to my boss. This report is written on police paper to inform my boss what I had done."

"So, if I had not had the good fortune to have a copy sent to me, I would never have learned of that last paragraph?"

"Yes."

"Then that, perhaps, is my good fortune and your ill-fortune. I will tell you for the future that it is utterly vital for a forensic scientist not to go outside observation, and to be totally objective when making examinations. There's an old adage in forensic science—'Failure to find is failure to look.'"

The young policewoman was excused from the hearing. She walked briskly from the courtroom, tears filling her eyes. The coroner's advice to her "for the future" was to be of little value. Less than four months later, she was to resign from the Northern Territory Police Force, claiming that she had been the victim of a vendetta by her superiors—a scapegoat for the senior officers she said had bungled the case.

After counsel from both sides summed up the evidence, only the finding of the coroner remained. And the way he said he was going to deliver it created a sensation. He was going to allow a television camera into the courtroom so that his decision could be shown to the nation. Lawyers around the country were astonished. In Australian State Supreme Courts judges are forbidden by their chief justices to allow cameras into a courtroom. Gordon Lewis of the Law Institute of Victoria said he had seen a televised murder trial in the

U.S., in Michigan, and he thought the prosecutor and defense counsel had behaved like prima donnas.

However, Mr. Barritt decided to proceed. "This has been a sensational case," he said. "It has touched, no doubt, on the emotions of a great percentage of Australians. It has clearly been a case which has crossed state borders and has captured the imagination, some of it all too fertile. It has been argued that televising the decision would add sensationalism to the situation. I think that the grounds of accuracy and the dissemination of this case in an accurate form exceed other arguments that have been advanced."

Coroner Barritt's findings, under the stark illumination of television lights the following day, would be historic. In less than twenty-four hours, the decision of this one man would put to rest one of Australia's most baffling mysteries.

Or would it?

VIII

Verdict

The television technician called, "Fifteen seconds!" The seventy people packed into the courtroom were hushed. "Ten seconds . . . five . . . action!"

Coroner Barritt, dressed in a patterned shirt and tie and wearing dark-rimmed spectacles, walked hesitatingly from the anteroom into the court, then sat in his blue chair. It was indeed a dramatic moment, but for viewers around the country the visual aspects of the live broadcast were quite unspectacular. No close-ups of the Chamberlains, no panning around the courtroom. Just the head and shoulders of the coroner, although the cameraman had a little leeway and was able to take in some of the bench. His eyes cast down at his prepared statement, Mr. Barritt spoke slowly and nervously, but his delivery was hardly noticeable. It was what he had to say that mattered, although it was to be some time before he came to the point of his summary. He went carefully and methodically through the whole story, beginning with the Chamberlains' journey from Mount Isa, to Lindy's cry, "My God, my God, the dingo's got my baby," to the discovery of the jumpsuit.

When the police were told, "commendable efforts" were made to preserve the scene of this discovery. It was the opinion of all who observed this scene on that afternoon that the clothes had been deliberately placed in that position and that the surrounding growth had not been disturbed. Such opinions, the coroner explained, were substantiated by the position of the clothing. The singlet was found inside the jumpsuit and the jumpsuit partly on top of the diaper. The booties were within the legs of the jumpsuit and all the clothing was within twelve to eighteen inches. The clothing was photographed in the position in which it was found, and also spread out on display.

Dr. Scott's evidence, in which the forensic scientist had said bloodstaining on the neck and back of the jumpsuit suggested the child was being held upright at the time of bleeding, led the coroner to his next statement.

"This evidence, incapable, I find, of no other explanation, coincides with the theory that Azaria was taken away by her head and neck in the mouth of a dingo, but is otherwise totally uncharacteristic of any other instance of an infant death. The facts that damage to the jumpsuit was slight, that no blood or tissue was found inside it nor dog nor dingo saliva adhering to it, appeared inconsistent with the controlled experiments conducted at the Adelaide Zoo. In accepting these inconsistencies, it would appear there are two alternatives —either Azaria met her death by another cause than a dingo attack, or else the dingo's possession of the child ended abruptly before it had time to set about devouring the child."

Referring to spray stains on the outside wall of the tent, Mr. Barritt said, "Of all the evidence pertaining to these stains, I am satisfied, and satisfied beyond reasonable doubt, the highest degree of proof recognized in law, that the sprays of blood on the exterior of the tent were sprays of arterial blood coming from Azaria's head or neck. Such an explanation accounts for the infrequency of the stains and is supported by the canine growl heard by Mrs. West."

Mr. Barritt recalled the evidence of Dr. Brown, the odontologist, who had been asked to show the possible correlation between the bite of a dingo and marks on and in various items of clothing.

"I am satisfied that Dr. Brown, an acknowledged expert on bite marks in humans, used his best endeavors to learn what he could of what had been, until the request had been made for his assistance in this case, an unknown field both for himself or indeed for anyone else. In the light of his straightforward admission that he has no experience in examining bite marks in clothing, I feel it would be dangerous to rely on his evidence in that regard. In any event, I accept the evidence of Dr. Scott that the singlet that Azaria was wearing on the night of her death was being worn the correct side out. This fact alone disposes of most of Dr. Brown's evidence. It reduces to mere speculation, and likely error, any hypothesis as to the origin of the small holes from which the absence of any blood or tissue staining eliminates the possibility of them being associated with any physical harm befalling the babe."

This rejection of Dr. Brown's evidence was to have its dramatic results. Meanwhile, Coroner Barritt was to level criticism in another direction. He recalled evidence by Dr. Newsone who had told the inquest that he regarded the seemingly tame dingoes at Ayers Rock as being potentially more dangerous than the wilder ones, which kept at a distance. Dr. Newsone had spoken of rangers at Ayers Rock trying to prevent the destruction of the tamer, but more dangerous dingoes; to keep them as a tourist attraction.

"It is not unreasonable to infer that the inclination of

Azaria Chamberlain. (NEWS LTD. AUSTRALIA)

A wild dingo. (NEWS LTD. AUSTRALIA)

Police sift through the sand at Ayers in the area where the incident occurred. (NEWS LTD. AUSTRALIA)

Lindy and Michael Chamberlain with their sons Reagan *(left)* and Aidan. (NEWS LTD. AUSTRALIA)

The Chamberlains' legal team arrives at the Darwin courtroom. John Phillips, QC, is at front, flanked by his assistants Andrew Kirkham, Stuart Tipple *(right)* and Greg Cavenagh *(left).* (NEWS LTD. AUSTRALIA)

Lindy and Michael leaving the courtroom in Darwin.
(NEWS LTD. AUSTRALIA)

Botanist Rex Kuchel with the Chamberlains and court officials examines the site at Ayers Rock where Azaria's clothing was found. (NEWS LTD. AUSTRALIA)

ABY'S CLOTHING FOUND NEAR HERE
-W CORNER OF ROCK

GENE
STOP

CHAMBERLAINS' TENT

BARBECUE AREA

DRAG MARKS IN SCR

An aerial view of Ayers Rock with key locations in the case indicated. (NEWS LTD. AUSTRALIA)

many at Ayers Rock to protect dingoes could provide a motive to conceal Azaria's body," said Mr. Barritt—words that were to anger rangers and residents at the Rock.

On all the evidence, said Mr. Barritt, he was certain that the accounts given by Pastor and Mrs. Chamberlain were true, accurate, and corroborated by truthful, independent eyewitnesses and the evidence of many experts. "Considering the evidence of Dr. Newsone and Dr. Scott, I am also satisfied that when the dingo was seen to be tugging at Azaria at the tent doorway, it was holding her by the neck or head and that, at that point, she would have sustained multiple fatal injuries to that region of her body. I conclude, from the absence of dingo saliva on the jumpsuit, that Azaria was being held by the head or neck at all times when possessed by the dingo. I accept the evidence of Sergeant Cocks that the cuts to the sleeve and neck of the jumpsuit were caused by a scissors whilst the clothing was under tension. On the probabilities, I find that at Ayers Rock a pair of scissors would be a tool used by a white person rather than an aboriginal.

"From the evidence of lack of damage to the clothing, particularly the singlet, which would have been a difficult garment for a dingo to remove undamaged, the absence of dingo saliva plus any large number of hairs, I find that the dingo's possession of Azaria was interrupted by human intervention on the night of 17 August, 1980. I am satisfied that at the time of such intervention, Azaria would have been dead. The cut sleeve may indicate that after Azaria was retrieved from the dingo, her body was placed at a safe height to prevent further attack and the scissors had been used to free the body. This, however, is speculative."

No one moved. No one so much as coughed. But

every person in that crowded courtroom and around the nation watching his delivery live on television was thinking about the coroner's words. What, exactly, was he driving at?

Mr. Barritt went on, neither emphasis nor emotion in his words: "I am satisfied that at some stage the clothing was buried in the plain or dune country, subsequently dug up, rubbed on undergrowth near the base of the Rock and placed by a person or persons unknown at the spot where it was later found. It may have been that whoever rubbed the clothing on the undergrowth had some knowledge of botany, but again, this is speculation. It would appear the clothing was meant to be found. This may have been to support the proposition that the child had been fully eaten, that it had been taken by a dingo having its lair or den in that area, thus concealing the offending dingo's identity, or for a number of other reasons."

Mr. Barritt went on: "The dingo is a dangerous animal and was known to be dangerous prior to 17 August, 1980. The conservation authorities had received reports of several instances of dingoes attacking children. The significance of a dingo's range and a dingo's territory was known and understood by the rangers. The existence and whereabouts of a number of their lairs were known and known to be in areas where children might be expected to wander while exploring the many areas of interest around the base of the Rock.

"The conduct of dingoes around campsites, together with their propensity to enter tents, was known, or ought to have been known. The propensity of a dingo, reared by Homo sapiens and treated as a pet in a domesticated environment, to violently attack children was known. Yet in the face of this knowledge dingoes

106

have been retained and indeed allowed to virtually in-
fest this area—'as a tourist attraction.'

"I would hope that as the moral responsibility to protect children visiting national parks would appear to
have been avoided in the past, the legal consequences of
such conduct in the future ought to lead to the elimination of any species dangerous to man from such parks,
or at least those areas frequented by tourists."

Mr. Barritt was reaching the closing stages of his
finding. His official verdict was coming. But he still had
a few more things to say about conservation and tourists.

"Every person in our community," he said, "is under
an obligation to conserve human life, and those charged
with the added task of conserving wildlife ought to remember and apply this primary tenet of our law. If
those charged with the protection of wildlife within national parks would rely on laws forbidding the destruction of such creatures, then they ought to be made to
publicize the inherent dangers that exist, and are permitted to exist, in such parks and also what medical
care would be available in an emergency in such remote
regions. Such publicity should be included in any tourist promotion to fulfill the requirements governing fair
advertising.

"This case clearly exercises that a choice has to be
made between dingoes and deadly snakes on one hand,
and tourism on the other. The two ought not to be
expected to coexist, creating hidden traps for decent
people, where formerly our forebears set hidden traps
for deadly creatures. Dingoes have not, and never have
been, an endangered species. Despite constant efforts by
man, they have held their position as the most dangerous carnivore of the canine species on the Australian
continent."

The death of this baby, said Mr. Barritt, in an area where previous attacks causing bodily injury had occurred, was too high a price, and a totally unnecessary price, to pay in the cause of conservation. And he recommended that all animals dangerous to man be either safely enclosed or eliminated from areas of national parks likely to be frequented by man.

Coroner Barritt had one further task—to briefly address Michael and Lindy Chamberlain.

Without lifting his head, the coroner said, "To you, Pastor and Mrs. Chamberlain and through you to Aidan and Reagan, may I extend my deepest sympathy. You have not only suffered the loss of your loved child in the most tragic circumstances, but you have all been subjected to months of innuendo, suspicion, and probably the most malicious gossip ever witnessed in this country."

And then, in legal language, Denis Barritt, who had presided over one of the most bizarre coroner's inquiries anywhere, gave his verdict:

"I doth find that Azaria Chantel Loren Chamberlain, a child then of nine weeks of age and formerly of Mount Isa, Queensland, met her death when attacked by a wild dingo whilst asleep in her family's tent at the top camping area, Ayers Rock, shortly after eight P.M. on 17 August, 1980. I further find that in attempting to remove this babe from the tent, the dingo would have caused a severe crushing to the base of the skull and neck and lacerations to the throat and neck. Such injuries would have resulted in a swift death.

"I further find that neither the parents of the child, nor either of their remaining children, were in any degree whatsoever responsible for this death.

"I find that the name Azaria does not mean, and never has meant, 'sacrifice in the wilderness.'

"I find that after her death, the body of Azaria was taken from the possession of the dingo and disposed of by an unknown method by a person or persons, name unknown."

So it was over. The coroner folded together his papers. Michael Chamberlain stood as if in prayer, hands clasped in front of him, staring at the floor. Lindy Chamberlain rose and stood beside him. They had been in the limelight for months, at the center of gossip. Now, vindicated by the coroner, they could resume their lives.

IX

Secret Investigations

Michael and Lindy Chamberlain walked out into the sunlight, arms linked. They grinned at the one hundred or so people waiting on the front steps. Somebody called "Congratulations," as if the couple had been on trial and found not guilty. One of their first moves was to unroll a poster-size photograph of Azaria. There she lay, six weeks old, in her mother's arms.

"This is to show how Azaria really was—to show the world that she was really a beautiful baby, for anyone who doubts this now," said Michael. As the cameras clicked, he looked at the picture and said, "This is our greatest treasure."

Those who had spread rumors about them, he said, did not understand the facts. "They will have to make peace with their God."

Now, he said, the family planned a new life. "This has been six months of disappointment, tragedy, and humiliation. We will go back to our children, have a holiday in New Zealand, and get back to our studies."

What about another child? "There are no special plans," said Michael, breaking into a grin. "But if we knew we could have another girl, we would have one tomorrow."

"Not quite tomorrow," said Lindy with a chuckle. It

was obvious they were in high spirits . . . a perfect mood in which to begin a new life.

While the coroner had "freed" the Chamberlains of further involvement in the disappearance, his findings sparked new developments in police circles. There had been, the coroner had decided, human intervention in the disposal of the child's body. Top policemen, in a hurried conference, agreed to try to find out just who was involved. Although he would not go into details, the Northern Territory Chief Police Commissioner, Peter McAulay, said, "Certainly the matter is not closed."

At Ayers Rock, many of the local people were outraged at the coroner's suggestion that one of them may have been involved in a cover-up after the death of Azaria. The park's chief ranger, Derek Roff, retorted: "There is no bloody way a ranger would have done it . . . no way." Aboriginals, too, he said, would tell the mother if they found the baby, because they had a remarkable love for children and great sympathy for the family unit. "Their tradition is that the spirit of the deceased child re-enters the body of the mother and is born again."

Less than a month after the coroner's findings Operation Ochre—named after the yellowish clay the aborigines use for their rock paintings—was put into effect. It was to involve the best detectives. And it was such a secret investigation that not a word leaked out. . . .

At the Seventh Day Adventist church college south of Newcastle, Michael Chamberlain had taken on the physical appearance of starting that new life he had talked about—he grew a beard, a dark brown that contrasted with his straw-blond hair. He lost himself amidst the college's six hundred students, studying for his master's degree. Lindy took up the study of physiology and hoped to teach at a secondary school when Michael found a new posting.

Australia might have just about forgotten the couple, had they not agreed to appear on television in May 1981, three months after the inquest. They said they still asked themselves why there had been conflicting reports on how Azaria's clothing had been found. Lindy emphasized that the policeman on the site, Senior Constable Morris, admitted at the inquest that he had picked up the clothes and then replaced them for photographs to be taken. But his version of the way they were found was "completely opposite" to that of a tourist who was there at the time. Another unanswered question, she said, concerned evidence that there had been no red soil in the area whereas the clothes were said to have been buried in red soil. It made her wonder if the burying happened in a dingo's lair instead of in the sandhills, as had been suggested.

Michael questioned the whereabouts of Azaria's matinee jacket. "If that had been found, it would have solved a lot of the unanswered questions," he said.

Although almost a year had passed since Azaria's disappearance, Lindy, in a public statement, criticized police handling of the case and raised the possibility of the habits of certain birds holding an answer to at least part of the mystery. No investigation at all was carried out on the possibility that birds such as crows or eagles could have dropped Azaria's clothing at the spot it was found, she said. And since the inquest she and Michael had received information that a bird's beak or talons were capable of inflicting the scissorlike marks on the jumpsuit.

The anniversary of Azaria's birth was a difficult time for the Chamberlains. As Michael put it: "All day long I looked around for something that would remind us of

Azaria. Then, late in the day, I saw two dozen roses in a florist's shop. The florist recognized me . . . gave me the roses free because of what we had been through. It was a beautiful gesture." The anniversary of the child's death was more traumatic, but they said they had both agreed to face the grief, go through it.

Said Michael: "For me, the grief process was delayed because I would not accept the fact that Azaria was really dead. If you can get through the grief process you will probably be a better person for it. In me, the grief process was delayed because I denied to myself I had lost Azaria. I have found the grief process runs through denial at first, followed by disorientation, then depression and anger, and finally acceptance of the fact that the person is dead. My problem was that I became stuck in a morass of depression and anger. Sometimes I would get very angry. 'Somebody must atone for this death!' I said to myself. People should not let their grief be denied to them. If they do, they will find they will become frustrated and angry.

"I got into a real self-pity state. I didn't care what happened around me. I just locked myself away from the outside world and brooded on my thoughts."

Lindy had more to say. It was almost as if the couple was taunting the police to look deeper. For the church mother said, "Police ignored a lot of clues and failed to follow up lines of investigation." The scientific tests conducted by the police, she said, were very doubtful. The tests with an effigy dragged through the bushes did not prove much. "Anybody with an ounce of common sense would realize a dingo holding something in its mouth would walk around bushes, not through them."

Once more, she referred to that missing matinee jacket. "Somewhere in a dingo's den at Ayers Rock are important clues relating to Azaria's death. One is the

113

matinee jacket she was wearing when I put her to bed. It was white with a pale lemon lining. It must be out there somewhere. . . . Perhaps somebody will find it someday."

Michael expressed the worry that his sons would be permanently affected by what had happened to Azaria. "Aidan wakes up screaming at night after bad nightmares in which a dingo snatches Azaria out of his arms. He has had other dreams in which the dingo attacks him."

Michael and Lindy confessed in their public revelations that Azaria's death had been hard on their life together. Statistics showed, said Michael, that many couples whose children died were separated within three years. "We knew the dangers our own marriage faced. It was something we both had to work at consciously together to preserve. Luckily, we have our friends and our faith to help us."

While the public hardened their opinions both for and against the couple, the undercover investigation that had begun in March went on slowly, methodically. Biologists were called in to help in Operation Ochre and scientists studied soil samples from relevant areas around the Rock.

And in London, a team of scientists probed through a heap of garments under the instructions of a middleaged, balding man. The garments were Azaria Chamberlain's clothing and the man was Professor James Cameron, who had a reputation as one of the world's top forensic scientists.

The clothes had been handed to him by Dr. Kenneth Brown, the scientist whose evidence had been virtually dismissed by Coroner Barritt. Dr. Brown had been concerned about the way his evidence had been received—he was an experienced and well-qualified man!—and he wanted to confer with Professor Cameron about his techniques. The professor, in Dr. Brown's estimation, was the only man to see. Consultant to the Home Office and Scotland Yard's detective training school, Professor Cameron had been involved in a range of other cases, including the mystery of a criminal's head found in the River Thames and the 1980 fire in which ten West Indians died when a firebomb was thrown into a house in one of London's southeast suburbs.

Handling Azaria's clothing with the greatest of care and applying the latest scientific techniques, the fifty-one-year-old investigator came up with a picture of what he thought had happened to the clothing. It was sensational. So much so that Professor Cameron's presence was requested in Australia. In mid-September he flew to Brisbane and, in complete secrecy, met the Chief Minister, Paul Everingham, and Northern Territory Solicitor-General Brian Martin.

The professor stayed for a few days. In that time he presented to the two men a lengthy and dramatic report. It was enough to convince them that a lot of things had not been done.

Four days later, on September 19, Paul Everingham officially ordered police to reopen investigations although, of course, they had in fact been under way for some months. But now the minister was able to announce that there was new information that had not been available at the time of the inquest.

The first event after the announcement was another visit to the Chamberlains by detectives, including Detective Sergeant Graeme Charlwood. Exactly what was said between Lindy and the detective was to be made public later—but it was to be shown that Lindy's recollection of events and those of the police officer were not entirely in harmony.

Once word was out about the new investigation and the subsequent visit to the Chamberlains by police, speculation began in earnest. A Sydney television station claimed that Professor Cameron's report showed that the baby might have been decapitated. That was quickly denied; from London a spokeswoman for the professor said the pathologist would never use the term *decapitated*. A spokesman for Paul Everingham put it even more strongly. The decapitation story, he said, was "bulldust."

However, other stories circulated. One had it that a human palmprint had been found by the professor under the armpit of Azaria's clothing, all but ruling out the theory that a dingo killed the baby. The palmprint, it was said, had been found as a result of an infrared technique used by Professor Cameron and the alleged discovery suggested that a human could have held the baby while it was bleeding. More details started to leak out. Police had seized the Chamberlains' car, the yellow Torana hatchback, from a repair shop in Hornsby, a Sydney suburb, where it was being repaired after having been involved in an accident in June.

As the police activity continued, Mr. Barritt, the Alice Springs coroner whose verdict now seemed to be in some doubt based on the events that were developing, agreed to break his silence. On the evidence he had before him at the time, he said, his had been the correct decision. And the evidence would have to be substantial to warrant any new inquiry.

Was he happy with the findings he had made? "No worries," said Mr. Barritt. "On the evidence given, I am quite happy with my finding." He thought it had quashed the rumors among all "but the most bigoted."

Speculation ripened that a new inquest would be held in the light of the still-secret new evidence. This was fueled by the fact that the Chamberlains' car was flown to Alice Springs by the Royal Australian Air Force. It was then wrapped in canvas inside a wire mesh cage and stored in a large tin shed at the police traffic section yard on the outskirts of Alice Springs.

All the pressure that Michael and Lindy Chamberlain had faced after their daughter disappeared came flooding back. Although the Chamberlains said little for public ears, a close friend, Colin Lees, also a student at the Avondale College, said the couple had little idea of what was going on among police ranks, although they had been preparing for the worst for a week. Lindy, particularly, he said, seemed to be suffering badly.

"She's looking older. It's not a nice thing to say, but she has more lines in her face. Whenever they go out people point at them and say, 'There they are. . . .'"

The Chamberlains' studies had also been affected—both had dropped a couple of subjects and would not finish their course that year. "Michael has come close to the end of being a nice guy. He wants to let off steam. He still has big depressions."

After taking possession of the Chamberlains' car on September 19, police called in a forensic biologist, Joy Kuhl, who was employed by the New South Wales Health Commission's Division of Forensic Medicine in Sydney. Holder of a Master of Science degree from the University of Sydney, she had had some four years experience in forensic biology and had earned the respect of Dr. Simon Baxter, the Health Commission's senior forensic biologist. The task given to Mrs. Kuhl was, it seemed at first, routine although the implications of her findings could be enormous for the Chamberlains. For Mrs. Kuhl was asked to examine the Torana car for traces of blood . . . baby's blood.

Assisted by Senior Constable James Metcalfe, Mrs.

Kuhl went over the car with a fine-tooth comb, centimeter by centimeter. Her search took three days as she carefully tested areas and took scrapes and swabs from all the interior surfaces of the car which had carried the Chamberlains over so many miles, so many rugged roads.

For her preliminary examination in the search for blood, Mrs. Kuhl used what is known as the ortho-tolidine test. Under this system, a dry filter paper is rubbed on the surface being tested and a drop of the reagent, or chemical substance, ortho-tolidine is then added to the paper. Should there be no change in color, a drop of hydrogen peroxide solution is added to the same area on the paper and the presence of blood—and sometimes other substances—is shown by the appearance of a bright blue color.

Mrs. Kuhl noticed a number of color changes on her filter papers. To confirm her belief that blood might be present she then scraped areas of the car and tested these samples by using various antisera. Each antiserum (a serum, or fluid constituent of blood, with antibodies in it) is designed to show a reaction to blood, or a component of blood. When these antibodies are brought together with antigens (enzymes and toxins) that are present in particular types of blood, there is a reaction; a visible band indicating a separation of the substances will appear. Mrs. Kuhl's tests with the anitsera were designed to indicate any types of blood that might be in the car.

In her further testing, Mrs. Kuhl used three different methods. One was the crossover electrophoresis which involves the use of an electric current passing across a glass plate containing the sample under examination. Another was the Ouchterlony, or immuno-diffusion, test, which also employs glass plates but not an electric current; instead the plate is allowed to stand in a humid chamber for twenty-four hours while particles disperse. Tube precipitation was the third test, in which antiserum is placed in a tube and the sample being tested is put in a solution and layered carefully with a syringe over the antiserum. In all the tests, a precipitation line, or band, will be formed—the result of reaction between blood and the antiserum.

For part of her testing the scientist used an antifetal hemoglobin antiserum. This is designed to react with a component in the blood of a baby. When born, a child's hemoglobin—the red coloring matter of the red blood corpuscles—is mainly, some 50 to 80 percent, of the fetal type. This hemoglobin rapidly declines during the child's first six months and from six months onward the child, except in exceptional circumstances, will have have less than 1 percent fetal hemoglobin, the remainder being of adult hemoglobin.

Azaria's blood contained about 25 percent fetal hemoglobin and 75 percent adult, so in order to distinguish between her blood and that of an adult—or even that of a child over six months—the test fluid had to be used in a way that revealed a 25 percent proportion of fetal hemoglobin.

Mrs. Kuhl went carefully through her testing procedures and came up with startling results.

On November 20, 1981, "the worst" happened for the Chamberlains. Justice Toohey, a supreme court judge sitting in Darwin, ordered a new inquest after hearing evidence from police. If the new evidence was accepted, he said, it was likely to prove that a dingo did not take Azaria Chamberlain. And he quashed the findings of the original inquest.

The new inquest was to be held at Alice Springs on December 14, 1981, with Gerry Galvin, the Northern

Territory's Chief Stipendiary Magistrate, presiding as coroner. The Chamberlains, although half expecting the news, were stunned.

On November 25 twenty police with shovels and sieves worked in small teams, excavating sand to the east of the now famous Ayers Rock campsite. They were looking, they said, for any metal object. Might it have been a spade? people were to ask much later. To assist them the police had a metal detector, but all they found on that first day was a pile of pull-rings from drink cans and two tent pegs. There were rumors they were looking for a spade or a knife. A soil expert from Alice Springs put samples on a white tile and analyzed them by tapping the tile. And, during the afternoon, a twin-engined Navajo plane made low sweeps of the area as police on board took photographs. There was a sense of last-minute urgency about the whole operation. Just what were the police up to? What did they have up their sleeve? It was a question the whole country was asking. Not to mention the two people most intimately involved —the Chamberlains.

Their nightmare was about to begin all over again.

X

Nightmare Relived

The Northern Territory Chief Police Commissioner, Peter McAulay, unfolded the letter and read its contents slowly. The postmark was Perth, Western Australia. The authors were a husband and wife who did not give their names. They claimed that while visiting the Rock they saw a dingo carrying what they first believed was a doll in its mouth and when the woman threw something at the animal it dropped the object. On inspection, they found it was a baby. The child was so badly mutilated, the letter added, that it was put in a plastic garbage bag, with the intention of burying it so the parents would not see it. The baby was buried in the bag after being stripped of its clothes. The letter said the couple then drove to Mount Isa and, after hearing on the radio about a search for a baby called Azaria, decided to get rid of the clothing. They drove back to Ayers Rock and dumped the clothing outside a dingo's lair. The confession was made out of fear that innocent people would suffer, the letter added.

Peter McAulay rubbed his chin. It was another rumor, fact, half truth—who knew?—to follow up along with all the other leads to be chased or dismissed.

On the Adventist Sabbath before the inquest was due to start the heavens opened, causing the worst flooding

Alice Springs had seen for nearly ten years. The Chamberlains spent that day in prayer at the college at Cooranbong but on Monday they were seated in the coroner's court half an hour before the start of the new inquiry. Michael was in a blue blazer with silver buttons, a blue-and-red-striped tie, light-gray trousers, and brown shoes. On his right was Lindy in a blue-and-white-striped jacket, a white dress, and white shoes. She was wearing just a trace of makeup; despite the recommendations of her religion, she allowed a touch of face powder and clear nail polish. To her right was Irene, a close Seventh Day Adventist friend.

The lawyers entered and took up their positions. On the right, as the Chamberlains looked at them from behind, was Des Sturgess, a Queensland barrister appointed to assist coroner Gerry Galvin. On his left was Sturgess' assistant, Michael O'Laughlin of the Alice Springs Crown Law Department. Then there was Phil Rice, the Adelaide Queen's Counsel who had represented Michael and Lindy at the original inquest. Next to him was his assistant, Andrew Kirkham, a Melbourne barrister, and finally there was Peter Dean, the Chamberlains' original solicitor.

Mr. Sturgess began by handing into the court two purple baby blankets, one of which, he said, had been partly bloodstained. A silver insulating blanket was submitted, followed by two green parkas belonging to the Chamberlain boys. A second insulating blanket was held up by Mr. Rice, who drew attention to some small holes in it. This blanket, he said, was significant. Next, the tent was submitted as an exhibit, although it was kept in a brown paper bag.

Next the baby's off-white singlet was tendered, followed by the jumpsuit, which, Mr. Sturgess pointed out, was "considerably bloodstained." But he said it also had a considerable amount of red sand in it. There was damage around the collar and around the area of the left arm. Handed to the court in separate plastic bags were the baby's booties, found inside the jumpsuit, and also the disposable diaper. Mr. Sturgess then showed the dress Lindy Chamberlain was wearing at the time of Azaria's disappearance. Police had taken possession of the blue, floral-patterned garment when Lindy returned from Ayers Rock to Mount Isa. The running shoes she had been wearing on the tragic night were also handed to the court.

Next, the coroner was shown a green sleeping bag. Lindy sucked on the end of a pencil as it was passed across to the Chamberlains for examination. Michael's running shoes were produced, followed by Aidan's sandals and Reagan's track shoes. Exhibit 24 was a red camp mattress that had been in the tent. It was cool in the courtroom and after a ten-minute break the coroner, who had been dressed in a shirt and tie, returned to his chair wearing a sweater. His style of dress illustrated the difference in formality between the outback and the city, where coroners wear suits.

The first witness, fair-haired Mrs. Sally Lowe of Hobart, cast her mind back to the night of August 17, saying she had not seen Lindy do anything that indicated she was not a "loving and caring mother." She described how Lindy had held the baby in its blankets close to her shoulder and had patted the child on its back. She had noticed the child had fought against Mrs. Chamberlain, as babies tended to do when they had wind. She had noticed that the baby's eyes were open, but had not heard the child utter any sounds. And there was "a bit of facial movement. It was only very, very slight." There had been another occasion at the barbecue area that night when she had seen the baby's feet kicking.

Mr. Kirkham asked, "Is it correct to say these were independent movements and not as the result of any action on the part of Mrs. Chamberlain?"

"Oh, yes—I had thought about that," said Mrs. Lowe.

And she was certain that the cry she heard later had come from the Chamberlains' tent. "It was a serious cry, but I would not say it was a scream of pain. It was something I would be concerned about."

Michael Chamberlain was called. He seemed subdued as he sat in the witness box and answered questions about the family's day at the Rock. But many of his answers about subsequent events were vague, as if he was suffering from a memory loss. He could not recall one of his sons' bags being cleaned before it was handed to the police and he was not sure whether it was his wife's or his own sleeping bag that had been lying on their bed when they spent the night in the motel, although he believed it had spots of blood on it.

Had he made any attempt to have his bag cleaned?

"I think I did, yes."

"What do you mean," asked Mr. Sturgess, "you think you did?"

"Sir, I have been under a considerable amount of stress and the things that happened to me make it difficult to recall at times."

Shown Lindy's blue running shoes, he said there had been blood on the uppers and around the toe area, and when handed Lindy's sleeping bag, he said he believed there had been blood on it, but could not recall.

Mr. Sturgess then turned his questions to the matter of the family car, the yellow Torana, which Michael had bought in December 1977. Asked whether he had had any accidents in it, Michael said, "I think probably three." Nobody had been injured, but Reagan had once traveled in the vehicle with a forehead injury received after falling down a flight of stairs; and Aidan had had a nosebleed. There was also a man who had been picked up after a road accident and carried in the car to the hospital.

The Queensland barrister asked Michael about a black camera bag produced in court. He had several camera bags, Michael pointed out, and the one shown to the court was not always used for camera gear. He usually carried the bag under his feet when he was driving so he would have fast access to the camera if he saw something to photograph at the side of the road.

Michael admitted he made no attempt to turn the car around to shine the lights in the direction the dingo had run, although he had tried to use the spotlight on the vehicle. It would not work because he did not have the keys to the car—the same reason he had not turned the car. Michael said he could not recall where the keys were, neither could he remember where he eventually got them from. They weren't in the ignition, of that he was certain, and they weren't in his trousers.

He said he had not joined the search the following day because he thought it best to stay at base so he knew what was going on. But he agreed that, following a request from a newspaper, he had decided to take pictures of the area and had gone to the camp store with his two boys to buy black-and-white film, returning to the camping area on the local bus. Asked why he had not used his own car, Michael said it was "messed up" —disarrayed with unpacked gear and opened cans of food. Apart from that, he added, "I didn't really feel like driving." He had arrived at the tent site at about 11:30 A.M. or midday and had remained about five minutes. He didn't want to look into the tent—"it seemed like a morgue."

Had he washed the car before going to Mount Isa? Yes, he thought he had washed the outside at Alice Springs and on arrival at Mount Isa he had cleaned the exterior and interior.

Michael said he did not remember taking the boys' sleeping bags to the dry cleaner's, but later recalled visiting the cleaner's and asking for a sleeping bag. He recalled, too, that when the bag was handed over to him he asked the woman assistant if all the bloodstains had come out. He recalled examining the bag and pointing out that the stains were still there. The woman had asked what the stains were and he said they were from his child.

Asked whether he had ever cleaned any blood out of the interior of the car, Michael replied, "I don't recall that."

Mr. Sturgess said he was not talking about a little speck of blood but "quite a quantity of blood." Had Michael ever noticed there was a considerable quantity of blood in the car and then set out to clean it up?

"I don't recall deliberately cleaning blood out of the car."

From time to time, he said, he and his wife cleaned the inside of their car, but he did not recall cleaning up a great deal of blood. He agreed, under further questioning, that there may have been quite a bit of blood in the car, possibly in the rear section.

"Do you recall cleaning blood off the seats?"

"I cleaned the seats regularly, but I do not recall specifically cleaning blood."

Michael Chamberlain was then handed a plastic bag containing a dismantled pair of toenail scissors. They were in the car when police took possession of the vehicle, but he could not be sure whether they were in the car on August 17, 1980, when Azaria had disappeared. His attention was drawn to a statement allegedly made by his wife in which she said he had come down from the Rock and cut his toenails—they were hurting him after climbing the Rock in his running shoes. They normally carried scissors in the car, he said, but where the scissors with which he cut his toenails came from he could not recall.

Michael's questioning completed for the time being, two technical experts were called to talk about the makeup of baby Azaria's jumpsuit and about the soil found around Ayers Rock. Then Mr. Sturgess turned slightly toward the row of seats immediately behind him and said: "I call Mrs. Alice Lynne Chamberlain."

The small figure of Lindy Chamberlain rose and walked briskly to the witness box, her dark hair, which had grown since the first inquest, bouncing on the shoulders of her brown jacket. Having taken the oath, she sat with legs crossed, coughed into her hand, and then began the task of identifying the clothes and camping equipment. It was when she was handed a blue blanket that she suddenly put her hand to her face and started sobbing. The coroner ordered a short adjournment and Michael walked across to the witness box to hand her a blue handkerchief and put his arm around her.

When they resumed, Exhibit 147 was produced for Lindy's perusal—the pair of scissors that Michael had earlier examined. Yes, they had a number of pairs of scissors and she thought these may have been one. There should have been a pair, too, in the first aid box and a pair in the console of the car, although the children sometimes took them out. She could not be sure whether the scissors she was looking at had been in the car or not. Questioned about Michael cutting his toe-nails with scissors, Lindy pointed out that she had not mentioned scissors in her statement to police. He had in fact cut his toes with nail clippers.

Had she assisted with the cleaning of the car? "No, I am not very fond of that job." Had she attempted to clean blood from the interior of the vehicle? Not since August 17, she replied.

The questioning of Lindy Chamberlain moved on to those who had bled in the family car. Aidan, she said, had had a nosebleed, but "not in copious" quantities. There would have been quite a number of other occasions when there had been bleeding, and she cited the time when the car had been used as an ambulance to carry an accident victim with a head injury. Reagan had once hit the dashboard, bitten his lips, and, while bleeding, touched the door handle. He had also had a nose-bleed. She also pointed out that members of the Pathfinders, a young people's group in the church, had also on occasion climbed around in the car with cut feet, cut fingers, and nosebleeds, because the car had been used as a first aid station. But she agreed that the baby had never been injured in the car.

Lindy, who now seemed relaxed in the witness box, was shown her husband's camera bag. At Ayers Rock, she said, it was used exclusively for his camera gear.

"Do you know of any way in which it could be blood-stained?"

"It was also used as a beach bag, and it is quite possible that there could have been blood on it from that because the children sometimes cut their feet on the coral."

Now the court was about to hear startling new evidence. It emerged from an alleged conversation Lindy had with Detective Sergeant Graeme Charlwood.

Lindy's recollection of events, it became clear, was different from the police officer's. But she agreed that as she drove with him to the police station at Toronto, near Newcastle, they had a discussion about the missing baby.

Mr. Sturgess: "In the course of that discussion, Mr. Charlwood mentioned the results of certain work that had been done by a Professor Cameron—is that so?"

"He did tell me some things, but he said he would deny all knowledge of having the conversation take place."

Mr. Sturgess said he wanted to relate to Lindy an account of some of the conversation. Did she remember Charlwood saying: "I'm aware of the advice given to you by a church solicitor in relation to making a statement and I'm not asking you to go against that advice"?

Lindy said that was not right. She had never been in contact with a church solicitor. What Charlwood had said was that he was aware of the advice she had been given by her lawyer.

The barrister assisting the coroner asked if the policeman had said, "There are certain things that I would like to put to you if you are prepared to talk to me." Lindy told Mr. Sturgess that the police officer said he had a question that he would have asked her in an interview if she had agreed to it.

Mr. Sturgess: "Did you say this to him, or something to this effect: 'I'll tell you what I can. What do you want to know?' "

"No."

"Did he say anything like this: 'It intrigues me why you or your husband never really queried why we wanted all the gear back that you took to Ayers Rock'?"

"His statement, as near as I can recall, is: 'You

haven't yet asked me why we're here,' and my answer was, 'No, I haven't, have I?' "

Mr. Sturgess asked if the detective had continued: "You recall me telling you that certain new forensic evidence had come to hand?"

Lindy Chamberlain replied, "He didn't mention any new forensic evidence till we were in the car. We had no idea of that."

Had Mr. Charlwood said: "I feel that you should be aware of what that [forensic] evidence is?"

"No, he asked me would I like to know what it was. He didn't say we should be aware of it." She had told him she was interested.

Mr. Sturgess asked, "Did he say this, or something to this effect: 'The baby's clothing has been examined by a Professor Cameron in London'?"

"That's correct."

"He goes on to say: 'He is perhaps one of the leading forensic people in the world.' "

"Yes, he told me he was rated somewhere around about sixth, or something like that."

Charlwood had continued in his statement that Professor Cameron's examination of the clothing had brought to light certain things.

Mr. Sturgess then asked: "Did he say this, or something to this effect: 'Well, his examination of the clothing has confirmed what others have already found. That is, that no dingo or dog was involved in the taking of, or the death of, your child'?"

"I don't think that's quite the way he put it. He said that his evidence indicated that there was no animal involvement at all." Lindy added that she had said she "didn't know there were any dingo experts in London."

Lindy said she did not recall Detective Sergeant Charlwood saying, "He doesn't profess to be a dingo

130

expert, but he has the expertise to say that no canine was involved in the death of the child nor with the disposal of the clothing."

Mr. Sturgess then asked, "Did he say this, or something to this effect: 'He has told us that your child died as a result of having its throat cut'?"

"He told me his tests had been— Sorry, I'll rephrase that. He indicated to me that Professor Cameron said the baby had been decapitated."

Mr. Sturgess said the policeman had added in his report of the conversation with Lindy Chamberlain: " 'He [Professor Cameron] has told us that your child died as a result of having its throat cut and the head possibly decapitated.' He put that to you, did he?"

"Yes, he mentioned decapitation."

"Did he say this, or anything to this effect: 'By various means and further to that, he has found on the clothing evidence of a human handprint'?"

"He mentioned human handprints in the underarm area."

"Did he say this, or something to this effect: 'He has told us that the handprint was a result of someone with wet, bloodstained hands touching the clothing when the hand was still wet with blood'?"

"He did indicate that, yes."

"And did he say this: 'And, more importantly, that this handprint is consistent with the handprint of a female'?"

"Yes."

Lindy Chamberlain said she thought she indicated to the detective that it was now rather obvious why the police had gone back to their house—"it was rather obvious from his discussion that I was suspected once again."

Mr. Sturgess then said, "The suggestion is that you

made no reply when he indicated it was the handprint of a female and there was a silence."

"No, I think that I did make a reply."

Mr. Sturgess went on to say that, according to Charlwood's account, he had said: "Do you realize the position that these findings could place you in?" Lindy, according to the account, allegedly replied: "Yes, I suppose I do." The policeman had added: "It puts you in what is sometimes called the hot seat." And she had said: "Yes, I can see that."

In the coroner's court, Lindy said she thought that conversation was relayed back to front—Charlwood was saying what she had said. The policeman had not been taking any notes at the time—he was driving. She said she had told Charlwood she hoped police were looking at other people who had been "involved" and were keeping an open mind.

"I named a person and he said, 'Who's he?'"

Mr. Sturgess asked, "Did you say this: 'What about [Senior Constable] Frank Morris?'"

"That's right. That's the person I named, and he asked me who he was." She told the court she had mentioned to Detective Sergeant Charlwood that Senior Constable Frank Morris's evidence about finding the clothing was contradictory to Mr. Goodwin's, the man who actually found it, and that when he was in the witness box at the last inquest he admitted handling the clothing before it was photographed.

Mr. Sturgess said, "Let me go on with this account. Did Mr. Charlwood say this, or something to this effect: 'You seemed to have missed the point, Mrs. Chamberlain. The handprints on the clothes are the same blood as your child's and were put there when the blood was still wet. The clothes were found a week later'?"

"Yes, that's correct."

"And after that there was silence?"

"No, there was not silence."

"You deny that there was a lengthy silence following that statement by Mr. Charlwood?"

"There was no lengthy silence in the car. There was some discussion about tampering with the clothes and methods of faking evidence, as I remember."

Mr. Sturgess asked if she was suggesting that Senior Constable Morris had tampered with the clothes.

Lindy Chamberlain replied, "We were talking then about finding the clothes a week later and faking evidence. I was suggesting that nobody has any idea what Mr. Morris did with the clothing from the time that the tourists left him until, by cross-referencing the statements of the other rangers, there is some twenty minutes in there when he was alone with the clothes; and it was indicated by them all that he had told them not to touch the clothing until it was photographed, and yet he had done it himself and not told anyone that he had done it—except that Mr. Goodwin had seen him do it, and mentioned it in the box."

"Now," said Mr. Sturgess, "let me proceed with this account. Did Mr. Charlwood say: 'Mrs. Chamberlain, did you kill your child?' "

"Yes."

"And did you say: 'You have asked me that before'?"

"No."

"Did Mr. Charlwood say: 'No, I asked you before if you knew what happened to your child'?"

"He said that was one question that he hadn't asked before. That he had asked me before what happened, but never had I done it."

"Did you say this, or something to this effect to him: 'Well, what are the implications if I tell you?' "

"That's correct."

"Did he say: 'It depends on your answer'?"

"No, that's not correct. I said that he had promised to keep conversations confidential before and he had broken his word. He asked me what conversation and I said that the— He asked me about hypnotism and then, in the box last time, he maintained that that was an official request when there was no indication of that given. I said to him: 'If I speak to you again like this, what guarantee have I got that I don't have this thrown up at me in court?' which obviously I am having right now."

"Why did you ask him that question: 'Well, what are the implications if I tell you?' "

"Because I had told him that our legal advice was not to give an interview and, although I've learned very fast how far to trust the police, I was still expecting them to honor their word. I was not sure what he considered an interview and what he didn't; and as I had no legal advice there, I was asking him the question. Unfortunately, I was given the wrong advice."

Lindy Chamberlain said she suggested to Detective Sergeant Charlwood that if the investigation was being reopened, everybody who was out at Ayers Rock that night should be thoroughly investigated if the police were going to do the job properly. "Otherwise the same thing that happened last time would occur; and you're trying to make a jigsaw puzzle up out of half the pieces."

Mr. Sturgess, continuing his questioning in the packed coroner's courtroom, asked, "Did you say this to Mr. Charlwood in the course of the same conversation I have been asking you about—'What about the rangers at Ayers Rock?' "

"Yes, certainly one of the rangers was mentioned in

the summary at the last inquest and I asked if they had
—were going to be further investigated as well."

"As possible culprits?"

"It is only logical if you are looking for a murderer;
everybody that had anything whatsoever to do with the
surrounding events would obviously be looked at."

Mr. Sturgess asked if the policeman had said: "Mrs.
Chamberlain, you haven't answered my question."

"Yes, that's correct."

"Did you say in response to that: 'No, I never killed
my child'?"

"In response to that question I said: 'No, I haven't,
have I?' I did at a later stage tell him most certainly that
I did not kill her."

"Did you go on and say this, or something to this
effect: 'You don't think if I did, I could have carried out
this charade all the time? Ask my friends. They'll tell
you I can't tell lies. I'm not that smart.' Did you say
that or something to that effect?"

"That's a mixture of a couple of sentences that I said.
I told him that I thought he was crediting me with some
brains that I didn't have, and he told me, 'Don't sell
yourself short,' and I said to him, 'Oh, come on, you're
crediting me with the brains to commit the perfect murder and get away with it,' and he said, 'Don't you sell
yourself short.' "

Lindy Chamberlain told the coroner that Detective
Sergeant Charlwood had said that one of the things they
would have liked to have done if she and her husband
had agreed to an interview was to have taken their
handprints. Lindy said she had told the police that was
fine by them, providing they got in touch with their
lawyers, and any interviews or handprints taken were in
the presence of lawyers.

Mr. Sturgess peered at Lindy over the top of his spectacles and asked, his words rebounding around the hushed courtroom: "Mrs. Chamberlain—would you be prepared to give to the police your palmprints?"

Her QC, Mr. Rice, jumped instantly to his feet before she could say a word. Mr. and Mrs. Chamberlain, he said, were not at the inquest to assert anything one way or the other.

"They are not here to volunteer any evidence. They have the right at all times—a right she exercised—to decline in the police station and I would have to protest at any demonstration one way or the other. I think the particular answer one way or the other is contrary to the conduct of a fair interview, let alone the examination of a person in the witness box. I don't care for this line of questioning—for this sort of request to be conducted. No one is obliged to comply with that request and refusal, of course, even on advice, might be misconstrued. My advice would be not to allow Mrs. Chamberlain to respond to that request, irrespective of what her state of mind might be."

Coroner Galvin decided to adjourn to allow Mr. Rice to advise Lindy on whether or not she should allow her palmprint to be taken. After the break, Mr. Rice told the coroner that Lindy was perfectly happy for her own part to provide the palmprint, "but on advice from the counsel, that request will not be complied with."

Mr. Sturgess said Lindy must claim the privilege herself. And, turning to her, he asked that question again: "Mrs. Chamberlain—are you prepared to provide a copy of your palmprints?"

Lindy replied; "I told Sergeant Charlwood and I say the same thing again—I would have been quite happy to have provided the palmprints to them, providing my lawyers agreed; and they do not agree that I give any palmprints at this stage. They know I'm not happy to give my palmprints."

Shortly afterward, Lindy Chamberlain stood down from the witness box. She was pale and exhaled visibly as she took her seat beside her husband, who was sitting with his fingers interlocked.

There was one more witness to be heard that day—Constable James Metcalfe of Darwin. He told the court that during a police search of the Chamberlain home he collected some scissors from the kitchen drawer and asked Mrs. Chamberlain if she had any other scissors at Ayers Rock. Only those she used to cut her hair, she said, but added: "While you are at it, why don't you check Sergeant Morris's knives and scissors?"

"Why is that?" Constable Metcalfe said he replied.

"He was left alone with the clothing for half an hour."

Constable Metcalfe then moved on to describe an examination of Michael Chamberlain's Torana hatchback, which had been involved in an accident and was under repair. In the console of the car, which had been removed and was on the backseat, he found a pair of scissors. He took four place carpets from the car and removed a number of items from the wheel-well area—a dirty rag, a pair of socks, a yellow towel, another dirty towel, a brown shoulder bag, and a small wooden-handled knife. Mrs. Kuhl, the biologist who had been assisting him, had made a cut into the carpet to test the bottom of the pile. He noticed staining on the handle area of the scissors and a dark brown stain on one of the surfaces of the cutting edge.

Constable Metcalfe, a burly man who made reference to photographs of the objects of which he spoke, said that when he unbolted the two front seats of the car and turned the passenger seat upside down, he noticed two stains on the metal cross-section. Under the bottom of a seat was a stain and running down the hinge was a second dark stain. On two metal clips holding the upholstery were two globular dark patches. On pulling back the carpet under the place where the passenger seat had been, food particles, nail clippers, and a ten-cent coin stuck to the floor by a heavy dark stain were exposed. A yellow towel, which was removed from beside the spare wheel and which had been wrapped around a flashlight, was also stained.

Further investigation revealed a stained area underneath a seat bracket. The policeman held up a close-up photograph of the bracket. He added that the bracket was removed from the seat to reveal a dark flaking substance around two bolt holes.

It was not to be long before the court heard an opinion of what those stains were—but in a town like Alice Springs, where gossip spreads like wildfire, many had already made up their minds.

XI

Blood in the Car

The yellow Torana was parked at an angle inside a wire cage in the vehicle shed at the Alice Springs police traffic department on the outskirts of town. The hood was up and the engine was missing. The seats had been unbolted and the rear hatch was raised. On the lowered sun visor were three badges—a motoring club emblem, a Queensland Justices Association badge, and a silver cross on a blue background. Under the cross was a single word: CLERGY.

A policeman raised a roller door and the coroner, Gerry Galvin, walked into the hot shed followed by counsel. Lost among the crowd were Lindy and Michael Chamberlain, in contrasting styles of dress. Her black dress, red high-heel shoes, red poppies on her belt, and red shoulder bag gave the impression she was ready for a dinner date; his sober white shirt with faint blue stripes, black and red tie, and dark trousers suggested he was about to lead a religious service.

The center of attention was a short, dark-haired woman—not Lindy Chamberlain this time. Entering the bizarre case that day was Mrs. Joy Kuhl, the forensic biologist who was often consulted by the New South Wales police when they needed help in crimes that involved the spilling of blood and other body fluids.

In the wake of Constable Metcalfe, who had described areas of the car where he had found dark stains, Joy Kuhl had presented sensational evidence to the coroner's court. Not so much that the stains were blood, for many in the public gallery had already guessed that, but that they had been caused by fetal blood, found in babies of six months and under. Joy Kuhl had raised gasps in court when she revealed the blood type.

On examination of the scissors in her laboratory, her tests had revealed the existence of blood of fetal origin on the cutting edge, in the hinge area and around the handle. She then went on to describe the areas in the car where fetal blood had been found: brackets, bolt holes and hinges around the front seats, and on the carpet.

Fetal blood, she said, had stuck a ten-cent coin to the floor. When asked the age of the blood, Mrs. Kuhl replied that it would have been at least twelve months old when she examined it in September 1981. She had also found fetal blood on the inside of a yellow container that held an imitation chamois leather. There had been positive findings of fetal blood, too, on the underside of the glove box and on the console.

The blood she said she had found under the glove box was to have major significance at a later stage. During Mrs. Kuhl's examination of the car in October a spray of some substance that was sticky to the touch had been found. No reaction was produced through the ortho-tolidine test and Mrs. Kuhl had suggested to Constable Metcalfe, who was assisting her, that the liquid might have been a soft drink or something similar. When reactions were obtained from the side of the passenger seat Mrs. Kuhl suggested to Constable Metcalfe that the area under the dashboard be examined further. As a result, a section of steel plate was cut from under the glove box and a sample of the spray pattern was delivered by Senior Constable Metcalfe to Mrs. Kuhl. When she tested it, she concluded that baby's blood was present.

Asked at the inquest before the court party traveled to inspect the car what was meant by the term *fetal blood,* the biologist explained how, after birth, fetal hemoglobin started to decrease and adult hemoglobin began to appear.

"This occurs up to six months and after that detectable amounts of fetal hemoglobin are not present in a normal infant," she said.

There were cases, she conceded, where fetal hemoglobin persisted through life as a result of a genetic condition. This was rare in Australia, but common in some Mediterranean cultures. In Australia, she said, she had come across only one case where fetal hemoglobin was detectable, in a twelve-year-old girl—and she was from Greece.

The blood in the car, said Mrs. Kuhl, was that of a child under six months old. She also told the coroner than an experiment was carried out with a car seat similar to the ones in the Torana to establish how blood had flowed to the bracket area. The seat, she said, would have to be occupied for the blood to seep through and the estimated quantity needed would be five milliliters (about two teaspoonsful).

Now, in the police garage, Mrs. Kuhl systematically went over the parts she had tested to confirm the presence of blood. The seats were taken from the car and laid out on a table while the coroner and counsel peered in at the dashboard, sweating under the heat of a portable lamp.

Mrs. Kuhl then pointed to areas on the console—which had also been moved to the table—where she had found blood. As everyone craned for a closer look, she took a scraping from a piece of vinyl that had been removed from a seat and placed it on a piece of filter paper. She then added a chemical which turned the paper turquoise, indicating, she said, the presence of blood. While the inspection went on, Lindy stood with her arm in Michael's. They didn't say anything to each other.

On the fifth day of the new inquest, Dr. Kenneth Brown, the Adelaide dental expert whose evidence on bite marks in clothing had been put aside by Coroner Barritt at the first inquest, stepped into the witness box. Holding the skull of a dingo, the bespectacled Dr. Brown started to explain the difference between animal teeth actions and those of a human. But then the Chamberlains' QC, Mr. Rice, rose to point out that the witness had been discounted at the earlier inquest because he had no experience in examining bite marks in clothing. Despite Mr. Rice's objections, Dr. Brown, whose pride in his work was apparent, was allowed to continue his evidence. He went on to point out facts such as the type of marks a tooth would have made in clothing compared with a sharp cutting edge. The odontologist —in his profession, he applied dental science in the administration of the law—was asked to approach the coroner's bench, along with counsel, to compare the jumpsuit used in the Adelaide Zoo test with Azaria's. The missing baby's suit was laid out on the bench, the legs dangling down, in full view of the public. It was a strange moment, evoking both horror and sympathy. In that grubby, white garment, with its dark stains around the collar, a baby had once lived.

The dental expert told the coroner that on May 27, 1981, he took the clothing to London and handed it to Professor James Cameron. "I had a discussion with him and left the articles in his possession," he said, giving nothing away. But Dr. Brown was asked to explain his reasons for taking the jumpsuit to Professor Cameron. He had done so, he said—and it seemed he spoke with some reluctance—because he was concerned about the interpretation of his evidence at the first inquest, and he wanted to consult some of his colleagues who would be at a conference at which he was to present a paper in Norway.

"I was concerned about the manner of the conclusions I had drawn, which were not accepted by the coroner," said Dr. Brown. He had applied to the police for Azaria's clothes—but denied he had taken them overseas for the purpose of conducting further investigations.

"I wanted to find out if I had reached a reasonable conclusion or one that was not reasonable," he explained.

"Your professional pride was hurt?" Mr. Rice suggested.

"I don't say it hurt my pride—I wanted to learn from these experts how I should have done it."

Dr. Brown said he believed Professor Cameron and a colleague, Mr. Sims, would be at the conference in Norway, but he found out on arrival in London they were not going. So he discussed the case with the two men in London.

For the second time that day, Azaria's jumpsuit was held up before the court, this time in the hands of Dr. Andrew Scott, the Adelaide forensic biologist who had given evidence at the first inquest. He told the coroner he had detected run marks of blood around the neck area that had spread out. This would have occurred, he said, while the garment was in an upright position. The mustachioed scientist then walked to the coroner's bench and held up the baby's singlet—so tiny in his hands, and so soiled. It was too much for Michael Chamberlain. He uttered a loud gasp and threw his body forward, burying his head in his hands. Lindy put her right arm across his shoulders and scratched at the back of his neck with her fingernails.

Azaria's jumpsuit was also to feature in evidence presented by the next witness, Sergeant Frank Cocks of the forensic science section at Adelaide police headquarters. He concluded that scissors had caused a cut in the arm and that the scissors were the curved pair the police had already taken possession of. Using a similar pair to cut into another jumpsuit of the same type as Azaria's he found that the pile, which was looped on the ends, lost small particles. In simple terms, he told the court, when the jumpsuit was cut, loops of material fell off. In vacuuming the Chamberlains' car, he said, he found looped particles on the passenger side floor mat and in other areas. Three small tufts had also been found in Michael Chamberlain's camera bag.

The last witness on that Friday afternoon added to the scientific evidence that was now dominating the bizarre affair. Dr. Anthony Jones, a forensic pathologist from Darwin, said that during an examination of the Chamberlains' car he had looked at a metal panel forming a support for the dashboard structure. Cutting out a section of the panel, he found that particles of staining on it showed positive response to blood tests. The staining was caused by droplets of blood with "tails" running in parallel lines "which is characteristic of spurting blood." There were droplets on the edge of the plate that faced the front of the vehicle, he said, but the direction of the spurts was from the front of the car toward the rear and, he considered, they would have come "from a small artery."

"While the heart was still beating?" asked Mr. Sturgess, assisting the coroner.

"Yes," said Dr. Jones.

The following day, the Seventh Day Adventist Sabbath, the inquest party gathered at the base of Ayers Rock, for Coroner Galvin, like Coroner Barritt before him, wanted to see for himself the area where the tent had been pitched and the place where the jumpsuit had been found. As the inquest party stood at the southwest corner of the Rock, Mr. Sturgess produced a color photograph said to have been taken by Michael Chamberlain. The picture was of lichen growing at the side of the Rock.

It was lichen in this same area that an Englishman named David Brett was to climb up over five years later and whose death was to result in the discovery of a vital clue that everyone in that inquest party that day, along with parties of searchers before them, had failed to notice.

Just why was to be questioned.

XII

". . . A Human Being with Wet, Bloodstained Hands"

"Your worship, I call James Malcolm Cameron."

Whispers ran along the public benches as the portly, sandy-haired man in the light-gray suit made his way briskly to the witness box. He took the oath and sat in the orange vinyl chair provided. His Glasgow accent penetrated the now-hushed courtroom as he confirmed his qualifications to Mr. Sturgess: Doctor of Medicine and Doctor of Philosophy from Glasgow University; Fellow of the Royal College of Pathologists; holder of the Diploma of Medical Jurisprudence; a member of the Worshipful Society of Apothecaries of London; a Professor of Forensic Medicine at the London Hospital Medical College and Saint Bartholomew's Hospital Medical School; the Ver Heyden Delancey Reader in Forensic Medicine of the Council of Legal Education, Grays Inn, School of Law, London; honorary civilian consultant in forensic medicine to the army; and honorary civilian consultant in forensic medicine to the Royal Navy.

On Monday, June 8, 1981, at the Department of Forensic Medicine at the London Hospital Medical College, he said, he received from Dr. K. A. Brown of Adelaide a dingo skull, a white jumpsuit, a white singlet that was turned inside out, a damaged plastic diaper, and two booties.

He had begun his experiments by taking photographs of a normal child of the same age as Azaria—nine to ten weeks old—dressed in a jumpsuit without a collar. This was to demonstrate in a life-size photograph the area of the neck that would be exposed in a child of that age.

"With such a photograph of a child in a similar age, I could find no possibility in my opinion of any member of the canine family gripping the child without damaging the top of the collar. In conjunction with Mr. Sims, I have been involved in a number of cases of assaults of humans by members of the canine family but, I might say right away, not any member of the dingo family."

He went on: "Given a normal opening of a canine mouth and working from the dingo skull which I had in my possession, I found difficulty in finding an area of skin exposed in a child that remained to be grasped without damaging the material of the neck of the garment. Examination of the jumpsuit which I was presented with confirmed that bleeding had occurred when the jumpsuit was buttoned up to the top and that the neck [of the garment] had been cut at or about shortly after by a cutting instrument such as scissors or a knife, but on closer examination it's more consistent with a scissors."

Professor Cameron said he relied entirely on Dr. Scott's report in which it was stated there was no saliva present on the clothing. He added that one of the interesting features of his study was that he could not detect any evidence of dragging on other areas of the jumpsuit. This indicated to him that it was not a member of the canine family that had carried the child—or if it had been it would have to be large, like a Great Dane. To carry a child of Azaria's size by the head or neck without dragging would necessitate the body being held at least twenty inches off the ground. In other words, he said, if the baby had been grasped by the neck, the feet would have dragged and he would have expected drag marks in the form of tearing or marking on the feet of the jumpsuit.

The forensic expert said that by looking at black-and-white photographs of the jumpsuit it was possible to see, apart from areas of bleeding, which were darker in color, that the top two snaps were undone when the garment was in contact with the reddish sand of the area. Surrounding the right-hand first snap a whitish area could be seen, confirming that the garment had been done up when the blood was flowing.

The court was fascinated by Professor Cameron's evidence. Crossing his legs and settling back in the chair, he proceeded to describe a special photographic technique—ultraviolet fluorescent photography—that helped to distinguish blood marks. In this method, since blood absorbed ultraviolet light, if there was no fluorescence, blood would show up dark in photographs. Sand, on the other hand, did not absorb ultraviolet light to the same extent, which meant blood would be more clearly defined. What fluoresced, he explained, was the white of the material, and it was possible to see a clear cut demarcation between blood and other staining. "The blood, in other words, is dark as compared to the other stains." He said he was assuming from Dr. Scott's report that there were only bloodstains and sand in the garment.

Professor Cameron went on: "The distribution of blood on the jumpsuit would suggest that the blood flowed on the collar from above, but all around the neck at one time and not from separate areas, as one would have anticipated from past experience were an animal involved. In other words, when an animal's teeth, or jaws, imprison the neck structures they would impinge on either side of the neck, so there would be two principal areas of bleeding, unless of course it was a chunk of tissue that had been removed. But in this, on examination of the jumpsuit, it appeared that it was right around the neck and it suggested that—or it confirmed to me—that it was not a two-pronged assault."

The ruddy-faced Scotsman said he and a colleague turned the baby's singlet right side out and ultraviolet photographs were taken. The distribution of blood the pictures showed confirmed to the two experts that the singlet had been on the correct way when the baby was bleeding.

Asked Mr. Sturgess: "In other words, the pattern on the jumpsuit is repeated, not exactly, but repeated sufficiently to enable you to express this opinion on the singlet; is that the situation?"

"Indeed. It appears that the singlet has been inverted or turned inside out on removal from a body, because the pattern produced by just looking at the inside of the cloth is the mirror image of that of the singlet. But when it is on the correct way it is the direct, or as direct as one can have, of a superimposed image."

Professor Cameron said that assuming dingoes acted much the same as ordinary domestic dogs, he would be surprised if there were no saliva or grip marks on the cloth. He would also be surprised about the absence of drag marks in particular.

Asked to turn his attention to the condition of the clothing, he said the only mark of significance, apart from those associated with the bloodstaining, were a cut in the right side of the neck of the jumpsuit collar and a slight tear at the seam attaching the right collar to the neck of the garment. His opinions on the cut were that it had been made by an instrument like scissors or a knife but, having had another look at the cloth and having talked with Sergeant Cocks, he was now convinced scissors were responsible.

Professor Cameron was asked to take Exhibit 15, the jumpsuit, to the bench in front of the coroner. Counsel, the coroner, and the British forensic expert gathered around the garment and Mr. Sturgess asked the professor to comment on damage to the right-hand side of the collar. That was where there were two layers of cloth, one having been cut through more extensively than the other. The barrister assisting the coroner asked Professor Cameron what he thought about staining in that area.

On looking at the cut, said the professor, it could be seen to be uniformly stained, but the inner lining of the collar was not bloodstained, or not as heavily bloodstained as the outside. This would suggest it was more likely to have been cut after the bleeding had stopped. There was a further hole with another cut that would confirm Sergeant Cocks's view that it was a double cut with scissors.

Professor Cameron put his finger on Azaria's jumpsuit.

"This tear here on the right side edge is more as if it's been pulled naturally, and not necessarily at the time of the incident, because that top stud, if done up, is rather tight to undo. And when the two are together one can see this line of thick bloodstaining, which is more suggestive that it was done up at the time."

He pointed to an area of blanching around the snap that would have been protected by the double snap. His finger ran to the inner seam leading up to the two snaps. That area, he said, was not stained like the rest of the garment in general "and therefore this staining of the garment, which is uniform, was produced on that garment, in my submission, when the two buttons, the top buttons, were undone. Now, if this garment was subjected to exposure to the sand or dust that is found on this garment, that sand or that staining is uniform. It's not as if it was done after the garments were folded. It's done when something was inside the garment."

Mr. Sturgess: "So assuming that the garment has been buried, your opinion is that the body of the baby was in the garment at the time it was buried?"

Professor Cameron: "It would have had to have been."

Mr. Sturgess asked the forensic scientist to comment on the damaged area on the left sleeve. Professor Cameron said it appeared to him to have again been caused by a cutting instrument like scissors or a knife and then torn. The interesting feature was that there was minimal bloodstaining around that area and, according to Dr. Scott's report, a total absence of saliva. There was no tissue staining that he would have anticipated had the damage been caused by any member of the canine family.

"How gross would the staining have been, both by tissue and blood, if a baby's arm had been in there, and that was done by a dog's bite or bites?" Mr. Sturgess wanted to know.

"I would have thought quite excessive."

Mr. Sturgess wanted an answer from the professor on the type of evidence that could be found if a child wearing the jumpsuit had been carried by the dingo, and the grip had been around the point of balance at the back.

"Well, the majority of members of the canine family carry a body by the center of gravity," said Professor Cameron, "and that in a child is in the small of the back or the lower part of the chest region . . . or in the side,

and in so doing, if it had been done I would have anticipated tearing in the clothing . . . at that point."

He added that in some material, bite marks might not
be seen. The singlet, he said, was of a different type of
material than the jumpsuit and this might be significant.
If the child had been in the jumpsuit and the garment
was gripped by the teeth, it could have torn because the
dingo was carrying about ten pounds. If the animal had
its teeth into the body of the child there would be bleeding points from those areas. But there was no evidence
of bleeding on the singlet that would have come into
contact with blood first in the "center of the gravity
point."

The professor and Mr. Sturgess were about to leave
the subject of clothing, but Coroner Galvin said, "Just
go over for me again your opinion that if the clothing
was buried, there was a body inside."

Professor Cameron said that if the jumpsuit had "not
been contaminated with sand, but had been just a normal garment with blood, and then folded up and buried
in sand, obviously there would be certain parts that
would have been more heavily stained than the ones
that are inside. But as it is uniform, it would suggest to
me that it is more likely that there was something inside
filling it up."

At this point, Mr. Sturgess asked Professor Cameron
to illustrate his findings with the aid of slides. A projector was switched on and a color slide of the front of the
vest showing the pattern of the bleeding appeared on a
screen. Professor Cameron said the blood was more
marked on the left side and also over the back of the
right shoulder. This indicated that it flowed from above
down, because it became lighter in the lower areas. The
second slide showed the back view of the vest, and it
again demonstrated the heavy bloodstaining over the

back of the right shoulder and, to a lesser extent, over the left shoulder.

Then two ultraviolet fluorescent photographs were projected, showing black areas—blood, the professor said. As the slides were being shown, the forensic expert pointed out areas of blood and at one point spoke of a "line of continuity in the bloodstaining of the neck when it is done up," which indicated to him that the jumpsuit was buttoned up when the bleeding started to come from the neck region.

"And as it is uniformly bloodstained around, it would suggest to me that it came all from above, from one point, rather than from two points; more circumferential, although I cannot exclude the possibility that the back was produced by pooling when lying on its back." Referring to a photograph of a tear in the jumpsuit, Professor Cameron said that if examined it could be seen that it was less bloodstained—if at all—from within, "suggestive that that occurred more likely after the blood had dried."

When the projector was switched off, Professor Cameron returned to the coroner's table with counsel to show them life-size photographs, in ordinary tones, in ultraviolet fluorescence and in color. He wanted to discuss further the marks he had pointed out in the slides.

There were marks at the back of the cloth of the jumpsuit, he said, that were consistent with fingerprints —four fingerprints of a young adult right hand on the underneath or over the left shoulder blade.

"Excuse me," said Mr. Sturgess, "you said 'a young adult'?"

"I'm differentiating that from a child."

"A child of four or six?"

"It's far too big a print. This is indicative of a hand placed in that position and then those vertical lines which I referred to appear to have been . . . superimposed."

Professor Cameron said the marks had been produced by "an adult human hand that was bloodstained and of the same blood group as the rest." The ultraviolet fluorescent photographs suggested a right hand of an adult gripping the left side of a child within the jumpsuit while the hand was bloodstained.

He went on: "If one looks also at the front of the right side there is this area here, which would be consistent with the thumb of an adult, and over the back of the right shoulder, the forefingers, but it is less well defined and one cannot be dogmatic on that at all. Now, having demonstrated that, if one goes back onto the ordinary black-and-white photographs, one can see that it's there even on that, and when one goes back to the color, one can see the similar sort of marks, but less well distinct, because one hasn't the benefit of ultraviolet fluorescence."

A naked child's doll was brought into court to enable Professor Cameron to demonstrate the gripping movement he was talking about. He held it up, thumbs at the front, fingers at the back.

Mr. Sturgess, referring to a mark on the back of the jumpsuit that was shown up by the ultraviolet fluorescence, asked Professor Cameron if he could point out further features. The Scotsman produced a magnifying glass for counsel and the coroner to look through. He told them they were looking at the middle finger, showing the first part of the finger with the joint of the first knuckle and the tip of the finger. He then took his description further, pointing out what he said was the index finger with its tip. Then he showed the tip of the middle finger, the tip of the ring finger, and the tip of the little finger. Professor Cameron said it was very difficult for anybody untrained in the use of a magnifying glass to follow the evidence "but to a trained eye it is relatively easy; but you need to sit down and look at it."

Referring to the "untrained eye," Mr. Sturgess asked the professor if it was true that he did a great many postmortem examinations. Yes, it was.

"About how many, approximately, per week?"

"Well, I average between 1,500 to 2,000 a year." He had been doing that work since about 1957.

Mr. Sturgess asked Professor Cameron for his final opinion in relation to his entire investigation.

"Well," said the eminent scientist, "working on the various samples that I was provided with, those in particular that were confirmed as being bloodstained, namely the jumpsuit and the singlet, show a blood group consistent with being a sibling of the union of Mr. and Mrs. Chamberlain and therefore are consistent with being the blood group of the child that is missing. There are no marks in the clothing, in my opinion, to suggest involvement with a member of the canine family and this is, in my submission, further supported by the absence of drag marks on the clothing and by Dr. Scott's evidence on the absence of saliva. I concur that the singlet, by its bloodstaining, suggests that it was on the correct way when the bleeding occurred and was turned inside out on removal from the body."

Professor Cameron went on: "I confirm that the jumpsuit had been done up to the neck at the time the bleeding occurred; and the top two studs had been undone prior to the jumpsuit coming into contact with the reddish sand, and only undone further for the removal of the booties when the clothing was found. Visual examination of the bloodstained jumpsuit reveals what would appear to be the handprint of a small right hand of an adult that was applied to the suit whilst the right hand was contaminated with wet blood of the same blood group as found elsewhere on the suit; whilst the jumpsuit was filled with the body at the same time, and the body was gripped by a similarly bloodstained left hand grasping the upper right shoulder within the jumpsuit, although one cannot be as dogmatic with the right hand as one can with the left."

The forensic expert said there was no evidence to suggest the hands came from two people. The evidence suggested one person held the jumpsuit "whilst the body was within that item of clothing and whilst the blood was either flowing or whilst certainly when the person holding the child [had hands that] were damp with blood. The distribution of the blood on the jumpsuit and on the singlet would suggest that the blood flowed onto the collar from above, all around the neck at one time, and not from two separate areas as one would have anticipated were an animal involved."

The professor went on: "There is little, if any, evidence of involvement with the jumpsuit, in my opinion, with members of the canine family. There is evidence, however, to suggest that a human being, with wet bloodstained hands of the same blood group as the blood of the infant, held the jumpsuit in an upright position whilst the blood was still flowing onto the clothing. That is to say that the blood, in my opinion, flowed circumferentially; that is, all around the neck and not from isolated points. The court has heard this blood is fetal in type and the bloodstained hands were stained with a similar blood of the same type."

Professor Cameron added that the sand staining on the garment would suggest that, after the blood had dried, the top two snaps of the jumpsuit were undone "and the clothing in that state, with the body still within it, came into contact with the sand." He said there was no evidence to suggest an uneven distribution of the sand on the clothing.

Regarding the possible causes of death, he said that in the absence of a body, they were unascertainable. He said, however, that it would be reasonable to assume that Azaria "met her death by unnatural causes, and that the mode of death had been caused by a cutting instrument, possibly encircling the neck or certainly cutting the vital blood vessels and structures of the neck."

The Scotsman said he had also studied a yellow towel, and he agreed with another specialist that it contained what appeared to be smear marks rather than a soaking of blood because they did not reach the base of the fibers.

The London-based forensic scientist, questioned by Mr. Rice about the blood marks on Azaria's clothing, insisted that the marks he saw on the jumpsuit were consistent with a human hand.

Mr. Rice asked whether there was a detectable fingerprint on any part of the clothing.

"When I examined the garment," said Professor Cameron, "there was an imprint but not a fingerprint. In other words, there had been a hand impression."

Professor Cameron stepped down. His evidence had been as dramatic as the rumors that had preceded his arrival. Now another witness was about to give evidence that was to further cast doubt on the dingo theory, evidence that was both technical and damning.

Professor Malcolm Chaikin, Dean of the Faculty of Applied Science and head of the School of Textile Technology at the University of New South Wales, was called to discuss the makeup of the fiber of Azaria's jumpsuit and singlet. Involved in textile research for thirty years, Professor Chaikin told the coroner that the

jumpsuit fabric was made up of cotton and nylon—
about 70 percent cotton, 30 percent nylon. He produced
for the court a plastic model of the weaving structure of
the jumpsuit cloth that, with its loops and bends, looked
like a tangle of blue and red miniature plastic coat
hangers.

Holes in the jumpsuit, he felt, had been caused by
cutting. He had carried out experiments in a similar
jumpsuit, both using scissors to make cuts and creating
tears by exerting strain. It was possible to readily distinguish between a cut and the torn part of the fabric. The
two incisions he paid particular attention to—on the
right side of the neck of the collar and on the left shoulder—were made by a cutting action, Professor Chaikin
said, basing his conclusion on "all the data I have been
able to collect."

His investigations, he said, had led him to the conclusion that two areas he studied on the child's clothing
had been cut rather than torn. If the fabric was cut
across the loops in the material, the loops dropped off.
If it was cut where the cotton worked its way into the
fabric—which would require a diagonal cutting action
—some cotton would still be attached to the fabric but
only loosely, "so that in subsequent brushing of the fabric against something, they will drop off." Cutting farther up, where the loops were more attached to the base
fabric, resulted in their remaining for some time. With
Azaria's jumpsuit, he said, he was able to remove some
of the small pieces that were still in the material. They
had the characteristics of the cut particles removed
from his experimental fabric.

Turning to the holes in Azaria's singlet—one was
close to the edging, the other in the middle of the back
—Professor Chaikin said that all he could conclude was
that they had been made by a pointed or blunt object

being pushed through, breaking the yarn, or that there had been a cut or a combination of the two. "And that is as far as I can say about them."

Professor Chaikin's evidence then turned to tufts found in the car and to the three tufts recovered from Michael Chamberlain's camera bag. He pointed out to the court that his microscopic examination involved looking for particular characteristics of surface and diameter to see if they matched experiments. Because tufts had been recovered by vacuuming a question arose: could the filter cloth, which was cotton, have confused his judgment? There was "no way" he and his colleagues could find similarities in the filter cloth, he maintained. In summary, he said that of the twenty-five tufts from the car, he rejected twenty-two for reasons including wrong size fibers, the intertwining of a synthetic material, and a lack of a twist. Of the tufts from the camera bag, he said all three could have come from Azaria's jumpsuit because there was a slight twist in the yarn, and the fiber diameters tallied with "something that could have come from cuttings from the jumpsuit."

Professor Chaikin told the coroner that he carried out experiments to find out if he could penetrate a singlet and jumpsuit with a canine tooth. He mounted the tooth into the metal finger of a specimen holder and material was stretched underneath. At one stage, he said, it was possible to puncture the underlying fabric of the singlet without puncturing the jumpsuit. Then he took the experiment further, putting the flesh of a freshly killed rabbit under the jumpsuit and singlet material. It was then not possible to puncture the fabric, even though the tooth was embedded to a depth below its gum line, because no tension had been applied to the material. "With a dingo tooth going into the flesh of a dead rabbit, you could have complete recovery without any breakages," said Professor Chaikin.

He agreed with Mr. Rice that a dingo's tooth, if it could create a cutting action like that of scissors, could cause the damage to the collar area. And he would not discount the possibility that the hole in the singlet was caused by a dingo tooth.

Professor Chaikin's recital of evidence was over. Just two more days had been set aside before the expected adjournment on December 23. Michael and Lindy Chamberlain sat back in their seats. It was impossible to know what they were thinking.

XIII

A Charge of Murder

The testimony of the remaining witnesses seemed almost incidental to the mound of evidence that had been presented to destroy, or at least throw serious doubt upon, the dingo story. But it did cast an even greater shadow of suspicion over the Chamberlains. A dry cleaner told of a friend of the couple bringing in a quantity of stained clothing. Another friend told of a pair of Lindy's running shoes with what looked like blood on them. Then there was British forensic expert Bernard Sims, a rotund man with gray hair and humor in his face who described himself as a senior lecturer in forensic odontology, which concerned the study of dental evidence and its presentation in court.

His studies enabled him to identify dead or living people by their teeth, and he could tell age or eating habits by looking at the wear on teeth. He also studied bite marks, such as in cases of sexual attack where teeth marks might indicate the perpetrator, and he pointed out that up to 40 percent of battered baby cases showed bite marks.

A dingo, he said, was typical of a basic carnivore of the dog family with its incisors, canines, premolars, and molars—the pattern of any dog's mouth. It had a long nose because it hunted by smell, and had very good muscle attachments which was a sign of a meat eater. The joint of the dingo jaw was a typical hinge joint, said Mr. Sims. The incisors were reduced and these were used to pick the meat off the bone. The main teeth were the canines, which did the biting, and he caused smiles in court when he pointed out that a snarling dog moved its lips out of the way because if it did not "it bites itself."

Mr. Sims said he had examined the clothing handed to him by Dr. Brown and it was his opinion that there was no evidence upon it to involve a member of the canine family, either by teeth marks or the presence of saliva "as one would expect."

All animals, he pointed out, secreted saliva and there were three glands that produced liquids. Basically, the function of saliva was to act as an antiseptic by covering and coating the gums—with a dry mouth, bacteria could get into the gums. Saliva also lubricated; without it, an animal could not swallow. His knowledgeable presentation was intriguing to the court. Mr. Sims spoke of enzymes in saliva that began the process of digestion and he pointed out that a dog, being a hunting animal, could not perspire through its fur but only through its mouth. This was why a dog always had its mouth open —it was the animal's only mechanism to maintain its fluid balance. And dog saliva, he pointed out, usually did not disappear when it dried.

He found no marks in Azaria's clothing that were, in his opinion, consistent with canine teeth. Normally, when one was bitten by a dog, human flesh would show two points of contact with the upper canine and two points of contact with the lower canine. There would be damage to the clothing at these points.

He had been shown the clothing used in the Adelaide Zoo experiment and in that jumpsuit he could see puncture marks that were typical of canine teeth. The experimental singlet had been considerably damaged because a dog would stand on an article and rip it; there would possibly be tearing with the claws as well. The odontologist, in reference to the search area, said he could only assume that a dog or a dingo would have to take "good purchase" on a heavy article; it would have to obtain balance as it made away and somewhere, he felt sure, drag marks and scuff marks would show. From the campsite to the base of Ayers Rock seemed a very long distance for a dog to have carried a baby in one go. He would have expected to have found marks consistent with the clothing being dragged as well as traces of vegetation on the clothing.

"Can you find any evidence whatsoever that a member of the canine family was involved?" asked Mr. Sturgess.

"No; in my opinion, no."

And then he was back, striding confidently across the courtroom—Detective Sergeant Graeme Charlwood, now stationed at the Darwin Criminal Investigation Bureau. He preferred to remain standing in the witness box, unlike others who had sat on the chair provided. He began by telling the court that his initial inquiries started several days after Azaria's disappearance. He was called in because the disappearance had been somewhat suspicious. The clothes had been discovered by the time he arrived at Ayers Rock to take statements from witnesses. He and six other police officers started searching in the area of the sandhills, near where the clothing had been found, and a comprehensive search was also made around the perimeter road and the Rock itself. The search went on for three and a half days, with six men from Alice Springs and two from Ayers Rock taking part, but nothing was found that could be connected with the disappearance of the child.

Initially, though, he said, three blood spots were located by Senior Constable Morris in an area above the Fertility Cave. A more extensive search was carried out farther up the Rock and a further nine spots were located. Swabs and rock chippings were taken.

When he went to Mount Isa to interview Michael and Lindy Chamberlain he was shown a parka, a sleeping bag, and a space blanket; other items were collected later. There were some small holes in the blanket that in his opinion appeared to be normal wear marks. Other articles collected were a white cane carry-cot, running shoes, a toilet bag, a cardigan, and two pairs of children's pajamas, the basic intention, said Detective Charlwood, being to take anything that was relevant. Blood was found on a sleeping bag which he believed was Lindy's and on one of the two purple blankets that had been in the tent at the time. The greatest amount of blood was on a parka, identified as Reagan's, which had smearing on the right sleeve, on the right side of the hood, and, he believed, on the upper sleeve.

On August 22, 1981, he had been called in by the commissioner of police who gave him "certain information." That was to result in his flying around Australia meeting scientists and other police officers until he finally took out a search warrant on number 17, College Drive, Cooranbong, the Chamberlains' home.

On the couple's Sabbath, Saturday, September 19, Detective Sergeant Charlwood, along with other officers, traveled to Cooranbong. At about 8:10 A.M., in response to a police knock on the door, Aidan answered. When Michael Chamberlain came to the door he was told about the search warrant. Michael Chamberlain invited Detective Sergeant Charlwood and another officer into the lounge room where he asked what the visit was about. Detective Sergeant Charlwood told him that fresh forensic evidence had come to light and, in view of that, the chief minister had instructed the commissioner to carry out further investigations. Michael Chamberlain was told that the purpose of the police visit was to obtain as many items that had been with the family at Ayers Rock as possible.

The search of the Chamberlain house, said the detective, started at the rear. Police took possession of a tent, a tent fly, and a sleeping bag. Then Lindy Chamberlain came from the hall with a plastic shopping bag, saying, "I thought you might be interested in these." She produced two ex-army "giggle hats." They had spots and stains on them, said the policeman, that appeared to be blood. Lindy told him they had not found the hats until they were unpacking between the two houses. They had once been right in the door of the tent at Ayers Rock.

The search continued and other items seized included another two hats, a yellow raincoat, a flashlight, a backpack, and a diver's knife. Detective Sergeant Charlwood said that when he entered a shed, Michael Chamberlain pointed out an orange and green tent with six segments of tent poles.

"I said, 'Where are the pegs for the tent?' He said, 'I don't know.' I said, 'They were given back to you,' and he said, 'Yes, but I don't know where they are.'"

The police officer said he asked Michael Chamberlain about shovels, and he said they did not have a spade. Asked about a folding utility camping shovel he replied, "No."

The policeman went on to detail other items found and seized at the house, which included two knives and twenty-five color slides from Michael Chamberlain's collection. Some, he said, were of Ayers Rock and some of the baby. Among them was the slide of the lichen; another was a view of part of Ayers Rock. Lindy Chamberlain had pointed out it was a view of the Maternity Cave. Michael had handed to the police a black vinyl camera bag carrying a sticker reading NATIONAL FREELANCE PHOTOGRAPHER.

Detective Sergeant Charlwood said that during the search one of the other officers found a machete on top of a wardrobe while Charlwood was standing in the driveway with Lindy Chamberlain. Aidan said, "There is another one," climbed onto the roof of the shed, and produced a large bush knife.

Sergeant Charlwood was on the point of giving the coronial hearing details of the conversation he had had with Lindy, but Mr. Rice objected.

Overnight, a decision was reached among the lawyers and the following day Mr. Sturgess told the coroner that he and Mr. Rice had agreed that Detective Sergeant Charlwood's statement detailing the conversation should be tendered as evidence, but that it would not be read out to the court. The hearing was adjourned until February 1, 1982.

The Chamberlains flew out of Alice Springs later that afternoon. The only indication of their plans had come from Michael earlier: "We are looking forward to spending Christmas with our sons."

They had sat listening to words that filled 609 pages of transcripts and had watched their daughter's clothing dangling several times in front of the crowded coronial courtroom. If there was a couple more than relieved to leave the chilled, clinical atmosphere of the Alice Springs Coroner's Court that day it was Michael and Lindy Chamberlain.

* * *

The inquest resumed with a bombshell statement by Mr. Sturgess. The evidence, though circumstantial, he said, painted a picture of complicity by both Michael and Lindy Chamberlain in the death of their child. Azaria, he suggested, had been killed in the family car rather than in the tent and her death had occurred in a period of between six and fifteen minutes after Mrs. Chamberlain left the barbecue area with the child and went in the direction of the family tent and car.

Michael Chamberlain had remained in the barbecue area in that critical period and so could not have been associated with the death. Azaria's blood had spilt onto a "person or persons" inside the car and had been deposited on objects inside the tent. Mr. Sturgess suggested that Lindy Chamberlain raised the alarm about the dingo and shortly afterward told her husband what really happened. There was ample opportunity during darkness, said Mr. Sturgess, for the baby to have been buried with its clothes on and also an opportunity later for it to have been dug up, undressed, and the clothing deposited at the base of Ayers Rock.

The camera bag, Mr. Sturgess suggested, played an important part in the events that night. When Pastor Chamberlain and his wife had driven to the motel with the nurse, the bag had remained under his legs and he had refused the nurse's offer to move it out of the way.

"My evidence suggests a prima facie case that the child was killed in the car and was in the car for some time before being buried," said Mr. Sturgess. With people coming and going during the search and in the general excitement and confusion of the night, there was an opportunity for the body to have been buried.

Coroner Galvin felt the evidence was largely circumstantial—"but it is my view that a properly instructed jury could arrive at a verdict."

And he committed Lindy Chamberlain for trial on a charge of murdering baby Azaria. Her husband was charged with being an accessory after the fact of murder. They sat with their heads bowed, as if in silent prayer, as the coroner spoke and granted them bail of $5,000 each.

The case was set for April, but the first of two dramatic events threw that date out of the window. For it was announced that QC Rice would be no longer acting for the Chamberlains, which would mean a delay in the start of the court proceedings. The case would now be heard in September, in the Darwin Supreme Court.

The second announcement was more sensational. Lindy was pregnant. When the case began she would be seven months into the pregnancy and if the hearing dragged on for its expected six weeks or more it was possible she would give birth while the trial was under way. But the Chamberlains were anxious for the trial to proceed. A date was set, September 13.

And already the proceedings were being described as "the trial of the century."

XIV

"The Trial of the Century"

At 11:38 A.M. on Monday, September 13, 1982, Ian Barker, Queen's Counsel, stunned the Darwin Supreme Court with these opening words:

"A baby was killed at Ayers Rock on 17 August 1980, between eight and nine o'clock. It was a Sunday. The child was just under ten weeks old. She was called Azaria Chamberlain. What will be proved largely from the scientific examination of the baby's clothing is that the child lost a great deal of blood from a major injury to her neck. She died very quickly because somebody had cut her throat.

"The Crown case is that the child was killed while Mrs. Chamberlain sat in the front passenger seat of the car. The Crown does not venture any motive for this case—we do not assess that Mrs. Chamberlain had any ill-will toward the child. We simply say to you [the jury] that the evidence we will put before you is that, for whatever reason, the baby was murdered by her mother."

As Mr. Barker spoke, Lindy Chamberlain, seven months pregnant with her fourth child, sat impassively in the dock dressed in a pink and white maternity dress with red dots. The dark flowing hair she had worn at the inquest was now short and her face was puffy. Behind her, supporting her back, was a colored cushion and beside her sat her husband in a fawn shirt and brown tie. The jury had been chosen—three women and nine men—and the Chamberlains had answered "Not guilty, Your Honor" to the charge that had been read to each of them. Lindy was accused of murdering Azaria, Michael with having been an accessory after the fact.

It was to be a day of courtroom dramatics, as first the baby's tiny jumpsuit was held up to the jury and then Mr. Barker walked up and down in front of the panel clacking together the jaws of a dingo skull—"that sort of mechanism," he declared, "would be impossible to produce a wound around the throat."

Mr. Barker pulled no punches. "The dingo story," he said as the Supreme Court judge, James Henry Muirhead, wrote notes, "is a fanciful lie, designed to conceal the truth that the child Azaria died by her mother's hand. The Crown does not assert that the father was involved in the baby's death. The Crown asserts that he became aware of the death shortly after it occurred and is an accessory after the fact." He went on to outline the Chamberlains' sightseeing expedition around Ayers Rock, and then told how Lindy Chamberlain had walked from the barbecue area toward the family tent with Azaria.

"When the mother commenced to walk to the tent, the child Azaria had not long to live."

They were chilling words that had many in the courtroom visualizing a mother striding through the darkness with her doomed baby.

"The only witness to the killing was the mother, Alice Lynne Chamberlain, and the Crown case is that she sat in the front of the car and cut the baby's throat."

The Crown asserted, said Mr. Barker, that there was a great deal of blood inside the car—the blood of a baby less than six months old. The blood that was later discovered was obviously just a small part of what was originally there. The blood inside the car had flowed freely, according to scientific evidence, and could not have been transferred there.

The discovery of blood in the vehicle after the police reopened the case later in 1981 was critical to the Crown's case. Mr. Barker said it would be "preposterous" to believe that a dingo took the baby into the car. In this case, he went on, there were two simple alternatives—either a dingo killed Azaria or it was a homicide.

"If you say the child was killed in the car, then you have to at once forget the dingo," he said to the jury. "Mrs. Chamberlain's story that she left the baby in a bassinet inside the tent wrapped in blankets was false. What had happened, the Crown asserted, was that the child was violently murdered and Lindy Chamberlain returned to her husband "which in the circumstances was all she could do."

The likelihood was that the child's body was in Michael Chamberlain's camera bag in the car when Lindy returned to the barbecue area; scientists had found fetal blood on the camera gag. During the night of August 17, the QC went on, somebody buried the baby's body, still in its clothes, near the campsite. Later, the body was recovered from the shallow grave, the clothes removed, and the body reburied.

The Crown, said Mr. Barker, found it remarkable that large volumes of blood were absent from the inside of the tent if the dingo story were to be believed. The Crown found it even more remarkable that a dingo could carry away an injured child, shake its head at the doorway of the tent as Lindy Chamberlain had claimed it to do, and leave only insignificant traces of blood. After the alarm had been raised, Michael Chamberlain had not used an "armory" of spotlights on his car to shine in the direction of where the dingo was said to have left the tent. And drag marks found leading one hundred meters over a sandhill were, to put it bluntly, a red herring.

The Crown began calling forward its witnesses to support its case. There was Mrs. Judith West of Esperance, Western Australia, who told of hearing the "throaty growl" of a dog and how, between five and ten minutes later, Lindy had called out that a dingo had got her baby. After the search had started, Michael and Lindy had walked away together for about ten minutes before returning to the vicinity of their tent where Michael had put his hands on his wife's head to give a blessing and say a prayer.

Then there was Mrs. Sally Lowe, the Tasmanian tourist who had chatted with Lindy while she nursed Azaria. When Lindy took Azaria, who had definitely been alive at the time, back toward the tent she was absent from the barbecue area for between five and ten minutes. After her return Aidan and Michael had said they thought the baby had cried out and Lindy had gone immediately to check. When she heard Lindy's cry Michael and Mrs. Lowe's husband had run off in the direction Lindy indicated.

A schoolteacher from Melbourne, Edwin Haby, told the court that he was one of the those who searched the desert with a flashlight that night and had followed dog or dingo tracks along the top of a sand dune near the Chamberlain tent. The tracks, which started no more than one hundred meters from the tent, led to an oval-shaped impression in the sand that "quite obviously" had been made by the animal putting something down. The impression indicated to him that the object was something like a knitted jumper or woven fabric. Beside the slight indentation was a drop of something that could have been saliva or blood.

The witnesses came forward, as they had at the two inquests, to describe their roles on the night of August 17, 1980, and afterward: Senior Constable Frank Morris, who had examined the jumpsuit, the police scientists—whose methods of procedure and deduction came under close examination by the defense team of John Phillips, QC, and Mr. Andrew Kirkham—and a new name, Mr. Keyth Lenehan of Cairns. He told of being picked up by the Chamberlains in 1979 after a road accident and how they had been for him "good Samaritans." He had, he recalled, been involved in a car accident fifteen kilometers south of Port Douglas, North Queensland, and had suffered a cut head. The Chamberlains had arrived at the scene minutes later and had cleaned away some blood. Then they had put him into their car through the rear hatch. Michael had driven and Lindy had been in the rear with him. The two boys were there, too, but he couldn't remember where. Mr. Lenehan, bleeding heavily, was taken between forty-eight and sixty-four kilometers to the Cairns Base Hospital in a trip of some forty-five minutes. Asked whether at any stage any part of his body was in the front part of the vehicle, Mr. Lenehan replied, "No."

Dr. Kenneth Brown, who had taken Azaria's jumpsuit to London, Sergeant Frank Cocks, who told of his opinion that cuts had been made with scissors, and forensic biologist Dr. Andrew Scott, who put forward the opinion that the head and torso of Azaria appeared to have been upright when the blood had flowed, all came forward to give their evidence to the hushed court.

Professor Malcolm Chaikin, the textile expert who believed that damaged areas of the jumpsuit had been cut with scissors, gave the court new evidence about

Michael's camera bag. Examining the bag some three months before the trial started he had found, he said, among other fibers, six baby hairs. He was able to tell them apart from dog hair because of their different characteristics, including taper and diameter, but he could not say whether they came from the same person.

When he began his cross-examination of Professor Chaikin, Mr. Phillips said the defense planned to show evidence that the Chamberlains had obtained the bag second-hand. "In those circumstances," he asked the professor, "do you find it at all surprising that you found baby hair in the bag?"

"Well, I'd rather not comment on that," said the professor. "All I know was that there was baby hair in the bag. I wouldn't know how it got there."

Mrs. Joy Kuhl, the forensic biologist from the Crime Laboratory of the New South Wales Health Commission, became the thirty-fifth prosecution witness to be called, and she spent much of the first day of her evidence showing the jury more than thirty slides demonstrating how scientists identified blood from other stains. She went on to say she had obtained positive findings of fetal hemoglobin on the side of the carpet under the driver's seat; on a yellow towel found in the rear of the car; on a ten-cent coin found in the floor well; on swabs taken from a stain on the floor well and around a blot under the front passenger seat; on swabs taken from a stain on a seat hinge; and on a chamois container taken from the car. Scrapings from a spray pattern under the dashboard showed blood of a child less than three moths old and she had also obtained an indication of fetal hemoglobin on a pair of scissors found in the car.

When she first carried out a screening test for blood on the dashboard spray she obtained a negative reaction and told a policeman examining the car with her that she thought it was probably soft drink. Then she had examined three scrapings the Northern Territory police had labeled as coming from under the dashboard. This time she concluded that the scrapings were blood of a baby less than three months old.

In what was one of the strongest attacks on a prosecution witness in the trial to date, Mr. Phillips asked Joy Kuhl, who had also testified that tests on the black camera bag indicated the presence of baby's blood around the buckle and a zip clasp, what had happened to the plates and slides used in the tests.

"They have been destroyed," she said.

Said Mr. Phillips: "Now you have come here and offered a number of opinions. The fact is that the hard evidence on which your opinions are based is all destroyed. The physical results of your tests, the slides, the plates, the hard evidence, is all destroyed?"

"The results aren't destroyed," said Joy Kuhl.

"The plates are destroyed?"

"Yes," said Joy Kuhl, explaining that it was standard procedure in her laboratory.

She also agreed that at the second inquest she had made a statement that was not scientifically correct concerning the content of adult hemoglobin in a baby while it was still in the womb. She had told the inquest that a fetus did not have any adult hemoglobin, but agreed under questioning from Mr. Phillips that it was detectable during the baby's eighth month in the womb. She had made the statement to make things simpler, she said.

The prosecution's last witness was the man they considered the most vital—the British forensic expert, Professor James Cameron. He summed up his conclusions by repeating that he had found no evidence to suggest that Azaria was killed by a member of the canine family —the bloodstains and damage to Azaria's jumpsuit indicated her throat had been cut by a person. The bloodstains were consistent with a cutting instrument across or around the child's neck. A child of some nine to ten weeks old would have a head circumference of fifteen inches on average, he said, and it would be very difficult for him to imagine a dog grasping the head from above.

"That would be the only way in which I think a dog could possibly grasp a child without damaging the collar. But in doing so I would have expected extensive bleeding, but not around the collar of the jumpsuit."

He explained his reasoning by adding: "When you get a head injury, rather than a soaked, bloodstained collar, you get rivulets of blood draining down and missing the collar. It goes down the front and down the back, depending on which way the head is bending. Certainly, you'll get bleeding around the back of the collar, depending on how the child lay afterward."

Azaria would have been alive when bleeding occurred, he said, because in his opinion it was primarily venous (from the veins) rather than arterial. It was an "ooze" and he would have anticipated it could be described by a "cut-throat type injury."

Prosecutor Barker wanted to know whether Azaria was lying down or upright at the time.

Said Professor Cameron: "Initially, it [the baby] would appear to be more lying down and then certainly there is an element of semi-sitting or sitting up. But then there is also the element of possible pooling by lying down. In other words, it's a bit of both."

The prosecution's forty-fifth witness showed the jury his ultraviolet fluorescent slides of stains on the jumpsuit and singlet, pointing out what he said were patterns consistent with a hand over a shoulder, with four fingers running down, and a hand under the left armpit with the four fingers in a line on the left of the back of the jumpsuit. He agreed that the evidence of a small adult hand print was his "impression."

Mr. Phillips, for the Chamberlains, then made a reference to a bizarre discovery in a case in London in 1972 when Professor Cameron had made an examination. The professor agreed that the letters "WANK" had been found in blood on the neck of a man found dead following a house fire. They could only be seen after a photograph of the neck had been blown up an enormous three hundred times.

"Would you not agree," asked Mr. Phillips, "that blood from an injury, purely by accident, can take up apparent shapes of objects?"

"By or against an object," said Professor Cameron.

"It can occur purely by accident—an apparent pattern of an object?"

"A pattern of an object can occur, certainly, yes."

Mr. Phillips put it to Professor Cameron that at the London trial of three men following the death of the man in the fire, he had given evidence without having a correct understanding of all the circumstances. The QC then suggested that Professor Cameron had done the same in the Chamberlain case.

"I was asked to examine the clothing, which I did, and passed an opinion," said the professor.

Mr. Phillips then moved on to the snaps on Azaria's jumpsuit. He reminded Professor Cameron that at the second inquest he had said that the top two snaps had been the only ones undone when the clothes were found. The defense counsel, referring to transcripts of evidence concerning the day the clothes were found, pointed out that they had not said the two snaps were the only ones undone.

Professor Cameron agreed that the fact he believed only two snaps were undone was an important factor in his concluding that a dingo or dog had nothing to do with the child's disappearance. He had, he agreed, regarded it as incredible that a dingo or dog could get a child out of a jumpsuit by undoing only two buttons.

"Well, have you given evidence under any other false impressions in this case, Professor Cameron?"

"Not that I know of."

He agreed that he had written a report in September 1981 in which he had stated: "Suffice to say, I have never known a member of a canine family leaving clothes in a neat bundle." That report, he agreed, had been written without his having seen a police photograph of the way the clothes were found. He had obtained the description of the clothes being in a "neat bundle" from Dr. Brown, the forensic scientist from Adelaide, and from other officers.

He agreed that in his report he stated that nobody saw Azaria alive, apart from an alleged kicking motion, after 3:30 P.M. on the day she disappeared.

Mr. Phillips then read part of the evidence of Judith West, who had testified that she saw the child at sunset.

"Do you agree," asked Mr. Phillips, "that that conclusion, having regard to Mrs. West's deposition, is a false assumption?"

"It is a false assumption if one negates, as I have apparently negated, Mrs. West's evidence."

Mr. Phillips asked, "Have you made any other false assumptions before you gave evidence, Professor Cameron?"

"Again, not to my knowledge."

Mr. Phillips then turned to Professor Cameron's reliance on Adelaide biologist Dr. Andrew Scott's findings that there had been no saliva on Azaria's clothing.

"You decided positively there was no saliva, in your view of his evidence, because he got a negative result, did you not?"

"Correct."

Mr. Phillips asked if the professor would agree with Dr. Scott who had said that one could never draw a positive conclusion from a negative result. It was good science, was it not?

It was scientifically correct, said the professor.

"You did not do that, though, did you? You did draw a positive conclusion from a negative result?"

"I work as a pathologist—not as a laboratory scientist," Professor Cameron replied coldly.

Wednesday, October 13, was to be a day of surprise and drama—surprise because Mr. Phillips announced that Michael and Lindy Chamberlain would go into the witness box and subject themselves to cross-examination by the prosecution; drama because two of the women jurors, seeing Lindy crying in the witness box, themselves broke into sobs, resulting in the judge's calling for an early lunch adjournment. It was a rare scene in a court, as if the case was not already well punctuated with the sensational.

The emotions had taken over when Lindy Chamberlain was about to be shown Azaria's bloodstained clothes, wrapped in plastic. As she reached out to touch the bag, she started weeping. Asked by Justice Muirhead if she was upset, Lindy indicated through her sniffles that she wanted to continue, but the jury foreman informed the judge that one of the three women on the jury was upset. At that moment, a second woman juror began to cry. As the court broke up at the judge's direction, Michael hurried across to the witness box where his wife, hands clasped in the lap of her well-filled blue and white maternity smock, was gradually

179

composing herself. When the court resumed, the three women members of the jury sat at the back of the jury box. A doll dressed in baby's clothes, used by Professor Cameron to illustrate how he thought Azaria had been held and which had sat on a table in the middle of the court, had been removed.

Her evidence often interrupted by tears, Lindy again described the night of August 17, this time for the benefit of a jury given the task of deciding whether she was innocent or guilty of murder. Her description of seeing a dingo, its head and shoulders partly out of the tent and its head shaking something vigorously, concluded, Mr. Phillips said to her slowly and clearly: "Now, Mrs. Chamberlain, the Crown claims that you did not put your baby to bed but that you took her to the car and, in the front seat of the car, you cut that child's throat. What do you say to that?"

For a moment Lindy looked directly at her lawyer. Then she threw her hands to her face and sobbed: "It's just not true!"

Some women in the court shifted uncomfortably in their seats. It was almost too much for them. But if Lindy found the early part of that day trying enough, there was to be a great deal more strain for the pregnant thirty-four-year-old. Mr. Barker, throwing the Crown's doubts at her, questioned her at length about the dingo she said she had seen coming from the tent. At times her exasperation showed through.

"Do you know why it was shaking its head?" asked Mr. Barker.

"If I went into that realm I would be going into the realms of a dingo expert," she retorted, suddenly brazen. "It is beyond my expertise and knowledge."

Mr. Barker suggested that when she was at the rail, the dog would have been within her vision. No, she said, it had gone before that. It left when she yelled at it, when she was about nine meters away.

"You watched it leave?"

"I watched it leave just a few feet, that's all; just a split second."

She did not see the baby in the dingo's mouth because its nose was below the light level from the barbecue and so was obscured by the scrub and the railing. She couldn't see what it was carrying as it went past the tent, because she could only just see the top of its head.

Lindy told the court that both Aidan and Reagan had bled in the family car, Aidan suffering from a heavy nosebleed while standing up in the backseat and Reagan bleeding from the lip after hitting the dashboard when the car stopped in a hurry. And she repeated what she had claimed before—that young people in the church group had been treated for nosebleeds in the car, where she had kept a first aid kit.

Those who thought emotions were running high on the first day of Lindy's evidence were to find the atmosphere positively charged with electricity on the second day of the case for the defense.

XV

"You Cut the Baby's Throat . . ."

"I put it to you that you sat in the front passenger's seat . . . that you held the baby in front of you, and that you cut its throat."

"No."

The question by the Crown Prosecutor could not have been more direct. The answer from the tense mother in the witness box, her body misshapen by the child in her womb, could not have been firmer.

It was another bitter exchange in the packed court during a day in which Mr. Barker hit Lindy Chamberlain with all that he had; in which Lindy, sometimes failing to hold back her tears, denied his every accusation. Again, her irritation showed through at times as she constantly denied murdering her baby daughter.

"Look, Mr. Barker, I wasn't there," she said at one point. "I can only go on the evidence of my own eyes. We are talking about my baby daughter—not some object."

Mr. Barker suggested to Lindy that blood from the child splattered the front of her pants. "Not while I was wearing them."

He suggested that drops fell on her shoes. "That's incorrect."

"That a spray of blood went up under the dashboard of the car in front of the seat."

"No."

"I suggest that you moved the child's body and blood flowed down the offside of the seat in which you were sitting."

"No."

"And that this is how the blood got under the hinge of the seat."

"No."

"Do you deny that?"

"Yes."

Mr. Barker suggested she had left the body in the car, either wrapped or inside the camera bag.

"No, that's pure fabrication, Mr. Barker."

The prosecutor went on to suggest that Lindy "entered the tent and that you left smears of blood in the tent from blood that was on you."

"No, definitely not."

"That you washed your hands in the tent."

"No."

"I suggest that you removed the tracksuit pants and that you went back to the barbecue."

"No."

"That your husband asked you to check the baby?"

"He did ask me to check the baby, yes."

"You did not hear her cry?"

"No."

"You went back to the tent and you invented the story of the dingo removing the child from the tent."

"I did not. I definitely did not invent that story and that's the truth, Mr. Barker."

"I suggest that for some time that night the body of the child was left in the front of the car."

"No."

"That at some stage you or your husband buried the baby in soft sand."

"No, that's completely untrue."

"That at some stage the child was disinterred and the clothes removed."

"No."

"That either you or your husband deliberately cut the jumpsuit with scissors with the object of simulating damage caused by a dingo."

"No."

"That the child's body was buried or otherwise disposed of."

"No, Mr. Barker, that's incorrect."

"I put it to you that you or your husband put the clothes where they were subsequently found . . ."

"No, that's incorrect."

". . . with the object of letting it be thought that the baby had been killed and eaten by a dingo."

"That's incorrect, Mr. Barker."

Mr. Barker referred to a statement Lindy had made to the police in which she said a dingo she had seen earlier on the day of the disappearance near Ayers Rock looked similar to the one she saw at the tent, a dingo that almost looked as if it was "chasing" the baby.

The QC suggested that Lindy attempted to implant the idea that the dingo had come from the region of the Rock in order to divert attention from the camping area to the place where the clothes were eventually found. No, said Lindy, but she was concerned that the Rock area appeared not to be undergoing a search.

"Do you think that is where it was likely that something would be found?"

"Well, there were dingoes there, and any area where there were dingoes I thought was worth looking at."

Mr. Barker wanted to know whether it was the blood

in the tent that led Lindy Chamberlain to the conclusion that the child had probably died. She said it was a combination of the blood, the weather, the dingo attack, and the effects of shock and exposure.

"Did you form the view when you entered the tent that the child had died before the dingo carried her off?"

"I wasn't sure about that, or that she was simply unconscious. I knew if she had been alive at all, she would have cried enough to hear her."

Mr. Barker then questioned the accused mother about positive reactions for blood in tests on samples taken from the car. Could she explain those?

People had bled in the car a number of times, said Lindy, but to offer any suggestion about how a spray pattern got under the dashboard would only be pure speculation—"I prefer not to speculate in court," she said.

Next, the QC moved on to the tufts of fiber found in the car and the camera bag; tufts, it was alleged, that were the results of cuts from fabric similar to the jumpsuit. They, she said, could have come from anywhere up to ten or a dozen jumpsuits her two sons had worn. She recalled cutting the legs off some jumpsuits so the boys could wear them as pajamas. The last of the jumpsuits had been cut about two or three months before Azaria disappeared and she had thrown out the last of the cut jumpsuits a few weeks after the baby's death, before the family moved from Mount Isa.

Lindy Chamberlain, whose voice began to fade to a whisper toward the end of a grueling day, told the court that in her opinion the dingo she saw at the tent entrance had the baby in its mouth.

"Well, is there any doubt about it?"

"Not in my mind."

"Is it merely your opinion or is it something you know as a fact?"

"It is something my heart tells me is fact. Other people don't think so."

The hours of torrid questioning and answering were almost up. Mr. Barker put forward the suggestion—one more time—that Lindy Chamberlain had invented the story of the dingo to cover up the fact that she had cut Azaria's throat.

"I definitely did not invent that story, and that's the truth, Mr. Barker," she said.

When at last the court adjourned for the day, Lindy rose slowly to her feet, Michael at her side to help. That, everyone believed, would be the last intense questioning she would go through over the disappearance of her daughter. She was tired of the questions—she had made that quite clear to the court only that morning. During one of her tearful outbursts, Justice Muirhead had asked if she wanted a break. No, she said, she preferred to go on—"It's been going on for two years and I want to get it over with."

With Lindy out of the witness box and back in the dock, the question of her state of mind after the birth of Azaria was raised when Mr. Phillips called Dr. Irene Milne of Mount Isa; she had attended the birth of Azaria in June 1980.

The GP explained she had some experience in postnatal depression, which could take a severe or mild form. In its severe form, the mother could become disassociated from her surroundings and totally disinterested in the child, and it could lead to the mother harming herself or the baby. In its mild form, postnatal depression usually lasted about four days and was manifested in the mother crying for no apparent reason. But there were no signs of either mild or severe postnatal depression with Lindy Chamberlain. Dr. Milne said that according to notes of a doctor colleague, Lindy had brought Azaria to the clinic after a fall in a supermarket, but there had been no injury. Dr. Milne said that Lindy Chamberlain had reported that Azaria had vomited on occasion—"she [Azaria] tended to vomit from birth," said the doctor.

A clergyman, Webber Roberts, was called by the defense to tell of his discovery of a spray pattern under the glove box on the dashboard of his car, a 1977 Torana hatchback, the same model as the Chamberlain car. Michael Chamberlain had been present, he said, when he inspected his car in March 1982 and saw the spray pattern. He gave Michael permission to cut the spray pattern, which was on a metal plate, from the car in the presence of a justice of the peace.

The defense continued to call forward experts to dispute the scientific evidence tendered by the prosecution. Professor Richard Nairn, professor of pathology and immunology at Melbourne's Monash University medical school, told the jury that he agreed with the evidence of Professor Barry Boettcher, from the Department of Biological Sciences at the University of Newscastle, who had disputed the findings of Mrs. Kuhl that stains found in the Chamberlains' car were fetal hemoglobin. In fact, Professor Nairn said he disagreed with the forensic biology evidence of the prosecution, including that given by Professor Cameron. He was asked by Mr. Barker, for the prosecution, if he was suggesting that the methods employed by biologists at the Metropolitan Police Forensic Science Laboratory in London were in some way inferior to those employed by research biologists.

"Some of them are, yes, because, as I say, they haven't the advanced equipment and they haven't got the very advanced training. Since forensic science laboratories were established, immunological courses were set up. Mine was the first in Australia and indeed one of the first in the world in which we actually train young scientists as immunologists. One day those people will filter into forensic science laboratories and then the problem will be solved."

Another professor, Hector Orams, a reader in dental medicine and surgery at Melbourne University, told the court that he believed damage on Azaria's clothing was consistent with having been caused by the teeth of a dingo. He had studied dingo teeth, but he conceded he was not an expert in fabrics. He also agreed he did not know exactly what Azaria's jumpsuit was made of and he could not exclude the possibility that a meat skewer, barbed wire, a nail, a knife, or scissors might have caused the damage.

A further conflict of opinion with prosecution evidence came from a Geelong pathologist, Dr. Vernon Plueckhahn, who said that Professor Cameron's findings that Azaria's throat had been cut were "completely unfounded." He had performed thousands of postmortems and the bloodstains on the jumpsuit could have been the result of a head injury. And of the evidence by Professor Cameron that he thought he saw impressions of a hand on the jumpsuit, Dr. Plueckhahn said, "With due respect to Professor Cameron's opinion, I cannot find any evidence whatsoever that would convey to me that these are imprints."

And of Professor Cameron's conclusions that the bloodstains could only have been caused by a cut throat, the pathologist said, "From my experience and from studying these clothes, I would say the conclusions of Professor Cameron are completely unfounded."

Michael Chamberlain was called to the witness box.

Within half an hour he had slumped forward, hands to his face, tears pouring. His reaction came when Mr. Phillips asked him why he had spoken to the media the day after Azaria disappeared.

"It was to me such a horrible thing that I . . . I didn't want it to happen . . ."

Mr. Phillips went on: "The prosecution case is that at some stage during the evening you became aware that your baby had been murdered by your wife. What do you say to that?"

"False."

"It is suggested that at some stage during the evening you buried the child somewhere near the area of the tent."

"Quite false."

"And it is suggested that either you or your wife then took the baby's clothes off and put them near the Rock, where they were found on 24 August. What do you say to that?"

"That is clearly false."

Mr. Barker, in his cross-examination of Michael Chamberlain, said, "I suggest that the whole story is nonsense and you know it."

"No."

The prosecuting QC asked Michael whether it didn't seem extraordinary to him that his wife did not see a baby in the animal's mouth as it came out of the tent.

"I thought about that, too, and I didn't know what to think on that point."

"Didn't it seem extraordinary to you that she didn't see a baby in a dingo's mouth as it walked past the tent?"

"It wasn't easy to understand."

"That fact that she didn't see the baby doesn't cause you any doubt?"

"Not really, no."

Michael said he could not account for the damage to the collar of the jumpsuit, and, when asked if he accepted that it was done by a pair of scissors, he replied, "I don't know."

"Do you accept that it was not done by a dingo?"

"That I don't know, either."

"Have you ever thought it was done by a dingo?"

"Yes."

"What about the damage to the sleeve—how do you account for that?"

"Again, I don't know."

"Did you cut it?"

"No."

"Did you cut the collar?"

"No."

"Did your wife cut the sleeve?"

"I don't think so."

"Did she cut the collar?"

"I don't think so."

Asked about the singlet being found inside out, Michael Chamberlain said he did not know whether it was inside out or not.

"You wouldn't suggest a dingo turned it inside out, would you?"

"I wouldn't suggest anything."

Asked whether he had buried the jumpsuit with the child in it, Michael replied, "No."

"Did your wife?"

"I don't think she did."

Mr. Barker asked Michael whether he had any knowledge of his wife going to the base of the Rock on the night of the disappearance. No, he said, he had no knowledge of that and he had not gone there himself.

"Are you prepared," Mr. Barker asked, "to say you

didn't, but you don't have any knowledge of your wife having gone there?"

"Yes."

"You are not prepared to say that she didn't."

"Well, I was asleep most of the night; at least, I was asleep some parts of the night, fitfully; but to my knowledge, she didn't."

Later Mr. Barker asked whether Michael Chamberlain's wife had said anything to him about his evidence. No, not anything in particular, he said, but when asked if he could remember anything in general he replied, "Yes: 'Stay calm.' "

"What else did she say?"

" 'Listen carefully,' I think."

Michael Chamberlain agreed that at the inquest he had said his wife suggested he might care to go to Mount Olga, near Ayers Rock, the day after the baby disappeared.

Mr. Barker asked Michael if he had sworn the day before his trial evidence that he did not search on the Monday because he was going to stay at the motel "in order that the police could contact you immediately there was something to be told"?

"That was my feeling, yes."

"Was that your wife's feeling?"

"Generally speaking, I think it was, yes."

"Why did she suggest you might go to Mount Olga?"

"The children were playing up and we just didn't know how we were going to keep them from continuing to play up. And we just felt very unhappy about them, the way they were feeling."

When Michael Chamberlain stepped into the witness box after the lunch adjournment the following day, Friday, October 22, he sat, clasped his hands, lowered his head, and closed his eyes. Some thought he was praying. A few minutes later Mr. Barker asked his last question in cross-examination.

"Mr. Chamberlain, have you and your wife ever discussed the possibility that something other than a dingo caused the death of your child?"

"Yes," said Michael Chamberlain, his voice just a whisper.

As if to follow the question, the Chamberlains' counsel, Mr. Phillips, asked him if he had heard rumors about what might have happened to Azaria.

Yes, he had. "One was a theory that an aboriginal person looking like a dingo or dressed in feathers might have tried to simulate an attack."

"And most of the others have been as fanciful as that?"

"Yes."

At last, the questioning was over. The trial had taken up twenty-eight days so far, the prosecution had called forty-five witnesses, the defense twenty-eight, and their evidence had filled 2,800 pages of transcript. The 140 exhibits had included the car where the Crown said the baby had had her throat cut and the tent from which Lindy said she was certain a dingo had taken her daughter. All that remained now was for the defense to make its final address to the jury, followed by the Crown. Then the judge would sum up and the jury would retire to consider its verdict in the case that had intrigued the nation.

Mr. Phillips was to spend more than a day in his address to the jury, an eloquent speech charged with emotion and packed with as many facts that contradicted the prosecution as he could draw from his briefcase. As far as motive was concerned, he said, the prosecution was "stone motherless broke." In fact, he said, "they are bankrupt. There is no other way to look at it. But we're [the defense] not bankrupt in this area of the case because we have been able to obtain from witness after witness, 90 percent of them independent of the Chamberlains, proof after proof of this mother's love and affection for her baby."

Mr. Phillips said Mr. Barker had never put to Lindy that she had cut her baby's throat for a particular reason. "It was never put because Mr. Barker, one of the best men in the business, just cannot think of any reason why she would do it. The prosecution have had two years and three months to think of a reason, any reason, good, bad, or indifferent, and they can't."

Mr. Phillips particularly attacked the evidence of Professor Cameron and Joy Kuhl. The professor's involvement was accompanied by a series of fundamental misunderstandings and false assumptions that led him to take one of only two alternatives. The defense lawyer reminded the jury that the London forensic scientist had admitted that he ruled out the dingo because of a complete misunderstanding as to the nature of the baby's clothes when they were discovered.

It was astonishing, said Mr. Phillips, that Mrs. Kuhl's "hard evidence" had been destroyed, denying experts engaged by the defense the chance to view scientific plates. "How would you like to be tried on the basis of opinions based on hard evidence which is destroyed?" Mr. Phillips asked the jury.

"The defense does not have to prove anything," he added. "I cannot stress that rule of law too much."

Now it was the turn of Mr. Barker to try to convince the jury.

"It was murder," he declared. "It was her mother, and there is no room for any other reasonable hypothesis." His words were pointed. Dramatic. Like an actor in his final scene, the prosecutor, who had been the first to enter the contemporary tragedy being played out in the Darwin Supreme Court, now directed his remaining lines at the jury.

"We don't have the eyewitnesses in the sense that anyone saw the child killed," he said, "so the whole case must be, in substance, a drawing of inferences from established facts. If those inferences point to the guilt of the accused, and if there is no room for alternative reasonable inferences, well, then, your duty is to convict." The Crown, he conceded, could not provide a motive for the killing. "We don't know why this happened. All the Crown is saying is that it did happen. You don't work backward by some strange process and find that a murder was committed and then say to yourselves: 'Well, we've found that out all right, but we can't find a motive; therefore we have a doubt.'"

Mr. Barker turned to the crucial evidence of Joy Kuhl who had identified baby's blood in the car. Neither he nor anyone sitting in that court was to realize it, but that evidence was to become even more crucial in the months to come. In the meantime, Mr. Barker reminded the jury that in carrying out standard tests and using standard techniques on old blood, she managed to get twenty-two positive results for fetal hemoglobin, "which said to her that she was dealing with blood of a child under three months old."

Referring to other witnesses who had supported her evidence, Mr. Barker said, "You've got Dr. Baxter, another government employee, checking the work of one of his biologists and he agreed with her twenty-two times, and you've got Mr. Culliford, totally detached from it all, checking her notes, her evidence, her work methods, and agreeing with her twenty-two times. Now clearly this is very prejudicial and embarrassing evidence to the accused. Clearly it is damaging to them to have a car with traces of fetal blood in it, to have a camera bag with fetal blood on it, and I notice that it's not suggested how that might have got there."

Mr. Barker then listed the places that Mrs. Kuhl had found fetal blood. "You remember the scissors and the inside of the chamois container. You remember under the dash . . . you remember under the passenger's side seat, the ten-cent coin, the stains around the bolt hole . . . you remember the stains down the vinyl of the passenger seat . . . and you remember the blood that she found under the hinge. Now you'd think, wouldn't you, that this would require a great deal of explaining even if it's adult blood. She says it is fetal blood, and I suggest to you that she ought to know, and Dr. Baxter ought to know what it is he's dealing with, because you know, really, if the suggestions made about their work in this court have any substance, people in New South Wales [where Mrs. Kuhl was based] are in constant danger of being wrongly convicted whenever there's some blood involved and it's really, I suggest, rather too ridiculous to contemplate that she would come into this, in the course of her daily work as a professional forensic biologist, and muck it all up, not knowing whether she was dealing with adult blood or the blood of a child under three months of age."

Lindy Chamberlain's story, he said, was an affront to the intelligence of the jury. "This preposterous story," he said, "has been seized upon by the accused to explain what is otherwise incapable of explanation." Having told the lie, Lindy had stuck with it. If a dingo had been on trial the case would have been laughed out of court. On the defense account, the dingo went into the tent, pulled the child from the bassinet, ran from the tent, buried the child, disinterred it, then carried it—on one account—some fourteen kilometers. It then, according to the defense account, took the child from the clothing, causing relatively little damage, turned the singlet inside out, and left the booties inside the jumpsuit.

If the accused was to be believed, said Mr. Barker, "we are dealing not only with a dexterous dingo, but a very tidy dingo." Lindy Chamberlain, he went on, had been deliberately vague about seeing the baby in the dingo's mouth—it was much safer to be vague because it meant the lie was more successful.

The Crown prosecutor turned to Lindy Chamberlain's description of the dingo she said she had seen at the tent. While she noticed, in a split second, the distinctive bridge on its nose and the hairs on the outside of its ears, she was unable to see, clutched in the animal's mouth, a human baby . . . her baby, dressed in white.

As for Michael Chamberlain's movements on the night, said Mr. Barker, it could be inferred he acted like a man who knew his wife had murdered her baby. He had shown a startling lack of curiosity about what exactly had happened to his child. "One would have thought that he would, beside searching, make the most intensive inquiries and would extensively question his wife with a view to determining what really happened."

Now it remained only for the judge to address the jury. Justice Muirhead remarked that inquests had come and gone and the tide of opinion and innuendo had ebbed and flowed but it was now the time for the jury to decide whether the Crown had established its case beyond reasonable doubt.

Evidence had shown that dingoes had prowled around the Ayers Rock area at the time the baby disappeared, that they were regarded as a potential danger, and that they were capable of carrying a nine-and-a-half-pound baby. Although the scientific evidence might help the jury, it was absolutely for them to determine whether a dingo took the child. They had to remember there had been dingoes in the area that had displayed aggression, there was blood in the tent, and there was a trail nearby, suggesting that a dog had dragged something and put it down. If a dingo had taken and mauled the baby, no one had the means of assessing how the dingo's jaws were applied to the clothing.

Turning to the evidence of Mrs. Kuhl, the judge pointed out that she had been working on blood that had been denatured. As for her admission that the plates she had used had been destroyed, that did not mean her conclusions were automatically invalidated. And as for Professor Cameron's evidence, the judge said the evidence of the handprint had to be treated with care.

"We are not in the realm of speculation; we are not in the realm of science; we are in the realm of proof."

This, he said, was a case of novel and unique circumstances—opinions were opinions; impressions were impressions.

Now, for the benefit of the jury, the judge summed up the essence of the case. It was the last time the twelve men and women were to hear anything from any of the court officials.

Events, said Justice Muirhead, began with a tired but happy mother nursing her baby to sleep at the campsite. Other people were in the vicinity. But, according to the Crown, instead of putting the baby to bed, she got into the front of the car and cut Azaria's throat with, perhaps, a pair of scissors. It would, remarked the judge, have been a "pretty bloody event"; but the Crown suggested she might have washed her hands in the tent. She went back to the car and got out a tin of beans and a can opener and returned to the barbecue area with

Aidan. The problem of concealing the killing lay ahead of her, said the judge, still referring to the Crown case. She went back to the tent and cried out: "My God, my God, the dog has got my baby," or words to that effect.

"If it was a plan to conceal a murder," said Justice Muirhead, "it was very quick thinking."

Until they went to the motel, observed the judge, there was a light close to the car which, on the Crown evidence, still had the baby and blood in it. Sometime during the evening, with caring women around her, some of whom would have been watching her, Mrs. Chamberlain and her husband were said to have taken the baby from the car and buried it. Sometime later they went out and located the burial spot, dug up the body, cut off the singlet, and reburied the body. The blood was mopped up in the car and someone put the blood-stained clothing or the body in the camera case. Despite extensive searching, the body was not found.

Once again pointing out the need for the jury to be satisfied beyond all reasonable doubt, the judge referred to Mr. Chamberlain hearing the baby's cry, as well as Mr. Lowe, who said he had heard someone mention a cry, and Mrs. Lowe, who testified that she heard it coming from the vicinity of the tent.

"It is for you to determine the accuracy of Mrs. Lowe's testimony," said the judge—perhaps, he suggested, she had heard an animal's cry in the bush, or perhaps she was lying, "because she cannot lead herself to believe that Mrs. Chamberlain would kill a baby like this."

The judge added: "You are not here to solve mysteries"—when they went to the jury room they were not going to consider what possibly happened, what might have happened, or whether they thought that Mrs. Chamberlain had probably done it. They were there to determine whether they were satisfied beyond reasonable doubt that Alice Lynne Chamberlain had murdered the baby and whether her husband was an accessory after the fact of murder. If they were satisfied, their duty was to convict; if they were not satisfied, they had to acquit.

It was 2 P.M. on Friday, October 29. In a few hours, at sundown, the Seventh Day Adventist Sabbath would begin. The jury filed out. Now there was only the waiting.

It was to be a long sojourn. Finally, at 8:30 P.M., the court orderlies indicated the jury had made a decision. The Chamberlains walked back into the dock, Michael in this red-and-blue-striped tie and white shirt, Lindy in a turquoise and white smock with white ruffled sleeves. Lindy sat on Michael's left, nearest the judge. She stared straight ahead at the empty witness box, but he occasionally looked around the court.

The accused couple watched tight-lipped as the nine men and three women, who held their future in the balance, took their places in the jury box. Three of the men glanced briefly at the dock on the opposite side of the narrow courtroom, but for most of those early moments they all directed their gazes at the judge.

"Mr. Foreman," said the judge, "would you be good enough to stand."

The man in the front row nearest the bench rose. Were they unanimous in their verdict? the judge asked. Yes, they were.

"Do you find the accused, Alice Lynne Chamberlain, guilty or not guilty of murder?"

"Guilty."

No one could know what Lindy Chamberlain felt at that moment. A mystery that had persisted for more than two years had been answered in a single word.

Apart from an almost undetectable inward gasp, a slight parting of the lips, her expression was stony. Then her eyes darted from the jury foreman to her QC, who was looking directly ahead at the papers on his desk.

And Michael Chamberlain. . . . His eyes squinted to the point where they were almost closed and then he slowly shook his head from side to side. He opened his eyes again and looked at the foreman and his expression suggested that if he were to say anything right then it would be the simple question "Why?"

The judge was speaking again while the pastor continued to shake his head. Did the jury find Michael Chamberlain guilty or not guilty of being an accessory after the fact of murder?

"Guilty."

Justice Muirhead addressed Lindy Chamberlain. She had been found guilty of murder, he said. There was only one sentence he could pass. "You will be imprisoned with hard labor for life."

Now the shock seemed to be hitting her. There was a frown, then a flash of anger in her eyes. Her husband looked disbelievingly at the two rows of people on the opposite side of the courtroom.

The judge was talking again, saying that Michael Chamberlain would be released and brought back to the court later so that submissions could be made on his behalf. An orderly opened the door behind the stunned Chamberlains and, as one, they rose and turned to their right and walked away from the sea of faces that stared at them from the public gallery. And now, in those last few seconds, Lindy looked close to tears.

Outside, it was dusk. Her Sabbath had just begun.

XVI

The Mystery of the Matinee Jacket

They took Lindy to Darwin's Berrimah jail, a bleak, sprawling complex surrounded by paddocks. Less than three weeks later, on November 17, she gave birth to her second daughter. Within hours, the child was taken from her, the authorities concerned that a woman found guilty of murdering once might be capable of doing it again. Lindy named the baby Kahlia, but none of the skeptics was able to find an interpretation for it. Those first few months in prison were far from easy. She was to recall later how, after having her new baby daughter taken from her, she was in agony as her milk dried up and her breasts swelled. She asked a prison officer for a breast pump without success and it was only when she almost fainted later that another officer took her to a breast pump. In an hour she lost forty centimeters from her bust.

Lindy and Michael—he had been given a suspended sentence of eighteen months on a $500 good behavior bond—appealed, of course: first to the federal court in Sydney, where they were turned down by all three judges, then to the High Court of Australia where they again lost, with three judges to two going against them. But there were many in Australia who were convinced that the Crown had not had a case and believed she was innocent. Public meetings were called to discuss action. Encouraging letters were sent to Lindy in jail, where she was now firmly engaged in the routine of mowing lawns, cooking breakfast for the other women inmates, and cleaning the administration buildings, for hard labor no longer meant smashing up rocks.

Heartened by the news that support groups had sprung up around the nation, Lindy began writing letters revealing her inner feelings. In one written in 1984 she admitted the total effect of the past four years on her life and that of her family was "permanent and far reaching." She added that "no one who has been touched by our tragedy and the subsequent events can claim to have been unaffected. I don't cry myself to sleep much any more. I just grit my teeth determinedly. Although I've felt broken at times, with God's help I've risen, armed for the fight. . . ."

In addition to the individuals who believed that Lindy should not have been convicted, scientists were working for her, too. Professor Barry Boettcher, the senior lecturer in biology at Newcastle University who had given evidence at the trial to dispute Mrs. Kuhl's findings of baby's blood, felt he should check the results of his tests, which he felt were vital to the defense. The professor, using the same antiserum to test for fetal blood that Joy Kuhl had used, had found that it also reacted to adult blood, at least he *thought* he had used the same antiserum, and just to make sure he flew to Germany to visit the manufacturers. He discovered that the batch he used was from the same batch used by Mrs. Kuhl—and to prove that a fetal reaction was possible with adult blood, he used his own blood in the experiment. This meant only one thing in Professor Boettcher's mind—that if Mrs. Kuhl had examined samples of adult blood, for example blood that had come from the accident victim, Mr. Lenehan, she could have had the same reaction from which she had concluded the blood was actually fetal hemoglobin.

Professor Boettcher felt so strongly about this flaw in the prosecution's case that he agreed to go on television with this critical appraisal of the jury: "The jury should have accepted the demonstrations that I provided that the reagent would react with adult blood. Since we now know that the demonstrations I provided in the Darwin court . . . were conducted with precisely the same reagent as was used in the Chamberlain car, we then should realize that the tests on the items from the Chamberlain car were not valid, or the conclusions from them were not valid."

In that same television program Greg Lowe, who along with his wife Sally had been chatting with the Chamberlains at the barbecue area, came up with something new—a vital piece of evidence about Lindy's movements that he said he had not included in his original statement because he did not realize its significance.

Said Greg: "I saw her not only approach the tent, I saw her kneel down to enter the tent with the baby. At that stage, Aidan was waiting alongside the tent, waiting for his mother to come out. I did see her come out, and she wasn't carrying the baby at that stage, and she proceeded with Aidan toward the car on the southern side of the tent." She did not have the baby with her at that time, he said. "She placed her left arm around Aidan and her right arm was unimpeded and there was no way known that she was carrying a baby at that stage."

Greg said he was advised that because he had not mentioned that observation in his original statement he should not refer to it at the trial—it might, he was told, be regarded as a fabrication.

Then Wallace Goodwin, the tourist who had found Azaria's jumpsuit, came forward to express his concern about the way the police had handled the evidence. Despite prosecution claims to the contrary, Mr. Goodwin said more than two snaps were open on the jumpsuit.

"The front was open to the waist, which exposed the singlet inside," he said.

Referring to it as a "gray suit," he said, "Most of the clips were open. . . . At first impression, the way the feet were sticking up on the gray suit and the way it was on its back, it gave the impression that the feet were still in the gray suit and the baby had been eaten out of it."

After he brought Constable Morris back to the scene, said Mr. Goodwin, he watched him kneel down, pick up the clothing, put his hand inside the leg of the jumpsuit, and pull out one of the booties. He told Mr. Goodwin that the bootie was the positive identification and then he asked the tourist to go and fetch another officer and notify the rangers. "When I left the area, Morris was standing there holding the gray suit in his hand."

The police officer arranged for two sets of photographs to be taken, one with the clothes in the position he said they were found in, another with the individual garments laid out. Mr. Goodwin said the jury became confused as to whether the clothes were found in a heap or neatly spread out. In fact, on his memory, the jumpsuit was laying with its legs slightly crumpled in, and the arms were almost spread fully, although they were also crumpled.

"When I was asked in court to show which one of the photos was the way the clothing was found, I replied, 'None of them are,' because I said that Morris had picked the clothing up." And he thought that even though he had laid the clothing out in court to demonstrate how he had found it, he did not think the evidence was fully understood by the jury. He thought the jury's reaction was to believe Constable Morris, not him.

Michael, looking after the children with help from his church and relatives, was also prepared to talk. He said that he'd always believed that if a system was good, it would eventually prove that a person was innocent. His and Lindy's case had been very complicated, with a lot of technical evidence that had been misunderstood by certain people. "If it had been correctly understood we would never be in this situation."

There was a point in continuing to fight, he said, "because the system has made a mistake in our case. We are innocent, and I affirm this and my wife would affirm it most strongly."

The campaign to prove that Lindy was innocent grew. There was ample copy for journalists who, believing she had been wrongly convicted, sought out those who shared their beliefs.

"A Prisoner of Prejudice?" asked one big headline over an article weighted in her favor. The Chamberlain Innocence Committee, headed by a number of prominent identities, pressed for a judicial review of the case in the Northern Territory; if that failed they would support Democrat Senator Colin Mason's bill for a federal commission of inquiry into the case.

Toward the end of 1985, the campaign really heated up with speculative reports that consideration was being given to Lindy's imminent release. These were dismissed by an angry Northern Territory Attorney General, Marshall Perron, who said such rumors gave false hope to Lindy and her family. Nevertheless, the pressure was on. Bob Collins, opposition leader of the Northern Territory, said he felt there had been a miscarriage of justice. A retired Victorian Supreme Court judge, Sir Reginald Sholl, expressed his doubts, as did retired former deputy chairman of the Commonwealth Conciliation and Arbitration Commission, Justice Frank Gallagher.

A syndicate of Seventh Day Adventist businessmen hired a legal team made up of John Lloyd Jones, QC, and two other lawyers. After carefully studying statements of all the witnesses from Ayers Rock, as well as employing a private investigator to talk to them again, Lloyd Jones concluded that there was ample material to show that Lindy's innocence was the only reasonable overall conclusion. Jones's team was backed financially by Chamberlain supporters around Australia and in California and they all held hopes that new demands for an inquiry into the case would be met by the Northern Territory government. But the government made a firm declaration: There would be no inquiry without new material and submissions and this must only come from lawyers instructed by the Chamberlains.

And solicitor Stuart Tipple, who had acted for the Chamberlains from the start—although it was the QCs who were always in the limelight—criticized the group by pointing out that they had foisted themselves upon Lindy. He had carried out a detailed examination of the material they had gathered and the evidence that had been submitted at the trial and he could not see anything of real significance.

"The material," he was quoted as saying in November 1985, "has got to be genuinely new. It cannot just be corroborative of something else. It has got to be completely new and something of sufficient cogency."

One hope of "something new" lay in tearing apart the scientific evidence. Professor Boettcher, having confirmed the weaknesses in Mrs. Kuhl's testing methods, obtained the support of other scientists who also pressured the Northern Territory government to set up a full inquiry into the Chamberlain affair.

Pressure was intensifying. Scientific opinions were pouring in, it seemed, from around the world. Professor Randall Bresee, associate professor of textiles at Kansas State University, put forward the opinion that although he agreed the damage to Azaria's jumpsuit was caused by cutting, "I strongly disagree that the most likely method used to produce the cutting of the jumpsuit has been shown to be the rather complex scissor mechanism shown by the prosecution." Evidence presented to him, he said, demonstrated clearly that canine creatures were capable of producing the type of cutting damage seen in the jumpsuit.

But the pressure was not merely confined to scientific quarters or interested individuals and groups.

On December 5, 1985, as a restless Englishman named David Brett fought with the devil in his stomach and told his flatmates they were evil, the Chamberlain boys, Aidan, now twelve, and Reagan, nine, sat down at their home in Avondale College, Cooranbong, and penned letters to the Northern Territory's Chief Minister, Mr. Ian Tuxworth, Prime Minister Bob Hawke, and Prince Charles and Princess Diana.

"Dear Mr. Tuxworth and Mr. Hawke," wrote Aidan (the original spellings are included). "I cannot understand why you are keeping my mummy in jail when I know she did not kill my baby sister Azaria.

"My mummy loved buby just as we all did and I was with mummy and talking to her the hole time. I miss my mum and Kahlia Reagan and Dad do to.

"Is there nothing you can do to help me?

"Yours Sincerly, Aidan Chamberlain."

Reagan wrote: "Dear Mister Tuxworth, Mr. Hawke, Prince Charles and Princess Diana,

"I can still remember the dingo walk on my chest. I loved my bubby Azaria and so did mumy. We need mumy at home so does kahlia need a mumy. Can you make them let my mum come home to me?

"From Reagan."

The children's nanny made the letters public "to show Australia there are two little witnesses who know their mother is innocent and are suffering by a mistake which has marred them for life." The letters, she said, were written "in desperation" after the boys' hopes had been buoyed by what they thought would be their mother's imminent release and then dashed by the decision to keep Lindy in prison.

From jail, Lindy kept up the psychological pressure on the authorities. In a letter to friends she wrote that she wanted truth, justice, and her name, and that of her family, to be cleared with a public apology.

Her parents, retired Seventh Day Adventist pastor Cliff Murchison and his wife, Avis, received a Christmas message from Lindy in which their daughter claimed she had been offered a deal if she was to say she was guilty and put it down to postnatal depression. Then they would let her out of jail.

"But she says she won't tell a lie—not even to get out of jail," said Mrs. Murchison. And she said she and her husband believed she would be released "in God's good time. That may not be our timing, but we must be patient and wait for Him to complete His work."

The Lord was at work. Journalists sympathetic to the Chamberlains and believing an injustice had been done continued to pump out stories about growing demands for an inquiry.

Early in January what was said to be new evidence was tossed into the debating ring—the Chamberlains' solicitor, Mr. Tipple, said that particles of what might be human flesh had been discovered during new tests on Azaria's jumpsuit. Although not claiming it was positively human flesh, Mr. Tipple pointed out that the Crown had relied on the evidence of textile experts who said Azaria's jumpsuit could only have been cut by scissors. However, recently the defense team had set up experiments which showed the Crown case was wrong . . . that dingoes' teeth could damage material in the same way the jumpsuit was damaged.

"The experiments have shown the damage is almost the same," said Mr. Tipple. "There are a number of features you can only get with dogs and dingoes and not other animals. During the experiments we started seeing some things we had not seen before."

In the test material, he said, flesh had been found imbedded. So they took a look at Azaria's jumpsuit "and sure enough we have found what we believe is evidence of flesh." However, he said, there was no point in the defense doing tests on the particles without the assistance of the Northern Territory government. What was needed, he said, was an inquiry similar to one held in Adelaide, which had led to the release of a convicted murderer, Edward Splatt.

Mr. Tipple's excitement was not shared by the Northern Territory government, which had already rejected defense claims of flesh on Azaria's jumpsuit. In a report the government said fragments were not seen under microscopic examination, or otherwise, by any of the experts who gave evidence at the trial. "In any event, it can hardly be flesh or any other body tissue dated from August 17, 1980, given the natural effect of deterioration, such as dehydration, in the intervening period."

Mr. Tipple said, however, "The conditions at Ayers Rock are similar to those in Egypt"—a reference to the climate that allowed mummified bodies to achieve near-perfect preservation. "There is no humidity. The flesh dries out and is preserved very, very well."

On Sunday, January 26, 1986, David Brett walked unsteadily through the scrub toward the southwest corner of Ayers Rock, the late afternoon sun beating down on his thinning pate. Bracken pulled at his clothes, the same type of bracken that had caught in the clothing of so many others who had trudged through the searing landscape searching for clues to Azaria's disappearance.

What drove David Brett, torn by inner conflict, to veer from his route to Perth and head for Ayers Rock? What led him to the southwest corner of that huge monolith, toward the place where Azaria's jumpsuit had been found five and a half years earlier? Why did he decide to climb over the lichen at that place? And what unknown force caused him to fall on the same day of the week and virtually at the same time that Azaria vanished from the family tent?

They are questions to be added to the legend and many mysteries of Ayers Rock. They will be asked along with one other burning question that was raised after searchers spread out from the spot where David's body was found. . . . It was a question that cried out for an answer when one of those who took part in the gruesome hunt for bones from the Englishman's body, apparently taken by dingoes, noticed something sticking out of the sand: Why wasn't Azaria's matinee jacket found until now, despite the numerous official searches and the amateur fossicking of curious tourists over the years?

In time, an eminent judge, the Honorable Trevor Rees Morling, was to comment on the mystery of why the jacket had not been discovered sooner.

"It is surprising," observed Justice Morling, "that the

extensive searches of the area on 24 August 1980 and subsequently, including police line searches, did not lead to the discovery of the jacket.

"The place where the jacket was found was one hundred fifty meters from the center of the search area. However, there is evidence that the bushes and grasses in that area would have been more dense, making it more difficult to see the jacket in August 1980 than in February 1986. It is possible that it may have been covered by leaves or mulch as the result of some animal activity."

In England, the mind of David's mother, Doreen, rang with his parting words: *"If you don't hear from me again, you'll know I've been sacrificed."*

Confused by erratic, exaggerated, and misleading reports about the Chamberlain case and defensive as any caring mother would be of the activities of her son, yet frustrated by distance, Mrs. Brett wrote an anxious letter to the Northern Territory police commissioner. Remembering other words of David, that he did not want to bring evil into the house and it was best he returned to Australia, Mrs. Brett said in her letter: "There are too many coincidences and something very strange about the whole case. I know all this sounds difficult to believe but had you known Dave you would feel as positive as we do and realize David was a courageous, experienced, and intelligent man whose main thought was to shield us. Dave said he had to go back to Australia and face it (the evil) to be free. We pleaded with him to stay in England. He had already booked his ticket from hospital to return to Perth next day. It was all so quick, as though he was being willed there."

Mrs. Brett wrote at a time when the police were already being beseiged by inquiries that had been sparked by a totally inaccurate television report that stated that engraved in the center of the Union Jack tattoo on David's buttock was the word "AZARIA." Such was the sensationalism that surrounded the discovery of the Englishman's body, but there was, of course, no denying the curious course of events that led up to his plunge from the face of Ayers Rock. Question after question arose in the Brett household. David cared a great deal about his sisters and he had told Annette, his would-be girlfriend in Sydney, that he intended to return to England in August for Gina's wedding.

"What stopped his plans?" Mrs. Brett asked her daughters. "We all know how much David loved us. And why suddenly veer off to go to Ayers Rock when he spoke about returning to Perth?"

One burning question begging an answer was David's reference to the men he said lived next door to him in the block of flats in the Perth suburb of Claremont. Prompted by numerous press inquiries and Mrs. Brett's letters, police set out to trace the men, but to no avail. Whoever had been living next door had moved on but there were a number of tenants prepared to confirm that "men in black" had been seen walking along the outside corridors of the apartment block. There had also been loud, hysterical chanting and mystical music in the dead of night. One tenant, Tony Venema, recalled that shortly after he had moved in he had been warned about strange people and black magic parties.

"I've been told stories by longstanding tenants about sacrifices in King's Park, and more," he said at the time. "It's bizarre. I don't know how true they are—and I don't want to know—but I've seen some pretty strange people around here. Several blokes are always dressed in black. First of all I thought they might have been bikies because they looked very heavy, but after hearing the stories I'm not sure what they are."

The caretaker of the block when David was there, Noel Mountney, knew nothing of strange happenings but pointed out there were more than two hundred tenants in the block and it was "pretty hard keeping tabs on all of them." But yes, he remembered David Brett, "a quiet type of guy, not outstanding in any way. But he left his flat in a terrible mess. I know, because I had to clean it out."

Three years on, resident Tony Tripp recalls the stories that circulated at the time of David's occupancy. Tony lived a few apartments along from David's, on the same floor, and what surprised him was that "these strange people in black, whoever they were," did not "target" *him*. Pictures of Hindu gods and other Eastern symbols adorn his flat and Tony believes he was a "sitting duck" for anyone dabbling in the occult. "I'm just a few doors along . . . why didn't they try to recruit me? I make no secret of my interest in such things. From the way other tenants have talked, it sounds like these people specifically went for David. Maybe they could see he was disturbed . . . I don't know. I don't suppose we'll ever know now."

While police were starting their inquiries into the troubled Englishman's background, the miracle that the Lindy Chamberlain support groups had hoped and prayed for was in the making. . . .

After hearing news of the discovery of the matinee jacket, the Chamberlains' solicitor immediately sent a telegram to the Northern Territory police commissioner. Mr. Tipple wrote: "Request immediate access for identification to jacket found at Ayers Rock and your undertaking that it not be subjected to any testing or further examination until then."

The most obvious step was to first ask Lindy whether

she could identify the jacket as the one she said her daughter was wearing on the night she disappeared.

"If this jacket is found to be Azaria's," declared Mr. Tipple, "there can be no murder case against her [Lindy]."

Identification would certainly blow a big hole in the Crown case. For the prosecution had insisted that Lindy had made up the story of the jacket to account for there being no dingo saliva or dingo hairs on the jumpsuit; her "story" was, said the Crown, that saliva would have been present on the matinee jacket. There was also the prosecution's conviction that patterns of blood on the jumpsuit were not consistent with the child wearing a matinee jacket at the time. Police made an immediate comparison with the jacket and the description given by Lindy. The freshly discovered garment was certainly weather-beaten but it was white with pale lemon edging around the collar and cuffs and light elastic around the wrists.

Prosecution lawyers thumbed back through her evidence, checking all her references to the jacket. One comment, made in an interview with Detective Sergeant Charlwood before the first inquest, now had particular significance. All the relevant clothing from the night of August 17, 1980, had been collected by the police, she had said, "except that matinee jacket, and it wasn't a tight one. It had light elastic around the wrists and the buttons were loosish. So there is as much chance of it being off on a bush, on the way from the Rock somewhere, as there would be down a den, and left away from the other clothes, I should think."

No one was surprised when Lindy, driven from Berrimah Prison to the Darwin police station, was shown the jacket and identified it as belonging to her missing baby. Trembling, she had looked carefully at the soiled garment, checking the label and the double-0 size. Yes, it was the one that a girlfriend had given her after her own children had grown out of it.

Police Commissioner Peter McAulay later announced that it had been agreed with Mr. Tipple that officers of the Victorian forensic science unit would be in charge of conducting further investigations of the garment. A search would also be made around the area where the matinee jacket was found. Soil sampling by police at the base of the rock, he said, had already uncovered a label, "organic material," and a button that belonged to the baby's jacket. The organic material had been found in soil under the garment. Questioned about the nature of the material, Mr. McAulay said the earth contained "grass, sticks, and other bits and pieces which we can't identify at this stage."

Mr. McAulay said he could not explain why the jacket was missed during meticulous searches of the area.

At Ayers Rock, Chief Inspector Terry O'Brien watched police and scientists sift through the earth around where the jacket was found. The renewed investigations, he conceded, might settle the Chamberlain affair once and for all. "I don't think anyone ever thought it was all over." And he agreed that the police were looking for anything—"naturally, I suppose we must be looking for the body."

On February 7 the miracle was fulfilled. Lindy Chamberlain was on a cleaning detail when Barrie Barrier, from the Northern Territory's Department of Correctional Services, called her into his office at the jail. "I've got good news for you, Lindy," he said. "You're being released."

Stunned for a moment, Lindy then broke into a grin.

The door was open. Not just to freedom but to proving her innocence.

After being showered with congratulations by other women prisoners, she changed from her blue prison dress into civilian clothes while the formalities of her release were completed. While that was happening, the Northern Territory government announced that on advice from the solicitor general and the police commissioner, an official inquiry into the Chamberlain case would be held. The government had decided to remit the rest of her sentence and set Lindy free with no strings attached. Whatever the outcome of any future inquiry, she would not go back to jail.

In a statement the Northern Territory's attorney general, Mr. Marshall Perron, said, "The decision follows advice received from the solicitor general, Mr. Brian Martin, and the Northern Territory police commissioner, Peter McAulay, on what they regard as significant new evidence. They have advised that the discovery of a baby's matinee jacket at the base of Ayers Rock, and its subsequent identification by Lindy Chamberlain, may have a bearing on the case. The government proposes to take whatever action is necessary, including possible introduction of legislation, to set up the inquiry."

Commissioner McAulay had told the chief minister in a letter: "I now believe that the discovery of the garment, and particularly the condition in which the garment now is, are matters which may prove to be significant new evidence in the case. I must point out that the significance of the find will not be fully comprehensible until the garment has been subjected to extensive forensic examination. I must emphasize that at this stage I am not aware of any facts connected to this piece of evidence which affects the veracity of the prosecution's original case, but that does not alter the fact that the garment, its condition, and the circumstances connected with its discovery are all significant matters which ought to be tested as evidence against the totality of other relevant evidence."

Lindy was smuggled out of jail under an elaborate plan of deception to avoid the press who had descended on the prison complex. Cars raced from the prison, giving waiting newsmen the impression that one of them contained Lindy, but she left the jail in another vehicle some time later. Even the lady waiting with a bouquet of flowers missed her.

What sparked Lindy's sudden release, when earlier the Northern Territory government had said that she would remain in jail pending new investigations? The answer, or certainly part of the answer, lies in a letter, highly embarrassing to the government, that had been leaked to journalists by the Northern Territory opposition. The letter had been sent to the Northern Territory solicitor general, Mr. Brian Martin, by the German chemical company Behringwerke—the firm that had supplied the chemical reagent used by Mrs. Kuhl to test stains found in the Chamberlains' car.

Like Professor Barry Boettcher, who testified for the defense, Mr. Martin had traveled to Germany to check the Chamberlains' submissions that the tests were faulty. Mr. Martin reported to his government that the tests were not faulty, but when the German company read his report they wrote to him saying that he appeared to have misunderstood some points in a report they had given him in September. In essence, the letter sent to Mr. Martin said the stains found in the car were not suitable for detection and determination of fetal and adult blood and the company could not guarantee that the antiserum would react only with HbF—a factor in fetal blood—in all test conditions.

"Referring to the HbF detection in the Chamberlain case, the results obtained in our view remain doubtful," said the letter. The fact that the press had got their hands on the letter put the government in a spin, and to lessen its impact Lindy was released.

At the Seventh Day Adventist Centre in Cooranbong a delighted Michael and his sons and three-year-old daughter Kahlia waited for Lindy's arrival. A hand-painted sign a kilometer from the main gate read WEL-COME HOME LINDY and scores of yellow ribbons lined the roadside.

After three and a half years in prison Lindy was about to be reunited with her family. And another episode in what is perhaps the strangest case of the century was about to begin.

XVII

A New Lindy

The Lindy who was driven home from Sydney airport with Michael at her side was a far different woman from the mother who had sat in the witness box at her trial and repeated the dingo story. Then she had been heavily pregnant, her face reflecting the hope in her heart that the jury would believe her. Now she was thin —thinner than she had ever looked since the Azaria saga began—and hardened. But she was free.

It was not easy for either of them at first in their brick veneer house in the Seventh Day Adventist College grounds. The children had matured. And Michael, married to Lindy for sixteen years, had to learn to start living with a stranger. Lindy, the former pastor's wife— he had given up the ministry for the time being—used words like *screws,* to describe the prison officers. She had, in fact, offered Michael a divorce while she was in prison, to give him the chance of starting a new life. But Michael had rejected the very notion. After her prison bed, she found difficulty sleeping in domestic surroundings. Even keeping her food down was difficult after three and a half years of prison food. Michael admitted that he found Lindy tougher. They had to learn to start living a marriage again.

In time, they started giving interviews to the newspapers, magazines, and television for undisclosed fees, but these, friends explained, would help offset their legal commitments. They hinted at the difficulties of starting again as husband and wife and talked of the way the two Chamberlain boys were coping with the years of stress. It was Reagan, said Lindy, who kept his feelings to himself, hiding them, perhaps, while he occupied himself playing with a toy. The Chamberlains spoke, too, of the police who, as one questioner described their activities, "pursued them." Lindy said they had to live with themselves. Their nature made them so suspicious of everyone that the best friends they had were themselves.

The Chamberlain boys had something to say, too. Reagan, who lost 90 percent of the vision in one eye when a bottle exploded at a backyard barbecue while his mother was in jail, said children still called out to him that his mother killed Azaria, but he ignored them because he knew it was not true. He still missed Azaria, he said, describing her as "my baby."

When she appeared on television Lindy told a nationwide audience that she loved "that little girl." And she denied having lied, asking: "Why should you lie when you can tell the truth? You shouldn't have to lie to get justice. . . . I have not wiped that night from my mind. I've got a very good memory. I can shut my eyes and see it all over again."

Nobody liked to be called a liar, she said, "and I've been told straight to my face that I'm the most fanciful liar that Australia's got."

Just what did the public think about her? A television station tried to find out. It asked its viewers: "Do you believe Lindy Chamberlain is innocent?" A total of 52,250 callers answered yes and 48,242 said no.

The terms of the inquiry into the Chamberlain affair,

announced by the Northern Territory government, revealed that it would be headed by Justice Trevor Morling, aged fifty-eight, a federal court judge since 1981 and a former president of the Australian Bar Association. A preliminary hearing was set for May and anyone who felt they had anything of use to put to the inquiry was invited to apply for permission.

By June, the Royal Commission was well under way and once again the familiar figure of Lindy Chamberlain was seen marching across the room at the former Darwin police station—venue for the hearing—to give evidence on her behalf.

She was asked by Chester Porter, QC, assisting Justice Morling, how confident she was that the matinee jacket that had led to her release was Azaria's. She started to describe the yellow pattern on the sleeves and the elasticized wrists, then suddenly started sobbing, leaning forward with her head in her hands. It was not an unfamiliar scene.

The judge asked if she would like a short break but she told him: "It's all right, Your Honor, I'd rather get it over with." She then went on to say how she had asked to see the label, which had turned out to be the same label she described to police the day after Azaria disappeared.

How *certain* was she about the jacket? Mr. Porter wanted to know.

"About 99.9," she said.

Waiting to give their evidence were the aboriginal tribespeople who lived around the rock—the traditional owner of the Rock, Nipper Winmarti, his wife, Barbara Tjikadu, and three other trackers, Impana (Kitty) Collins, Nui Minyintiri, and Daisy Walkabout. Two of the six aborigines who had tracked around the Rock the night and day after Azaria disappeared had died and those men who survived were now white-bearded, in their sixties or seventies.

When it was her turn to give evidence, Barbara Tjikadu said that dingo tracks she saw around the tent and on a sandhill were made by the same animal whose tracks had been seen near Azaria's jumpsuit a week later.

"A dingo is a dingo," she said through an interpreter. "If it wants to feed it will kill and eat."

At times the difficulties of trying to bring two cultures together through questions and answers proved trying, to say the least. When Michael Adams, representing the Northern Territory government, asked Barbara why she had said she knew the dingo had carried the child off, she replied, "Because I know if it kills a joey [baby kangaroo], it will take off with it, carry it."

"So this dingo could have had a joey?" asked Mr. Adams.

The interpreter asked if Mr. Adams would like to hear the answer Barbara had given. "Yes," said Mr. Adams, "it won't embarrass me if it was a stupid question."

The interpreter said Barbara had replied: "You are talking your way with your ideas and you are talking about lies."

The judge then asked the interpreter to ask whether the dingo could have been carrying a joey.

"Was a kangaroo living in the tent?" was the brazen answer.

One by one, week by week, the witnesses, many of them familiar with the questions from previous inquiries, some of them new, came forward to give their evidence. And, in time, the $200,000-a-week inquiry became bogged down by the vital but complicated issue of whether there was baby's blood in the Chamberlains' car. That there was some form of blood in the vehicle was to be generally agreed upon, but its significance in the Azaria Chamberlain mystery came under question.

Opinions were diverse but what became abundantly clear was that the "routine" tests carried out by Mrs. Kuhl, although properly executed, had their "traps." There was the age of the blood—which could cause it to go through a denaturation process under which its properties would be altered—the various temperatures it had been exposed to in the car, and the suitability of the antiserum used by the woman scientist. In Mrs. Kuhl's tests on the Chamberlains' car, the inquiry was informed, she looked for a precipitation band, the result of a reaction when antigens and antibodies are brought together. Sometimes, the inquiry heard, some other form of chemical action can cause a reaction even when blood is not present, known as a nonspecific reaction. The question was, were Mrs. Kuhl's methods and her experience sufficient to distinguish between nonspecific and specific reactions?

At the request of Justice Morling, the car was examined by Michael Raymond, Biology Division Manager of the Victorian Forensic Science Laboratory. Scraping and rubbing, just as Mrs. Kuhl had done five years before him in 1981, Mr. Raymond obtained positive responses to the ortho-tolidine screening test. Then he subjected thirty-two samples, including one from Azaria's jumpsuit, to the crossover electronic test against various antisera. There were reactions from eighteen samples, confirmed by additional Ouchterlony tests, under which samples are exposed to various antisera in a humid chamber. Only one of these reactions, however, produced lines indicating a true reaction, and that was from the jumpsuit. What this meant in Mr. Raymond's experience was that the remaining reactions were nonspecific; in other words, in 1986 there was a substance in the car that was not necessarily blood but that was capable of giving a reaction. The scientist was not able to tell the commission whether similar reactions would have been obtained in 1981 when Mrs. Kuhl went over the car, but he did point out that there were areas where mistakes might be made if there were no proper controls or if the scientist involved was not fully competent.

Mrs. Kuhl's ability to distinguish between specific and nonspecific reactions came under further question during the evidence when it was revealed that bands of precipitation she found to be "fuzzy" were recorded as a positive finding of baby's blood. According to another scientist, Peter Martin, head of the biology division of London's Metropolitan Police Laboratory, these fuzzy bands would be inconclusive in confirming the presence of fetal hemoglobin.

There was, it became clear, another problem with Mrs. Kuhl's testing: the antiserum produced by the German company Behringwerke was not designed for routine laboratory work. Rather, it had been manufactured as a research product and its diagnostic use was limited. In addition, Mrs. Kuhl had not carried out any testing of the antifetal hemoglobin antiserum, whereas a number of experts believed it was necessary to test it against a range of adult and infant bloods under various dilutions. And there was also the question of the crossover electrophoresis test, in which an electric current is passed across a plate containing the samples. All the plates she used had been destroyed and the question arose whether the band of precipitation Mrs. Kuhl said she saw was the result of blood—or a reaction to something else.

A major blow to the Crown's case arose when the so-called arterial spray under the dashboard of the car was discussed. Although Mrs. Kuhl had at first been unable to get a blood reaction from it, a later test led her to conclude that baby's blood was present. Now the inquiry heard that the spray pattern, at least a sample of it on a steel plate cut from under the dashboard, was not blood at all but sound deadener that had seeped through a hole during manufacture of the Torana.

But apart from the flaws in the tests for blood there still remained the overriding question of whether it really was possible for a dingo to have carried the baby off. Dingo experts from the Commonwealth Scientific and Industrial Research Organisation testified that it was highly unlikely that Azaria was taken by a dingo. There was evidence that there was no blood in the child's carry-cot and no trail of blood leading from the tent. Neither was there any sign of bleeding in the area where her clothes were found. One witness, who claimed to have seen the remains of a baby allegedly killed by a dingo, testified that a skeleton had remained even after days of gnawing by Australian wild dogs in the Great Sandy Desert.

While the inquiry wound on, another hearing slipped by almost unnoticed at Alice Springs.

Coroner Denis Barritt, who had presided over the first inquest into Azaria's death and who had believed in the dingo story "with human interference," now opened another inquest strangely linked with the Chamberlain affair. It was the inquest into the death of David James Brett.

Lindy and Michael had already publicly expressed sadness that someone's death had led to the discovery of the matinee jacket—God never intended anyone to die, said Lindy, adding that if He wanted the jacket to be found He could have got somebody simply to trip over

225

it. As for the occult stories linking David Brett's death and the jacket's discovery, Michael described them as being beneath contempt.

Now Coroner Barritt was assigned to give his opinion on the circumstances of Brett's death. He called forward the investigating police officer, Sergeant Michael van Heythuysen, stationed at the Alice Springs police station.

Sergeant van Heythuysen told the court how at about 9 A.M. on Sunday, February 2, 1986, he was contacted by a Jack Coppinger of the Conservation Commission at Ayers Rock and advised that a decomposed body had been found at the base of the rock, on the southwest side. When he went to the scene, Sergeant van Heythuysen had found David Brett lying in a small depression at the base of the rock with a backpack still attached to his body. The police officer said the right arm, left hand, and right foot were missing and personal belongings were scattered in the immediate area. The sergeant said he spoke to Sharon Gray, the Conservation Commission ranger who told him of seeing Brett walking into the park on the afternoon of Sunday, January 26.

Photographs of the dead man were taken and the immediate area surrounding the body was examined. Scuff marks were noticed on the face of the rock directly above the body. Brett was taken away and a search of the area was organized in an attempt to locate the missing limbs. Line searches were carried out with the assistance of the Conservation Commission rangers and Northern Territory Emergency Service volunteers. The search failed to locate any missing limbs and a further search was arranged for the following morning. In that search, two bones were located. Despite the discovery of Azaria's matinee jacket during the search, Sergeant van Heythuysen made no reference to this in the report he read to the coroner's court.

"Investigations carried out have not revealed any suspicious circumstances in relation to the death of Brett," said the police officer.

Sergeant van Heythuysen agreed that in compiling his report he had received two further reports from Chief Inspector O'Brien. But the coroner said he did not want them read into the court transcript: "I take the view about this particular . . . I know I differ somewhat to what other people might think, but I take the view that all this stuff about witchcraft and stuff like that is just an irrelevancy," he commented.

Then the coroner asked Sergeant van Heythuysen: "The part where the deceased apparently attempted to climb the Rock is not necessarily unclimbable, is it? A good climber would apparently probably have a look at it and say, 'I reckon I could climb that from that angle?'"

"There was part of it toward the base of it," said Sergeant van Heythuysen, "that was quite easily accessible, Your Worship. As it got higher it became steeper."

"Yes, but he would have completed climbing a lot of the really difficult part, do you feel, by the time he fell?"

"From indications, marks on the lichen, the moss area, he was going across one of the more difficult parts higher up on the face."

The policeman told the coroner that it was possible to climb up a fair distance and from observations of the lichen it appeared a shaly piece of rock had possibly broken away when Brett was trying to move across one of the difficult areas.

"By the fact that he climbed there and fell off there," asked the coroner, "you wouldn't necessarily conclude that when he started out . . . to climb from that angle that he intended to commit suicide?"

"No."

"It could have been just an accident?"

"That's correct."

Shortly afterward, Coroner Barritt gave his verdict: David James Brett, aged thirty-one, met his death on or about January 26, 1986, when he apparently slipped and fell from the side of Ayers Rock. His body was not located until February 2, 1986, and when examined it was discovered death was due to multiple injuries consistent with a fall from a height.

"The deceased was apparently observed attempting to climb the Rock from an unauthorized locality late on January 26, 1986. His actions were reported to rangers who went to the area but could not see the deceased on the Rock. The Rock was not unclimbable in the area where the deceased was observed. It appeared the deceased left scuff marks on lichen on the side of the Rock above where his body was discovered.

"It appears the deceased had been suffering from mental illness during the latter years of his life but there is no evidence to indicate his fall was a deliberate act on his part. Accordingly, I find the deceased died by accident. . . ."

February 1987 saw Lindy under questioning again as the Royal Commission of Inquiry ground on. As before, she displayed a mixture of emotions ranging from tears of sorrow to supreme confidence. The tears came just thirty seconds after she entered the witness box and her counsel, John Winneke, QC, asked if she had killed Azaria.

"No, I did not," she said, her voice strong but shaking.

The tears started rolling down her face as she described the joy she and her family experienced when Azaria was born.

Had she always wanted a girl?

Sobbing loudly, Lindy took a deep breath and replied, "It was one of the happiest days of my life." And yes, she loved Azaria; the whole family had derived pleasure from her during her short life.

It was a much more composed and confident Lindy who took to the witness box the following day to face questions from Ian Barker, QC, the counsel who had led the Crown case against her at her trial and who now represented the Northern Territory government and the Territory's police. Mr. Barker closely examined Lindy on minute details of her statements relating to the presence of dingoes around her tent the night Azaria disappeared. Several times during his questioning Lindy told him she thought he was "nitpicking" and finally she let him have the full blast of her frustrations.

"I don't like you, Mr. Barker," she said firmly. "I never have liked you. If you expect me to be polite to you, don't. I don't like your form of law and I don't adhere to it. It's the reason for these courts in Australia being in such a mess."

Thunderous applause broke out among the spectators crammed into the room. The court orderly was forced to call for order several times as the clapping continued. Justice Trevor Morling said he would not tolerate the public's conduct in his court.

"I can understand you are under stress," he said to Lindy. "You have very competent counsel representing you and you may be assured that if Mr. Barker is acting unfairly in his questioning your counsel will take the necessary steps."

As expected, the questioning came around to whether the Chamberlain boys had anything to do with Azaria's death. Mr. Porter, assisting the inquiry and referring to Reagan, asked, "I take it it would be ridiculous to suggest he had anything whatever to do with Azaria that night?"

"Totally ridiculous," said Lindy.

Mr. Porter went on: "From time to time the suggestion has been made that possibly Aidan killed the child and you covered up for him."

"I have heard that rumor," said Lindy.

"What do you say to that suggestion?"

"Aidan never harmed his little sister."

"Are you quite happy for this commission to consider the case on the basis that that particular possibility can be entirely excluded?"

"It can be completely excluded," said Lindy. "He absolutely adored her."

When Michael went into the witness box, it was not an easy time for him. For he was questioned about "gilding the lily" in the account of events given by Lindy. Michael told the inquiry that he heard Lindy say, as she walked over to the tent to check on Azaria, "Get out" when she saw a dingo at the tent—evidence he said he had not previously given. Mr. Porter reminded Michael that when he gave his opening address for the inquiry in June 1986, he said Lindy had yelled at the dingo to go away but no one seemed to have heard her.

"You seem to fill the missing gap, don't you?" asked Mr. Porter.

Michael said it was not intentional. Mr. Porter remarked that anyone could understand a person in Michael's position telling a story many, many times; it would vary between accounts or at least be different here and there.

"But on the other hand," Mr. Porter went on, "there

were some things that are indicative of a deliberate attempt to gild the lily or exaggerate, and I'm putting to you that having had so many opportunities before various courts and in various statements to have told people that you heard Lindy say 'Get out,' to then say it after I have drawn attention to that defect in your case is, to say the least, highly suspicious. What do you say to that?"

"That was the last thing that was in my mind." His recollection, he said, had become hazy, but there was no intention to try and mislead or embellish anything.

"How do you know a dingo did take your baby?" asked Mr. Porter.

"As far as actual real knowledge is concerned, I don't know," said Michael.

"It is only what your wife has told you?"

"It is only from what my wife has told me, and what I believe to be very strong corroborative evidence since, that I am confirmed in my mind it must have been a dingo."

In March, the inquiry wound up. Mr. Winneke left Justice Morling with the submission that the case in which the Chamberlains were convicted in 1982 had been discredited because of the fundamental errors in expert opinion evidence. The police, he said, had displayed an "almost paranoid" attitude toward the Chamberlains and police hostility had prejudiced them.

For the Crown, Mr. Barker conceded that evidence had changed and mistakes had been made. Taken overall, however, the facts pointing to murder remained. The Crown case hinged on several different aspects— Azaria's disappearance, her violent death, the state of her clothing when found seven days later, bloodstaining of the clothes, the mother's lies, the incisor wounds Azaria suffered, blood found in the tent, and blood found in the car. And if the last two points—blood in the tent and the car—were thrown out, the other six points were capable of proving that Mrs. Chamberlain killed Azaria.

So another deep-searching inquiry was over. Now the Chamberlains, whose fortunes had changed so often in the past six and a half years, went home to their church center to await the findings of the Royal Commissioner, Justice Morling.

After ninety-two days of evidence from 145 witnesses, with a further nine days taken up with submissions from counsel—plus volumes of written submissions—the judge would now begin writing his report and declare, once and for all, whether Lindy Chamberlain murdered her baby and whether her husband helped her in a cover-up.

XVIII

Erosion of a Case

There were few who had been touched in any way by the Azaria Chamberlain mystery who envied Justice Trevor Morling's task of sifting through the mountain of evidence in order to come up with the definitive conclusion.

He put his findings together carefully and in logical order, aware that the scope of his role as Royal Commissioner was confined to a section of the Crimes Act 1900 (New South Wales) that states:

> Whenever, after the conviction of any person, any doubt or question arises as to his guilt, or any mitigating circumstances in the case, or any portion of the evidence therein, the Governor on the petition of the person convicted, or some person on his behalf, representing such doubt or question, or the Supreme Court of its own notion, may direct any Justice to, and such Justice may, summon and examine on oath all persons likely to give material information on the matter suggested.

Well, they had all been summoned and had given their material information. Now the judge had to ask himself whether the evidence persuaded him *beyond reasonable doubt* that the Chamberlains were guilty or that the evidence at their trial was free from doubt.

What he was required to do, in fact, was consider the entire evidence that had been put before him and, without looking for proof from either the Crown or the defense, decide whether there was a doubt about the Chamberlains' guilt. He had, he was well aware, an advantage over the trial jury for he had been presented with much more extensive evidence than they had heard and, in some important respects such as the question of blood, the evidence was different to that presented at the trial.

So the judge's task came down to a simple question: Is there enough doubt in the case against the Chamberlains to find that they should not have been convicted?

Justice Morling began his close examination of the Azaria affair by examining the claims made by the Crown and the evidence presented by new witnesses in regard to the events that had occurred around the time Azaria disappeared.

He looked back over the evidence of a Mr. and Mrs. Andrew Demaine who lived in a caravan in the top camping area and who were told about Azaria's disappearance at about 8:30 P.M. Responding to a request by Mrs. Chamberlain that their dog, a red setter cross, help in tracking the baby, Mr. Demaine took the dog to the passenger side of the car. Mrs. Chamberlain picked up an article of Azaria's clothing from the back of the car and put it under the dog's nose before Mr. and Mrs. Demaine set off to assist in the search.

It would have been foolish, the commissioner considered, for Mrs. Chamberlain to have acted as she had if she was aware that fresh blood had been spilt shortly before. At the trial the prosecution had told the jury they should conclude that Mrs. Chamberlain had endeavored to keep people away from the car. The Demaines were not called to give evidence at the trial. Their evidence, the judge decided, would have greatly weakened this part of the Crown submission.

On September 19, observed Justice Morling, the police took possession of the Chamberlains' car with their consent and it was examined carefully by Mrs. Kuhl, who tested, inch by inch, every inside surface, including the ceiling, over a period of three days. The three main questions that now had to be answered by the judge were whether the tests Mrs. Kuhl carried out established the presence of the blood of a young baby; whether any blood at all was found and in what quantities and where; and, if the presence of blood was established, was its quantity and location consistent only with it being Azaria's or was there any other reasonable explanation?

Justice Morling devoted a great deal of time looking at the difficulties that arose over the nature of the blood tests. He was aware that the type of tests carried out by Mrs. Kuhl were normally carried out in forensic laboratories within a relatively short time after blood was shed. But if Azaria's blood had flowed in the car, it would have been at least thirteen months old by the time it was tested by Mrs. Kuhl. And if any of the blood tested was that of Mr. Lenehan, the road accident victim the Chamberlains had picked up in June 1979, it would have been at least twenty-seven months old. There was also the possibility that any blood in the car was exposed to very high temperatures, possibly as high as 176° F., and the question arose whether the immunochemical tests used by Mrs. Kuhl could have produced reliable results. The judge recalled the evidence of a Dr. Siegfried Baudner, production manager of Behringwerke, the German company that made the antisera for the testing of fetal hemoglobin, who said that if blood was exposed to a temperature of 176°F. for half an hour it would not produce any immunochemical reaction.

And there was the evidence of Michael Raymond of the State Forensic Science Laboratory of Victoria, who found that temperatures above 140°F. had a deleterious effect on the composition of blood.

Although Mrs. Kuhl might not be expected to have been aware of all the difficulties posed by the age of blood in the car and the temperatures to which it had been exposed, the judge concluded, they did raise doubts as to the reliability of her immunochemical results and, in particular, those depending upon the use of the fetal hemoglobin antiserum. The scientist, he observed, had not carried out any testing of the fetal hemoglobin antiserum before she used it. She had relied upon the general system of testing antisera as new batches arrived at the laboratory but up to the middle of 1981 there was no set practice for testing.

Justice Morling decided that the task Mrs. Kuhl was called upon to perform in testing the Chamberlains' car and its contents posed substantial difficulties for even the most highly skilled and experienced forensic biologist. It was much more apparent before the inquiry than it was at the trial that there were many traps for the unwary in carrying out immunochemical tests upon old samples that had been exposed to severe conditions. It was apparent that the Health Commission's system of destroying the plates upon which tests were conducted not only had adverse consequences for the defense but also put the Crown in the position of having to depend upon Mrs. Kuhl's skill and experience to support the conclusions drawn from what the judge thought were "these difficult tests."

Justice Morling next turned in detail to the evidence of the discovery of baby's blood and noted that Mrs. Kuhl had spoken of some twenty-two samples from various parts of the car in which she found baby's blood. A part of the car that had come under scrutiny was an area under the dashboard next to the glove box. A spray pattern there felt sticky to the touch and after testing and getting no reaction Mrs. Kuhl suggested to Senior Constable Metcalfe, who was involved in the examination, that the spray was soft drink or something similar. However, when she tested a sample of the spray later, Mrs. Kuhl concluded that baby's blood was present. She also concluded that baby's blood was present in another area under the dashboard. But an analysis carried out by the Victorian State Forensic Science Laboratory revealed that the spray pattern was in fact a sound-deadening compound that had been sprayed during manufacture of the car into the wheel well upon the outside wall of the passenger compartment, passing through a drain hole in the wall.

This evidence was a blow to the Crown case, the judge reflected, bearing in mind the evidence of Professor James Cameron. He had told the trial that if the spray was blood, it was consistent with a small arterial or blood vessel spurt. He had testified that this could be caused after death by squeezing the cardiac region, but the pattern suggested to him bleeding rather than squeezing.

Justice Morling concluded that the fact that Mrs. Kuhl decided baby's blood was present under the dashboard when the substance was very probably sound deadening cast doubt upon the accuracy of her other results and the efficacy of her testing generally.

If that comment alone seriously undermined the scientific evidence against the Chamberlains, there was more to come as Justice Morling turned his attention to other parts of the car where baby's blood was said to have been found. Mrs. Kuhl, the judge recalled, had found baby's blood in a sample taken from the carpet on the floor of the car in front of the driver's seat. However, other scientific evidence had cast doubts upon her definite conclusions and the judge decided that it was apparent on the weight of the expert evidence that a conclusion could not be drawn that baby's blood, or any blood, was present on this piece of carpet.

He also decided it had not been established to his satisfaction that there was baby's blood, or any blood, on the hinge or vinyl behind the hinge of the passenger seat. There was no reliable indication of the presence of human blood on the bracket beneath the hinge, or on the ten-cent coin found in the floor well. It was clear there were fundamental objections to the acceptance of Mrs. Kuhl's findings of baby's blood in the area of the offside rear hinge of the passenger seat and the floor beneath.

Now Justice Morling turned to the objects in and associated with the car that had been said to have been touched by blood—the nail scissors found in the console, the cotton towel in the trunk, the synthetic chamois in a plastic container also found in the trunk, and Michael's camera bag. And one by one he knocked down their significance as evidence against the Chamberlains. He could not even find that the scissors were in the car at Ayers Rock in August 1980. And if the towel was used to wipe a murder weapon or to clean up blood from the car, it was difficult to accept that the Chamberlains would have left the towel in the trunk for over thirteen months. The lack of a sensible explanation for such strange conduct would raise doubts about the evidence of baby's blood on the towel, even if the results of the tests were much more acceptable than they were. It had not been established that there was baby's blood on the chamois and its container, and the judge noted that one witness had said he would not have even tested the items because the chamois was damp when Mrs. Kuhl removed it from the container; humidity and heat were most conducive to denaturation of bloodstains.

As for the camera bag, the judge noted that Mrs. Kuhl concluded that baby's blood was present on both the zip clasp and the buckle although there was also evidence that there were no proper controls for her tests. The results could not be relied upon, the judge decided, and he decided it had not been established that baby's blood was present on the camera bag.

Despite the Royal Commissioner's "negative reaction" to Mrs. Kuhl's findings, he was aware that the accuracy of her conclusions was given considerable support at the trial by Dr. John Baxter, former senior forensic biologist of the New South Wales Commission, and by Bryan Culliford, deputy director of the Metropolitan Police Laboratory, London.

However, there was a hitch. The approval Mr. Culliford expressed at the trial of Mrs. Kuhl's methods and her conclusions could not be explored further because he was too ill to give evidence to the commission. His successor at the Metropolitan Police Forensic Laboratory had testified that although he had not read all of Mrs. Kuhl's evidence, he found her work notes extremely confusing and on the information before him it was impossible for him to pass judgment on the reliability or accuracy of her testing procedures.

As the judge went carefully over the evidence presented to him at the inquiry, he went into a detailed examination of the important ortho-tolidine test. This screening test was relied upon by the Crown as establishing the presence of blood in a large number of places in the car. In her evidence at the trial, the judge remembered, Mrs. Kuhl described the reaction to this test in many areas of the car as "strongly positive for blood"; she also referred to substances obtained that reacted strongly as blood. The ortho-tolidine test had come under close scrutiny at the commission and there was evidence from James Fowler, a forensic scientist at the South Australian Forensic Science Centre, who carried out tests on surface scrapings and dust containing copper compounds which had been obtained in Mount Isa, where the Chamberlains used to live. He found that the reactions were similar to those given by bloodstains although in general the rate of reaction was rather slower. Mr. Fowler felt that in his opinion the results were such that an experienced forensic analyst would be unlikely, on the basis of this test alone, to distinguish readily between blood and copper compounds.

And there was Dr. Andrew Scott, who agreed that the reactions to copper dust could be mistaken for blood. And Professor Barry Boettcher tested washings from the floors of three vehicles from Mount Isa and obtained weak positive ortho-tolidine reactions from many locations on the floors.

The Crown relied at the trial upon the ortho-tolidine result alone as showing that blood was present in the Chamberlains' car. Now Justice Morling felt that even if the reactions observed were the product of blood, it could have been of such a small amount that its presence there would not justify the drawing of any inference adverse to the Chamberlains.

So far, in considering the evidence presented to him, Justice Morling had found many weaknesses in the scientific side of the Crown's evidence. He continued his study and was unable to conclude there was evidence of blood on the window handles of the car or a hinge of the driver's seat. Neither was he able to conclude that there was blood on the zip clasp and buckle on Michael's camera bag. Even if it were shown that a small amount of blood—not shown to be baby's blood—was present, this could be readily explained by the use of the bag by someone with a minor cut to a finger.

Next, the judge turned his attention to the offside hinge of the passenger seat and the floor beneath. The Crown had claimed that all the staining in these areas came from the same source—blood dropping from above the hinge and flowing down to the floor and then on to the ten-cent coin.

Now, for the first time, the Crown was to find some support in its case. Justice Morling felt he would not be able to conclude beyond a reasonable doubt that blood was present in the car, even upon the hinge area of the passenger seat. However, he felt that the number of positive results from the various tests conducted by Mrs. Kuhl on the area of the hinge of the passenger seat and the floor beneath showed it was more probable than not that, at the time of her testing, some blood was present in those areas. But in contrast to the evidence before the jury that there was a wide distribution of significant quantities of blood, the commissioner concluded that if blood was present in the car, it was there in very small quantities.

Whose blood was it?

Justice Morling summed up his examination of the evidence relating to the car by deciding that none of Mrs. Kuhl's tests established that any such blood was Azaria's. The blood shed by Mr. Lenehan could have been the source of stains in the area of the hinge of the passenger seat and beneath. And the presence of a small quantity of blood would not justify the drawing of any inference adverse to the Chamberlains.

It was the Crown's case, the judge recalled, that Azaria was killed in the car. But he felt it was absurd to suggest that Mrs. Chamberlain carried Azaria's bleeding body from the car back to the tent, where she would have been under Aidan's observation. The presence of Azaria's blood in the tent, unless it could be shown to have been transferred there upon Mrs. Chamberlain's person or clothing, was inconsistent with the Crown's case. And he felt that the blood found in the tent was as consistent with dingo involvement as it was with the murder of the child in the car.

Just where Azaria was injured—whether in the head, neck, or both—was something the judge was unable to decide upon, but he was firm in discounting the evidence of Professor James Cameron, who had stated that in his opinion Azaria had been killed by having her throat cut.

He concluded that the pattern of bloodstaining on the clothes did not support the contention that the baby's throat had been cut with a blade with an intent to kill the child. This was not to say that the pattern of bloodstaining was inconsistent with a more tentative cut to the throat or neck, whether done by a blade or other means.

And because of the diversity of opinion, the judge felt he was unable to conclude whether the damage to the child's jumpsuit occurred before, during, or after the bleeding.

But what of those human handprints that Professor Cameron said he had been able to detect on the back of the jumpsuit? Upon his own examination of the infrared photographs and of the jumpsuit itself, the judge had been unable to discern any such pattern. He concluded, therefore, that there were no detectable prints of hands or fingers, whether in blood or any other material, upon the clothing.

The staining on the clothing, when considered on its own, did not provide any positive support for the dingo theory, he felt. However, in contrast to the evidence given at the trial, the staining, considered on its own, provided no positive support for the allegation of murder, either.

The damage to Azaria's clothing also came under close scrutiny by the judge as he assessed the enormous amount of evidence. In essence, the Crown had attempted to establish at the trial that Mr. or Mrs. Chamberlain had cut Azaria's clothing to imitate dingo damage and thereby give credence to their story that a dingo had taken her. Two separate questions had arisen —whether the damage to the clothing *was* caused by dingo teeth or some kind of human interference; and whether, if humans were involved, the Chamberlains were responsible.

The judge reminded himself that the jumpsuit was found seven days after Azaria's disappearance about four or five kilometers from the camping area and at a location some two hundred meters off the road on the southwest side of the Rock. There was a dingo den about thirty meters to the west and there were dingo tracks around the vicinity of the den, which was far too narrow for a human to enter. The main damage to the jumpsuit consisted of a roughly circular severance in the left sleeve measuring a few centimeters across with the circular piece missing, and a V cut to the right collar. There was a similar cut in about the same position on the right collar of the matinee jacket after its discovery five and a half years later.

Justice Morling recalled the evidence of Professor

Chaikin at the commission who described what was known as "planar array"—the phenomenon of nylon fibers lying together in the same plane with evenly matching ends, indicative of knife or scissor cuts in fabric. However, this could only be seen properly under a special scanning electron microscope.

The judge made up his mind that, because of differences in opinions between the experts, he was unable to adopt the planar array test as a reliable one for distinguishing between canine teeth cuts in fibers and cuts caused by a knife or scissors. And after considering comparisons between Azaria's clothing and other clothing damaged by dogs or dingoes, he believed it could not be concluded beyond reasonable doubt that the damage to the baby's clothes was caused by scissors or a knife, not by the teeth of a canine. As for the circular severance in the left sleeve of the jumpsuit—which Sergeant Frank Cocks of South Australia sought to demonstrate had been caused by the use of scissors—the judge felt the evidence was too speculative to be of much value.

Turning to the damage to the diaper, the judge pondered that if a dingo killed Azaria, it was surprising the diaper was not bloodstained. It was torn and there were pieces of wadding lying nearby but there was no bloodstain on it. However, the absence of staining seemed consistent with the paucity of staining on the lower half of the jumpsuit. It was conceivable that the diaper could have been pulled off the child before being ripped apart and before any injury was caused to the lower half of the body. The appearance of the diaper was yet another puzzling feature of the evidence, he believed. On balance, it seemed to support the theory of dingo involvement. But he did leave the possibility open in his mind that a dingo from the nearby den could have damaged the diaper after a human being had removed it from Azaria's body.

Could a dingo have removed the baby from her clothes without causing more damage?

The judge now had to consider a gruesome scenario as he examined the evidence put forward. The fact that the top button of the baby's matinee jacket was done up when found did not of itself preclude dingo involvement, the judge believed. If a dingo had consumed the child, it may have done so by first devouring the head. In this event, the jacket, jumpsuit, and singlet would all have been more easily removed from the body. Further, it was demonstrated that if, for example, a dingo placed its paws on the feet of the jumpsuit so as to steady its prey, it could have extracted the child, leaving its booties in the legs of the jumpsuit, where they had been found, the judge recalled, when it was discovered.

However, he thought that if a dingo had consumed the head first, or if it had inflicted severe head or neck injuries—as it must have done—then the absence of extensive collar damage to the jacket and jumpsuit seemed surprising. Yet he concluded that although a dingo would have had difficulty removing Azaria's body from her clothing without causing more damage to it, it was possible for this to have happened.

The question of whether Azaria's clothing had been buried before discovery was also considered by Justice Morling, who recalled Professor Cameron's evidence that when he examined the jumpsuit in September 1981 he noticed that it appeared to be almost uniformly stained with sand except under the arms. The professor had concluded from this that the jumpsuit had been buried in sand and, since he observed no fold marks showing variations in the staining, he believed it was possible that the clothing had been buried with the body in it. Professor Cameron had also concluded from the variation in staining down the front of the garment that only two of the snaps were undone when the jumpsuit was covered with sand. This evidence, along with geological evidence about the source of a small quantity of soil found in the jumpsuit, had been relied upon by the Crown to found a submission that Azaria's clothed body had been buried by the Chamberlains on the sand dune immediately east of the campsite on the night she disappeared.

But Justice Morling made his mind up otherwise as he went back over the evidence presented to him. That evidence told him that it appeared that most of the soil in the jumpsuit could have come from a large number of places in the Ayers Rock region, many of them in the sand dune country lying generally in an easterly direction from the campsite. And as one expert had said, his findings would not be inconsistent with the jumpsuit being dragged across the sand dunes in that area. The geological evidence, too, did not further support the suggestion that the clothing had been buried, as opposed to being dragged along the surface.

Samples taken from around the Uluru Motel area clearly did not match the soil in the jumpsuit. The closest place from which a reasonably matched sample was taken was from under a desert oak about one kilometer from the motel. This indicated to the judge that there was no support for any suggestion that Azaria's clothed body may have been buried near the Uluru Motel late on the night of August 17, 1980.

There had also been the suggestion that fragments of plants were deliberately rubbed upon the jumpsuit and singlet by human hand—Sergeant Cocks had given evidence that the fragments of parietaria upon both items of clothing were consistent with their having been rubbed directly on that plant. Some fragments were so far imbedded that it seemed they had become attached to the clothing from the inside back of the jumpsuit, within the V formed by the undone top snaps—an indication that Azaria was not in the suit at the time.

However, Justice Morling decided that the evidence concerning the soil and plant fragments on the clothing was consistent with the clothed body of the baby being dragged through sand on the dunes east of the camping area and through low vegetation. On the other hand, if the clothing had been merely taken from the car, buried, disinterred, and later placed at the Rock by the Chamberlains, he could imagine that it may have picked up some plant material but it was difficult to conceive how it could have collected the quantity and variety of plant material found on it. While the evidence did not exclude the possibility of burial, the judge decided, neither could it support a finding of burial. At the same time, while it was not inconceivable that the plant fragments came upon the clothing by a deliberate dragging by human hand through a variety of low-growing vegetation, in the absence of other evidence, this did not seem likely.

Azaria's clothing, the judge reminded himself, was found about two and one-half kilometers from the Uluru Motel and one-fourth to one-half kilometers northwest of the Fertility Cave. Did the Chamberlains have the opportunity of returning there after the child disappeared and leaving her clothes there? Yes, the judge decided, they did. The motel had still been serving drinks until well into the early hours of Monday, August 18, but there was a period of two to three hours afterward when the Chamberlains' absence from the motel would not have been noticed. Although the starting of a car might have attracted attention, Mr. Chamberlain at least would have been able to walk or jog to where the clothes were found and return unnoticed.

But, the judge asked, why would they have chosen to place the clothes where they were found? The Crown had suggested, of course, that the clothes were placed in the vicinity of a dingo den, but there was no evidence to suggest how the Chamberlains could have known about this den. Also, the judge wondered, why would the Chamberlains have placed the clothes so far west of the Fertility Cave, where Mrs. Chamberlain said she had seen a dingo on that Sunday afternoon?

As for the evidence of the trackers, who had told of animal tracks leading from the tent and a depression in the sand where the baby would have been laid down, Justice Morling remembered the importance of keeping in mind the fact that the Chamberlains had never carried the onus of showing that a dingo took Azaria, or that the tracks seen near their tent and on the nearby sand dune were made by a dingo. The tracking evidence had to be considered as part of the overall pattern of evidence, and what the commission had heard gave greater credence to dingo involvement in Azaria's death than did the evidence at the trial.

The Chamberlains won further support from the judge when he examined everything he had been told about what had been alleged to be blood on Mrs. Chamberlain's tracksuit pants. There had been four versions put forward at the trial—the tracksuit pants were splattered with Azaria's blood at or about the time her throat was cut by Lindy; there were no bloodstains on the pants; the pants were lying on the floor of the tent when a dingo took Azaria and spots of the baby's blood fell onto the trousers as a result of her injuries; the pants became spotted with blood when Mrs. Chamberlain, who was wearing them later in the evening, crawled into the tent after Azaria had been taken by a dingo and the pants came into contact with bloodstained items.

The judge remembered a statement Lindy had made, long after the event, that the stains may have been caused by the spillage of food or drink. The Crown had relied on this as demonstrating that her testimony on the nature of the stains was not worthy of credence. But the judge felt that this criticism did not carry much weight since it was not unreasonable for Lindy to have suggested, even belatedly, an alternative cause of the stains. Further, he thought, the possibility of blackcurrant juice having caused part of the staining on her running shoes was mentioned by her to the police at the first opportunity, on October 1, 1980, and it seemed not unreasonable on her part to infer that there was staining of a similar kind on the tracksuit pants.

The judge was far from satisfied that the pants were bloodstained. In fact, on the whole of the evidence, he was of the view that the marks on the tracksuit pants were not bloodstains.

The judge had some interesting thoughts about Greg and Sally Lowe, who had been with the Chamberlains at the barbecue. Giving evidence to the commission, Greg Lowe had described for the first time how he saw Mrs. Chamberlain leave the barbecue area and enter the tent with Azaria, before emerging without the baby and then going to the car with Aidan. The judge decided that he could not safely rely upon Mr. Lowe's evidence because he may have been anxious, subconsciously, to support his wife's evidence. And as for Sally Lowe, the judge decided she had been an honest witness but that she was prone to exaggeration and embellishment. The discrepancies in her various descriptions of the cry she claimed to have heard did not inspire confidence in the reliability of her testimony. However, the judge accepted that she was convinced she heard a baby cry.

Justice Morling had gone over a great deal of the evidence. It was taking him many weeks to sift through it all and write it up for his official report.

There were now only two witnesses left whose evidence had to be examined and assessed with care—that of Michael and Lindy Chamberlain. So far the judge had come down heavily against the Crown submissions. Now the detailed evidence of the Chamberlains was about to come under the spotlight for the last time.

XIX

Final Opinion

"It is not possible to do justice to the Crown case without referring to some of the unsatisfactory features of Mrs. Chamberlain's evidence," Justice Morling wrote in his report at the outset of his detailed examination of the couple's versions of events.

According to the Crown, the judge noted, a fatal flaw in her story was that she did not claim ever to have seen Azaria in the mouth of the dingo supposed to have taken her. Her explanation that the dingo's mouth was obscured by the post-and-rail fence was unconvincing, the judge noted, and she had given varying accounts of the direction taken by the dingo after she had frightened it away.

Her statement that she believed the dingo had the baby when she first saw it was not easily reconcilable with another statement she made that she "dived straight for the tent, to see what had made the baby cry." The Crown had also contended that because she only saw the dingo at the entrance to the tent and did not see the baby in its mouth, she could not have known that the dingo had taken the baby when she cried out that it had taken her.

These were all-powerful considerations, the judge thought. Yet he believed it was not difficult to find explanations consistent with Lindy's innocence for many of the problems raised by her evidence.

The Crown, he recalled, had submitted that it was unbelievable that Mrs. Chamberlain could have had such a clear view of the alleged dingo as to be able to describe its face and head with great precision yet be unable to see Azaria in its mouth. This was, he thought, a very powerful submission if the assumption were made that there was only one dingo at or near the tent at the time. It was rendered even more powerful by the circumstance that the child was clad in white clothing. But the submission lost its weight if it was accepted that two dogs or dingoes might have been at or near the tent. On the evidence, Justice Morling did not think this possibility could be ruled out.

The Royal Commissioner recalled that the Crown had claimed that some statements made for the first time by Mrs. Chamberlain in her evidence before the inquiry demonstrated a willingness on her part to make untrue statements in support of her claim of innocence. But the judge felt that if any of her more recent statements were incorrect, and they might well be, their inaccuracy could be due to frailty or confusion of memory or a desire to obtain redress for an unjust conviction.

Some of Mrs. Chamberlain's actions when she returned to Mount Isa, observed Justice Morling, were extraordinary if she had murdered Azaria in the manner alleged by the Crown. It would have been foolhardy, for example, for her to have volunteered the statement that she had washed blood off her track shoes if she had killed the child.

What he thought was a "minor matter" relevant to Mrs. Chamberlain's credit was the discovery of the matinee jacket. She had at all times maintained that Azaria was wearing the jacket when she disappeared and its discovery proved this to be the case.

The judge turned to the evidence of Michael Chamberlain, having decided that he was not only a man of excellent character but also a good father, well educated, and devoted to his children. The most crucial part of his evidence, the judge observed, was his statement that he heard Azaria cry after his wife returned to the barbecue, a claim corroborated by Mrs. Lowe. The judge saw this as the most crucial part of Michael's evidence because, if it was correct, his wife must be innocent.

It was highly improbable that Michael knew before the alarm was raised that his wife had already killed Azaria—if in fact she had—and the opportunity Lindy had to converse with him in private and tell him that she had killed Azaria was virtually nonexistent in the first fifteen minutes after the alarm was raised and extremely limited in the half hour or so afterward.

The Crown had submitted, the judge remembered, that it could safely be inferred from Michael's conduct after Azaria's disappearance that he knew his wife had killed Azaria and that there had not been any dingo involvement in her death. There was his alleged failure to make an urgent and sustained search of the sand dunes, his failure to use the headlights of his vehicle to assist in the search, his premature acceptance that Azaria would not be found alive, his failure the following day to inquire about the progress of the search, his failure to exhibit great grief, and his willingness to talk to the media along with his decision to leave Ayers Rock on the morning of August 19.

Although he felt there was considerable force in some of the Crown's criticisms of Michael, Justice Morling did not share all of the Crown's attack. However, he did consider that Michael's willingness to be interviewed by the media and to talk about the tragedy was extraordinary.

He wrote in his report:

> Perhaps the most extraordinary aspect of his conduct was the request he made of Constable Morris that he be permitted to photograph the jaws of a dingo which had been shot by the police. Strange though this request was, it was not of itself incriminating. The request, like some of his other conduct, was equally extraordinary whether Azaria was murdered or taken by a dingo.

> To my mind, the most suspicious aspect of Mr. Chamberlain's conduct was the statement he made so soon after Azaria's disappearance that she would not be found alive. . . .

> There is much in the evidence to justify a conclusion that Mr. Chamberlain has a tendency to describe events in theatrical language. I think he also enjoys having an audience. These characteristics . . . may account for some of the embellishments and exaggerations in his evidence. It is these exaggerations and embellishments which give some of his evidence a ring of unreality. In one of his interviews with the media he said that the great quantity of blood discovered in the tent led him to conclude that Azaria's death must have been swift. This statement was patently ridiculous and could not have deceived any person who saw inside the tent. The Crown relies upon it as showing that Mr. Chamberlain is a liar, but I think the statement does no more than reflect his proclivity for hyperbole.

The judge took the defense of Michael further:

> It was part of the Crown case that he or his wife buried Azaria's body on the sand dune to the east of their tent. Of course, he denied this. At the trial, it did not emerge

clearly, if it emerged at all, that Azaria's body was probably not buried until at least two and a half to three hours after her death, if indeed it was buried. The consequence of this is that, if Mr. or Mrs. Chamberlain buried the body on the sand dune, they probably could not have done it until about 10:30 to 11 P.M. at the earliest. This circumstance raises a not inconsiderable difficulty for the Crown in its claim that Mr. Chamberlain falsely denied that Azaria had been buried on the dune.

On the Crown case, by the time Azaria's body was buried it had remained undiscovered in the car for at least two and a half to three hours. By 11 P.M. Mr. Chamberlain had a reasonable excuse for taking his distressed wife and children to the safe haven of a motel, where he would have a better opportunity of disposing of the body than if he remained at the campsite. The camping area was alive with activity, and no doubt he and his wife were the cynosure of all eyes. Why he would run the enormous risk of taking the body out of the car and burying it on the nearby sand dune is not apparent. No one saw him or his wife acting suspiciously at the time. It is to be remembered that there were up to three hundred people searching the dune. Moreover, if the body were buried and disinterred later in the night, it seems probable the disinterment would have occurred after midnight. It seems improbable that if he had succeeded in burying the body before midnight without being detected, he would have returned to the grave very soon thereafter, disinterred the body, and carried it back to the car.

At midnight the Chamberlains went to the Uluru Motel, some two or three kilometers from the dune. If he had returned to the sand dune by car after midnight it is almost certain that he would have been observed since the search continued until 3 A.M. If he had returned by foot, he still ran the risk of being seen carrying the baby's dead body back to the motel. Quite apart from the risks involved, the difficulty in finding an unmarked grave on a dark night on a sand dune well covered with vegetation would have been not inconsiderable, unless the grave were quite close to the road. . . . The difficulties inherent in this part of the Crown's case are very considerable indeed. Compared to them, the difficulties the defense has in explaining the Chamberlains' conduct, although of a different kind, are minor.

Justice Morling had now completed his examination of the evidence. It was time for him to summarize the entire case against the Chamberlains and make his conclusions.

He had invited, he recalled, counsel for the Crown to indicate a place, other than the front seat of the car, at which the murder might have occurred. The prosecutor had been unable to suggest an alternative location but submitted that it was not incumbent upon the Crown to specify and prove the particular place where Azaria was killed.

The judge agreed with that, but noted that the trial was conducted upon the basis that the child was murdered in the car. The new scientific evidence cast serious doubt on the reliability of all the findings of blood in the car. If there were any blood, it was present only in small quantities in the area of the hinge on the passenger's seat and beneath, but it had not been established that any such blood was Azaria's. Taken in its entirety, the judge assessed, the evidence fell far short of proving that there was any blood in the car for which there was not an innocent explanation.

The judge believed that in the light of the new evidence, the opinion expressed by Professor Cameron at the trial that the pattern of bloodstaining on the jump-

suit was consistent only with a cut throat could not be
safely adopted, nor could it be concluded from the pattern of bloodstaining on the clothing that Azaria's
throat had been cut with a blade. In addition, Professor
Cameron's evidence that there was an imprint of a hand
in blood on the back of the jumpsuit had been weakened, if not totally destroyed, by new evidence that a
great deal of what he thought was blood on the back of
the jumpsuit was, in fact, red sand.

And, in the light of the new evidence, the judge decided, it was difficult to conceive how Azaria's clothing
could have collected the quantity and variety of plant
material found upon it if it had been merely taken from
the car, buried, disinterred, and later placed near the
base of the Rock. It was more consistent with the new
plant and soil evidence that Azaria's clothed body was
carried and dragged by an animal from the campsite to
near the base of the Rock, rather than being buried on
the dune and later carried there.

Regarding the damage to Azaria's clothing, the judge
felt it could not be concluded beyond reasonable doubt
that the damage was caused by scissors or a knife, or
that it was not caused by the teeth of a dingo or dog.
And there was no reason to doubt that when Azaria
disappeared she was wearing the matinee jacket that
had been discovered in 1986. The jacket would have
covered much of the jumpsuit and the failure to detect
dingo saliva on the jumpsuit was now more explicable
than it was at the trial.

So, were there doubts as to the Chamberlains' guilt?
It was the vital, final question that Justice Morling now
had to consider.

The jury, he surmised, must have disbelieved Lindy's
story about the dingo. The effect on her credit of her
inability to explain the presence of blood in the car and

how the alleged spray of blood came to be on the plate under the dash could not be known with certainty, but it was probably disastrous.

Looking at the "unsatisfactory features" in Lindy's account of having seen a dingo, the judge felt it could be fairly said that there were inconsistencies and improbabilities in her story and in the various versions she had given of it. But there were possible explanations and the obstacles to the acceptance of the Crown's case were both numerous and formidable. The judge took this thought farther: "Almost every facet of its case is beset by serious difficulties."

The Crown, he recalled, was unable to suggest a motive or explanation for the alleged murder and if Lindy left the barbecue with the intention of killing Azaria it was astonishing that she took Aidan with her. It was even more astonishing that she should have murdered Azaria, as the Crown purported, a few feet from where her son was awaiting her return to the tent. It seemed improbable that Lindy, having murdered Azaria in the car or elsewhere, would have returned to the tent with so much blood on her or her clothing that some of it dripped onto articles in the tent. Unless she did, there was no explanation, except the dingo story, for the blood found in the tent.

It was extraordinary, the judge thought, that those present at the barbecue area at the time of and immediately after Azaria's disappearance accepted Mrs. Chamberlain's story and noticed nothing about her appearance or conduct suggesting that she had suddenly killed her daughter, and nothing about Mr. Chamberlain's conduct suggesting that he knew that she had done so. She must have been a consummate actress, the judge thought, if, having killed her daughter, she was able to appear calm and unconcerned when she returned to the barbecue a few minutes after the murder.

The short period during which Lindy was absent from the barbecue made it only barely possible that she could have committed the crime of which she was accused. On the Crown case, in the five to ten minutes she was proved to have been absent from the barbecue she must have returned to the tent; carried out whatever was necessary to make sure that Aidan did not follow her; put on her tracksuit pants; taken the baby to the car; got hold of a murder weapon; cut Azaria's throat; allowed sufficient time for Azaria to die; hidden the body; carried out at least some cleaning up of blood in the vehicle; taken off her tracksuit pants; obtained a can of baked beans for Aidan; returned to the tent; gone into the tent and done whatever was necessary for several articles in it to be spotted with blood; collected Aidan and returned to the barbecue.

On the Crown case, recalled the judge, the length of time that must have elapsed between Azaria's throat being cut and her death was of some importance. It seemed probable that if Lindy murdered the child she would not have returned to the tent before she was satisfied the baby was dead. If both Azaria's cartoid arteries were severed it probably would have taken about two to three minutes, with a minimum of half a minute, for her to have died. It would have taken up to twenty minutes for her to have died if her jugular vein had been severed. The bloodstaining on the jumpsuit indicated an absence of arterial bleeding.

It was surprising, the judge thought, that if Mrs. Chamberlain had blood on her clothing, nobody noticed it in the hours after Azaria's disappearance. If Azaria's body was left in the car after the alleged murder, it was foolhardly for Mrs. Chamberlain, in the presence of the

Demaines and their dog, to open the car door and give
the dog the scent of Azaria's clothing. The risks involved in the Chamberlains burying and disinterring
Azaria when there were so many people who might
have observed them were enormous. It was also difficult
to explain how the variety of plant material found on
Azaria's clothing could have got there if she had been
murdered. It seemed improbable that, the murder having been so cleverly accomplished and concealed, the
clothing would have been so left as to invite suspicion.

Coming to the end of the examination of all evidence,
the judge wrote in his official report:

I am far from persuaded that Mrs. Chamberlain's
account of having seen a dingo near the tent was false
or that Mr. Chamberlain falsely denied that he knew
his wife had murdered his daughter. That is not to say
that I accept that all their evidence is accurate. Some of
it plainly is not, since parts of it are inconsistent with
other parts.

But if a dingo took her child, the events of the night
of 17 August must have been emotionally devastating to
Mrs. Chamberlain. Her ability to give a reliable account
of the tragedy may have been badly affected by her dis-
tress. The inconsistencies in her evidence may have
been caused by her confusion of mind. Where her evidence conflicts with the Lowes' account of what she
said and did in the few seconds after she commenced to
run back to the tent, it may be the Lowes' recollection,
not hers, that is at fault. The belief that people might
unjustly accuse her of making up the dingo story might
have led her, even subconsciously, to embellish her account of what happened, and this may explain some of
its improbabilities. Her failure to see Azaria in the
dingo's mouth is explicable if, as is quite possible, there
were two dingoes, not one. These considerations afford
at least as convincing an explanation for the apparently

unsatisfactory parts of her evidence as does the Crown's claim that she was lying to conceal her part in the alleged murder. Having seen Mr. and Mrs. Chamberlain in the witness box, I am not convinced that either of them was lying.

And now, after months of evidence at the inquiry and weeks of careful examination, Justice Trevor Morling, who had undertaken the task of assessing guilt or innocence in the most talked-about case in Australia, was ready to officially declare his findings.

"In my opinion," he decided, "if the evidence before the commission had been given at the trial, the trial judge would have been obliged to direct the jury to acquit the Chamberlains on the ground that the evidence could not justify their conviction."

So the Crown's case against Lindy Chamberlain had completely collapsed. The scientific evidence, the thrust of the prosecution, had been totally discredited. The legal system had failed, and failed dismally, leaving open the question of how many others convicted on scientific evidence were wrongfully lingering in jail.

There was little doubt that each scientist had gone about his or her task to the extent of their relevant skills, but it had not been enough. While there were factors indicating blood had been in the car, there was no conclusive proof it was Azaria's or even that of a baby. It *may* have been baby's blood, as the initial tests had indicated—but it might equally have been an adult's blood as later tests had shown. And with such a doubt existing, the Crown had no case. For it was not enough now for the Crown to fall back on the circumstances that surrounded the night of August 17: nobody saw Lindy go into the car with the baby; nobody saw her brandishing a knife or scissors; nobody saw her dashing from car to tent; nobody saw Michael lifting the baby's body from the camera bag; nobody saw either of them burying the child's body. Without the scientific evidence to back up the supposed sequence of events, it was the end of the case against the Chamberlains.

The judge's findings were greeted with wild enthusiasm by the Chamberlains and their supporters—who then hesitated. It was good news, certainly. But there should be more, surely? A total exoneration . . . a recommendation of a pardon. . . .

There was nothing more. Justice Morling's job had been to decide whether there was a doubt as to the Chamberlains' guilt and he had done that.

The Chamberlains decided to fight on for a pardon and the quashing of their convictions. The Northern Territory government met their demands halfway and issued them a pardon.

"Now we fight on to clear our names completely," said Lindy, who still remained a convicted murderess. However, she had made a new friend in Helena Mantz, whom she had met in Berrimah jail. Also released, Helena moved in with the Chamberlains to help Lindy with the children and housework.

The Chamberlains were left holding a legal bill of more than one million dollars, which they owed to their church. Their only hope was to continue to fight the Northern Territory government for compensation.

Michael was far from happy with their treatment by the government, describing their actions in granting a pardon without quashing the convictions as "mean and despicable."

What they had been through, said Michael, was a nightmare that had scarred them and all who had had anything to do with their case. But there was a silver lining to the dark clouds that still hovered over them. Actress Meryl Streep agreed to play Lindy in a multi-million dollar movie about the affair because she felt a great injustice had been done. Lindy, she believed when she had read through all aspects of the story, was innocent. When, toward the end of 1987, she met Lindy, she considered her to be harder than she had expected, but that soon passed. The two women became good friends and it was said they had decided to invest in real estate together, purchasing land in Queensland for a resort development. The money that Lindy received as an adviser on the film would go, said her friends, toward paying the legal bill.

The money, though, was not the problem. It was the unsettled matter of the convictions still standing that concerned them.

Yet there were few who doubted that the Chamberlains, who had been to hell and back despite their belief in God, would win the day and be officially declared innocent of involvement in the death of baby Azaria. That day finally arrived on September 16, 1988, when the Northern Territory Court of Criminal Appeal in Darwin officially declared them innocent and cleared them of all charges. The Chamberlains' eight-year ordeal, at last, was over.

But one thing was certain: They would never be the same private couple who set out with their young family on the road to Ayers Rock on their Sabbath day in August 1980.

For that was the day they entered the realm of legend.